Hannah Roberts holds a PhD in War Studies from King's College London. She is Head of Sociology at Godalming College.

'This book offers a historic and chronological overview of the WRNS with particular attention to the role of the individual. It is a solid piece of historical research which makes a genuine contribution to knowledge in the field, and has some lovely colour from the oral interviews conducted.'

Corinna Peniston-Bird, Senior Lecturer in Gender History, Lancaster University

'A new way of seeing naval history has arrived. This book does for the navy what Lucy Noakes has done for the army. It's analytical, combative, and aware of how gendered norms shape military organisations and the women within them in wartime and beyond.'

Jo Stanley, University of Hull, author of
From Cabin 'Boys' to Captains: 250 Years of Women at Sea

THE WRNS IN WARTIME

The Women's Royal Naval Service
1917–45

HANNAH ROBERTS

BLOOMSBURY ACADEMIC
LONDON • NEW YORK • OXFORD • NEW DELHI • SYDNEY

BLOOMSBURY ACADEMIC
Bloomsbury Publishing Plc
50 Bedford Square, London, WC1B 3DP, UK
1385 Broadway, New York, NY 10018, USA

BLOOMSBURY, BLOOMSBURY ACADEMIC and the Diana logo
are trademarks of Bloomsbury Publishing Plc

First published in Great Britain by I.B. Tauris 2018
Paperback edition published by Bloomsbury Academic 2020

A catalogue record for this book is available from the British Library.

A catalog record for this book is available from the Library of Congress.

ISBN: HB: 978-1-7883-1001-7
PB: 978-0-7556-0198-1
ePDF: 978-1-7867-3325-2
eBook: 978-1-7867-2325-3

International Library of War Studies 22

Typeset in Garamond Three by OKS Prepress Services, Chennai, India

To find out more about our authors and books visit
www.bloomsbury.com and sign up for our newsletters.

CONTENTS

Acknowledgements

With thanks to my parents, Colin and Janice Roberts, for their constant support throughout the long journey to create this book; to Rosie Ballantyne-Smith for always cheerfully proofreading; to Jo Stanley for taking the time to read and comment on my work; to Dr Alan James, my PhD supervisor at King's College London, for his supportive direction over the years; and to the Wrens who shared their stories with me.

LIST OF ILLUSTRATIONS

Plates

Plate 1 Dame Katharine Furse inspecting VAD officers. Credit: Alamy.

Plate 2 Sir Eric Geddes. Credit: Alamy.

Plate 3 WRNS on German U-boat, November 1918. Courtesy of WRNS Benevolent Trust.

Plate 4 World War I recruitment poster for WAAC and WRNS. Credit: Alamy.

Plate 5 Betty Calderara. Courtesy of Betty Calderara.

Plate 6 Jean Atkins née Aitchison and her sister Mary, a topographical Wren. Courtesy of Jean Atkins.

Plate 7 Jean Atkins née Aitchison having completed her Officer's training at Stoke Pogues (first from right at the back). Courtesy of Jean Atkins.

Plate 8 Met Office Staff at Machrihanish, Scotland. Jean Atkins née Aitchison with Commander John Simmonds, better known as 'Seaweed'. Courtesy of Jean Atkins.

Plate 9 Sheila Rodman. Courtesy of Sheila Rodman.

Figure

Tables

ABBREVIATIONS AND TERMINOLOGY

ATS	Auxiliary Territorial Service (World War II)
FANY	First Aid Nursing Yeomanry
IWM	Imperial War Museum
M/T	Motor transport
NMRN	National Museum of the Royal Navy
P/O	Petty Officer
QMAAC	Queen Mary's Army Auxiliary Corps
RN	Royal Navy
SD (Special Duties) X	Those Wrens who worked in or around Bletchley Park as part of the code breaking operation
SD (Special Duties) Y	Wrens who worked in the listening stations on the coast of Britain, intercepting signals and communications from German ships and U-boats
VAD	Voluntary Aid Detachment
WAAC	Women's Auxiliary Army Corps (World War I)
WAAF	Women's Auxiliary Air Force (World War II)
WRAF	Women's Royal Air Force (World War I and 1949–94)
Wren	A woman who served in the WRNS
WRNS	Women's Royal Naval Service
WSPU	Women's Social and Political Union
W/T	Wireless Telegraphist
WVR	Women's Volunteer Reserve

INTRODUCTION

The history of the Women's Royal Naval Service (WRNS) is relatively unknown. As the smallest of the women's services it has not received the media and academic attention of its larger, army counterpart (the WAAC in World War I and the Auxiliary Territorial Service or ATS in World War II) and its air force equivalent (the WRAF in World War I and the Women's Auxiliary Air Force or WAAF in World War II).[1] The WRNS was created, disbanded and recreated under a number of different social, political, military and cultural conditions, at different points in British history. The official histories of the service have only traced its key events.[2] This book explores why the Women's Royal Naval Service was created in 1917 and disbanded in 1919; why for 19 years, between the two world wars, women had no official involvement in the Royal Navy; why it was recreated in 1938 and the roles it undertook during World War II.

'From the late seventeenth century into the mid nineteenth century the presence of women aboard ship was common, although their presence was officially ignored or even hidden.'[3] In this quote, Suzanne Stark shows that the exclusion of women from being aboard ships was a relatively new phenomenon. Women had always been part of the navy in some form and this only stopped in the middle of the nineteenth century before the convention was overturned in November 1917. Nevertheless, she notes the 'ancient and ubiquitous' notion that women held no place at sea because they were regarded as weak and a distraction to the sailors.[4] Where the histories of the WRNS are limited, writers including Stark and Jo Stanley have outlined the record of women at sea in detail.[5]

In the age of sail these 'hidden' and 'ignored' women were aboard ship in one of three roles. The largest category was made up of hundreds of prostitutes who shared the quarters of the sailors in the lower decks whilst a ship was in port. The second group were the wives of warrant officers who may have spent years at sea with their husbands. These women were often very active members of the ship's community, participating in warfare as nurses and the rearming of guns. The practice of having women aboard ship 'was officially tolerated in peacetime, and certainly survived in time of war'.[6] It was understood that any woman aboard had to either be elderly or dress plainly, so as not to be 'disruptive' to the sailors.[7] The final group was made up of a small proportion of women who dressed as men and served aboard ship as sailors.[8] Stark regards these women as significant because 'they prove that manual seafaring tasks were not necessarily beyond women'.[9]

In 1731, the Admiralty issued the first set of 'Regulations and Instructions', stating, '[a captain] is not to carry any women to sea ... without orders from the Admiralty'.[10] This was because women aboard ship were typically seen as disruptive. Dudley Pope talks of how women sat all day gossiping and drinking.[11] Stark remarks that in many instances women and dogs were, to the navy, in the same category.[12] A memorandum by Horatio Nelson stated his intention to rid his ships 'of all the women, dogs and pigeons'.[13] He was one of the few admirals who flatly refused to allow women aboard his ship.

Women aboard ship in the Age of Sail was therefore not uncommon. And there is evidence to suggest that women were taking active roles within the community of the ship, participating during conflict by rearming guns and by adopting nursing roles.[14] Yet the role of women was not that of a sailor. Traditional female social roles were still upheld, those of wife, nurse, steward, carer, but not of sailor or warrior. Despite women having gone to sea with the navy in the Age of Sail their role aboard can hardly be compared to that of the Wrens who went to sea in 1990 first and foremost as sailors of the Royal Navy, for whom there might be every possibility of being deployed in combat.

There are similarities to women in the army. Noakes's work provides an effective point of comparison to the WRNS.[15] Like the RN, the army had a long tradition of female participation in the form of nurses and non-combatant camp followers.[16] These women, who were often the wives of serving men, carried out the important task of maintaining the camp, stores and providing meals. According to DeGroot and Peniston-Bird: 'the camp follower ... was in fact an essential component'.[17] The inclusion of field nurses since Florence Nightingale's breakthrough in the Crimean War of the 1850s cemented the links of the army with essential women workers. However, the professionalisation of the military in the nineteenth and twentieth centuries meant that women became increasingly excluded from the support functions they had performed, and these were taken over by men.[18]

Similarly, Barton Hacker argues, 'the end of the Napoleonic wars, at the beginning of the nineteenth century, which completed a cycle in military history, brought with it both the elimination of the last vestiges of non-military support services and the total exclusion of women' in the navy.[19] The Royal Navy had, by the start of World War I, become the military institution recognisable today. No longer would you find a woman aboard a RN ship. This separation in the acceptable roles of women and men in conflict reflected wider social norms about the spheres of responsibility for the genders. Other than as nurses, women were excluded from the realm of conflict.

Officially, it was not until 1917 that women were allowed to join the Royal Navy as auxiliary members of the WRNS. During World War I, the role of Wrens was limited and restricted to the concept that it would only be for 'the duration'.[20] Wrens 'were considered to be *of* but not *in* the Navy, even though they *felt* they were *in* the Navy, not just in the naval *services*'.[21] Between 1917 and 1919, around 7,000 women served in some 75 locations.[22] The service was predominantly confined to Britain and land service only. The women were initially employed in clerical and domestic occupations, maintaining the traditional roles of womanhood under the slogan 'Never at Sea'. By 1919, when the WRNS was disbanded, they had assumed many roles previously maintained as male domains, for example, acetylene welders, air armourers and cylinder cappers. 'But when the armistice was declared, it was reasoned that there was no longer any need to retain the service, and so, despite their enormous contributions and successes, the WRNS was finally disbanded in October 1919.'[23]

During the interwar period there was no official female, naval service, although low-level readiness was maintained by groups of volunteers. The spirit of the service was preserved by the Association of Wrens and, arguably, from 1920, through the creation of Sea Ranger units as part of the Guide Association. Many of these groups were led by former Wrens, including both of the first Directors: Katharine Furse and Vera Laughton Mathews. Furse, the World War I Director, was appointed head of the Sea Rangers in 1922.

The WRNS re-formed again in 1939 under the growing threat of a new European war. In World War II there was once again recognition that men would have to be freed for sea service and personnel numbers increased. It had again become politically and socially expedient to allow women to assume roles that had hitherto been regarded as the domain of men. Initially it was overseen by the Civil Establishment branch of the Admiralty, which meant that until April 1941 it had a civilian, rather than military status (although it would remain civilian in law by not coming under the Naval Discipline Act), which was different to what it had been in World War I and unexpected to its new leadership who regarded it as holding a military remit. Again, the WRNS were part of the naval service rather than being in the navy. Despite the fact that this status was being maintained until it came under the Naval Discipline Act in 1977, Wrens felt that they were in the Royal Navy, with only very few reflecting on this distinction in their testimonies.

The role of the WRNS was far greater in World War II. At the war's height the numbers of Wrens totalled around 72,000 members in some 200 shore establishments in the UK and 50 international bases. The branches of the WRNS had almost doubled by the end of World War II, with certain roles allowing women to train and assess male sailors. Wrens increasingly formed part of the decision making process in the RN, performing an instrumental role in the dispatch of RN warships. Wrens, in some instances, 'were responsible for issuing charts, typing and issuing sailing orders and allocating berths to ships'.[24] Some would even serve aboard the monster troopships as the war progressed, sending and receiving coded messages. There were also around 500 Boats Crew Wrens who worked on the small boats in harbours from 1943 to 1945, the most coveted and iconic WRNS role. The role Wrens came to play in the operational duties of the RN was shut down at the end of the war. Once again, the roles of women and men in the military were demarcated between that of combatant and non-combatant.[25] This distinction, which had emerged with the modern navy, would be maintained for over a century. Women could not serve on RN ships because it overstepped the acceptable bounds of females in military roles.

Studying the Women's Royal Naval Service

Following the maintenance of the service in 1945, it would take 45 years for the WRNS to gain parity with the Royal Navy (RN) (when women were allowed to serve at sea for the first time in 1990) and three more years for the separate service to be amalgamated with its male equivalent. Cultural sensitivities have maintained the combat taboo (the exclusion of women from military roles) until very recently. In fact, much of the information about the decision to allow women to serve in the Royal Navy has to still be obtained via a freedom of information request.[26] The WRNS acts as a distinct case study to explore the exclusion and inclusion of women in the British military, with this book being the first step in forming a full history of the service, from its first formation to the end of World War II.

Within the current academic literature, the WRNS is often supplementary to the history of women's experiences in World War I and World War II, or that of the other women's auxiliaries.[27] Accounts of Wrens are used to form comparisons with other women, building a broader narrative about feminine identities in war.[28] More recently, Wrens have been present in fictional or documentary accounts of Bletchley Park as the story of this most secret war work has become popularised. In these accounts, former Wrens have been interviewed and the photographs included show their work on the 'bombes'.[29] The presence of the WRNS in the accounts of Bletchley Park are perhaps the most widespread current inclusion of the service beyond its own histories.[30]

On the whole, the image of Wrens is positive in cultural memory. They are presented as 'good-humoured, no-nonsense' and 'pretty',[31] in their smart, naval uniforms, which linked them fundamentally with the 'senior service' of the Royal Navy.[32] Such images have come to embody the service in its memorialisation. This image was carefully maintained through the standards its leaders established from the start, rather than it being a fictionalised, romanticised later addition.

The establishment of the Women's Royal Naval Service in November 1917 during World War I, almost nine months after the Women's Auxiliary Army Corps (WAAC) had been established in March, was a natural consequence of a Britain gripped by total war; it was in no sense due to emancipatory sentiment, as its disbanding in 1919 attests. Its subsequent history, following its reformation in 1938, was shaped by a series of immediate, political and practical decision making, although this was increasingly affected and led by the women in the organisation itself.

The WRNS developed a sense of purpose, directed by strong leadership that made it a very independent force and which complemented the RN. It ultimately gained greater freedom than the ATS in its ability to make its own decisions, despite retaining a civilian legal status. The army did much to control the remit of the ATS, in part due to a whispering campaign about its reputation in the media. This ultimately led to the Markham Report in 1941.[33] Whilst this report debunked many of the rumours of the 'Cinderella' service, the ATS was always far more restricted in its remit and more 'domestic' in the roles it offered women.

The WRNS' distinct identity also came from it not needing conscripts, upon which the ATS relied.[34] The ability to select volunteers gave it a very different image, which the service used to its advantage, creating an aura of respectability.[35] As Jeremy Crang indicates, there was always a 'pecking order' among volunteers for the auxiliaries. Membership of the WAAF was always the most sought-after and '[t]he WRNS was also a popular preference. It was the smallest service and had a reputation for being highly selective'.[36] This could lead to an assumption that the service was more middle class and discriminating of women from such backgrounds. Undoubtedly, the service was more preferred by middle-class women, as is indicated in an official 1941 survey that found 30 per cent of women in category B class (middle class) would prefer to enter the WRNS if they had the choice, compared to 4 per cent of category D women (working class). For those wishing to join the WAAF, the numbers wanting to join the service was spread across classes B, C (skilled working class) and D at 36 per cent, 38 per cent and 27 per cent respectively.[37] However, this finding hides the meritocratic nature of the service, where skills and experience overturned social status.

Far from being the domain of middle-class women, the WRNS was very much focused on capability, looking for women who were intelligent or who showed the capacity to learn. Its leadership was not interested in promoting young women from the 'right' families; instead, they wanted women who could do the best job. Unlike the other services, all new-entry Wrens served on the 'lower deck' as ratings before being considered as potential officers (there were very few direct entrants), and good connections did not really enhance the potential of promotion. In fact, the WRNS allowed many women to become socially mobile.

The WAAF was similar to the WRNS in this respect, as the RAF, Martin Francis argues, 'appeared substantially less socially exclusive than the two other services'.[38] Unlike the other two women's auxiliaries, as Tessa Stone identifies, the WAAF was uniquely administered by men as part of the RAF, with women and men working alongside each other in mixed RAF commands, rather than being a separate service. This, she argued, led to full integration in the workplace with women and men's roles being interchangeable.[39] It meant the meritocratic nature of the RAF was transferred to its female sections. The assumptions that Wrens were more middle class, as will be explored in Chapter 5, was because many were educated to a higher level (in part due to the necessity of their roles) and because the Royal Navy was class-ridden, with male officers undoubtedly coming from middle-class backgrounds and far less likely to allow for social mobility through the ranks.[40]

The author has family experience of this, as her paternal grandfather, who joined the RN in the early 1930s, had to modify his Welsh accent to be recognisably southern. He was also stopped from referring to himself by his very recognisably Welsh middle name, Glyn. David Roberts faced a great deal of stigma for his social background, which he had to overcome in the early years of his service life. Men experienced many pressures in the RN to conform to the class expectations embedded within it, although, interestingly, as the war progressed, David would be promoted through the ranks to end up as a Lieutenant Commander, demonstrating that even this middle-class bastion would come under threat of the 'egalitarian structures of a so-called "people's war."'[41]

Whilst the WAAF was unprecedented in the workplace equality it experienced in the RAF, it did not have the same autonomy as the WRNS. The naval auxiliary pushed the bounds of what women could do whilst also being led by women. It decided to be meritocratic, despite being connected to a bastion of class division. This self-sufficiency, in part, came from its initial dual identity in the World War II that forced it to be independent, having been granted, somewhat unintentionally, greater freedom in decision making.

This led to its leadership building relationships with the various Commanders-in-Chief of the British and international naval bases, which resulted in the impromptu creation of new military roles for women. It allowed the service to widen its role internationally, militarily and within covert roles, subverting the combat taboo of female exclusion much as the other women's auxiliaries did to various degrees. The WRNS predominately challenged the taboo through covert operations such as boom defence – a cover for Operation Outward action of the release of balloons with trailing incendiaries – and by sending coders aboard monster troop ships. The ATS stationed servicewomen in its mixed-sex anti-aircraft batteries although they were not allowed to load or fire the weapons owing to the visibility of their role. And the role that directly contravened the exclusion of women from military roles were the female SOE agents who were sent undercover into occupied France.[42]

A wide range of sources have been used to form the history of this organisation, with particular importance placed upon the 21 original, oral histories conducted for this research, which bring to life the voices of actual women who were Wrens.[43] Other sources include official documents of the time; autobiographies of its leaders; over 60 memoirs held in the Imperial War Museum; and accounts in the BBC *People's War* archive.[44] The range of sources reflects the 'boom in memory' that Geoff Eley argues has occurred over the past 15 years.[45] We have become fascinated with all aspects of conflict, their impact, the people that experienced them and their legacy.

This cultural memory is extremely important in the way we view history and wartime experiences and events. It places the subjectivities and intersubjectivities of individuals within the culture of the society being explored.[46] More simply, it places facts, such as being an officer within the WRNS, alongside what it actually meant to have this role. In doing so it enables a greater complexity of experience to be exposed. It is closely aligned with the oral history tradition that became popular in the 1970s. Often regarded as a method of researching 'history from below', oral history and personal testimony — whether in autobiographical or memoir accounts held in archives, shared with magazines, or in media sources such as the BBC's *People's War* website — have become important sources to understand conflict and people's lives. Housden and Zmorczek state that 'telling one's life story, either formally through reminiscence and oral history, or informally with family and friends, is an essential part of exploring and developing one's sense of identity throughout life'.[47] We all have a narrative of our lives in our heads and these are often shared with other people. The author believed it was very important to gather the memories of women who were Wrens to be able to reflect on their experiences.

Nineteen of the interviewees were women who had served in World War II; two others were husbands of former Wrens. The latter could be regarded as part of the growing nature of family memories where stories are maintained within families who are able to share artefacts and accounts their family members shared with them.[48] The interviewees were aged between 83 and 95 when they were interviewed in 2010. The interviewees were encouraged to trace their lives back before they joined the WRNS, to reflect upon their family lives, education, previous work and then explore the nature of their service lives and the later impact, or lack thereof, on their future lives. The interviews were required to be flexible because of the challenge memory posed for some.

Specifics, such as where the women served and for how long, were returned to throughout the interview as stories about their different jobs arose. To the author they provide a direct link to the past, with an interview process that resulted in what appeared to be very honest accounts, particularly when many of the women discussed personal or taboo subjects, such as the woman who felt she was not as good a parent because being in the service had made her more independent minded, or the lady, who out of the blue, brought up the issue of lesbianism in the service. There was a definite sense that many of the interviewees saw their role in passing on their memories as important, and they enjoyed the opportunity to do so, for which the author is grateful.

There were problems with the cohort, however, as most were relatively young when they joined the service, meaning that the highest rank was one Second Officer. This meant there was no direct link to the decision making of higher-ranking officers. Archived official documents, memoirs and the autobiography of Vera Laughton Mathews have therefore had to be relied upon to help understand the nature of the service in the early years of World War II. In the history of World War I scant personal reminiscence has been recorded, which has resulted in a more 'traditional' historical account. However, this lacks the type of cultural memory present in later chapters.

The book adopts an interdisciplinary approach to form this history of the WRNS, a convention that has become increasingly more common in histories of gendered experiences of the world wars.[49] In doing so, it combines social history, as personified in the work of historians like Arthur Marwick, with feminist approaches that have sought to recover women's hidden histories, and broader gender histories of the wars that have, more recently, increasingly placed the experience of women alongside men, believing them not to be 'polarised or antithetical'.[50] These newer historical approaches use cultural memory as an important source. This identifies the family stories, and the popular and material culture that has come to form the legacy of the two world wars.[51] The book also addresses broader issues, as it is not possible to understand changes in gender roles within the military without appreciating the complex intersection it has with the culture of British society, the social position of women, political and military decision making and the national security situation throughout the two World Wars and the interwar period.

It does this by drawing on the work of sociologist Mady Segal who is concerned with determining the conditions for the inclusion of women in the military.[52] She has proposed the most important contribution to understanding the inclusion and exclusion of women from the military, providing a systematic theory of the variables that affect the degree and extent of female participation in the military.[53] Segal's theory focuses upon military changes from the 1980s onward. This makes the applicability to a historical study of female military involvement possibly challenging. However, as the first wide-ranging model to understand the reasons for the increase and decrease of female military inclusion, it is very useful.

She argues that women can only participate in the military under a number of conditions: the military come to see women as having a value within the armed forces; women change in ways which make them seem more suited for military service; or, the situation facing the nation is so critical that it is necessary to allow women to assist the military even if this contradicts the dominant cultural values of the society.[54] Segal contends that gender is a social construction, something that is repeatedly being renegotiated and re-formed. Women's military participation also does this, being based on cultural values of a particular society, within the context of social circumstances of the time. She sets out three conditions, which she argues determine the level of contraction and expansion of women taking on military roles, depending on the interaction of each. None are mutually exclusive; at times they will overlap, and in particular circumstances one could be completely overridden.

These three factors are the military, social structure and culture. The military includes the nation's security situation and aspects of military organisation and activity that affect women's roles, including technology, force structures and the combat to support ratio. The social structure pertains to demographics, aspects of women's civilian roles, including female participation in the labour force and social structural variables that affect women's roles, such as family structures. The cultural dimension includes how gender and family roles are socially constructed in society and what values are held toward female military participation. Segal suggested it was likely within any future research into the social construction of women's military roles that other conditions will need to be included. In a piece of research conducted in 2002, the theory was expanded by a group of sociologists, including Segal herself, exploring female military participation in Zimbabwe, Australia and Mexico.[55] In this expanded theory, the dimension of the political was included so that the leadership of the country and public policy surrounding gender roles is taken account of, as in Figure I.1.[56] The way in which the national security situation is addressed by political leadership is also included, relating to the way in which most countries have armed forces that are executively controlled by a government.

These factors will form important dimensions within the coming chapters. They place the formation of the WRNS in the two World Wars within their context to identify the particular circumstances that were necessary to create and grow the auxiliary.

Segal's theory provides points of focus to develop a deeper understanding of the WRNS as an institution. However, it neglects the individual biography of those involved or their interpersonal relationships, as advocated by historians engaged with cultural memory.[57] Segal herself addressed this as a need for future research. In addition, her theory may not pursue the historical context of events to the extent that historians such as Marwick have done. He suggested that there is no point in studying the effects of war without first grasping the essential features of the society.[58]

The combination of Segal's model with cultural memory approaches is used to build this history of the WRNS. The services

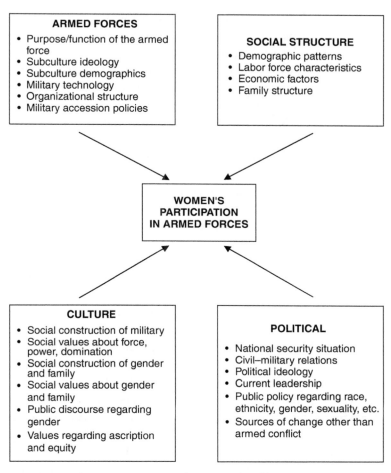

Figure I.1 Iskra et al.'s expansion of Segal's model of female military inclusion.

of World War I and World War II developed out of particular social structural and political conditions, influenced historically. These had shaped their leaders' own particular notions of identity that were imbued with cultural discourses relating to gender, the identity of the military organisation to which they were tied, and national identity. A few individuals, influenced by the social structure, who in turn had an influence on the lives of women who joined the auxiliaries, created the organisations. The individual biographies of those who made the decisions and the experience of the women who worked within the institution are therefore essential to understanding this process.

Each chapter seeks to explore the interlinking themes developed in the approach, using it as a way to consider a multiple range of factors that came to form, and in the case of World War II, grow and maintain the WRNS. The first chapter will explore the cultural, political and military conditions under which it was possible to form the first WRNS, concluding that political expediency in the face of a massive labour shortage in 1917 became the key reason for the formation of the service. It demonstrates the crucial role of the First Lord of the Admiralty, Sir Eric Geddes, in creating the service. His reorganisation of the Royal Navy's bureaucratic practices resulted in the subcultural ideological shift needed to form the first WRNS. The inclusion of his biographical details in this book is part of the modern way of placing the experience of men in wartime alongside women in order to understand gender. Chapter 2 continues the story of the World War I WRNS, showing the importance of Katharine Furse in the formation of its distinct identity, and a service which came under less scrutiny than its army equivalent. It will be argued that she established the high reputation of the service, which would be maintained as part of its ethos in World War II.

Chapter 3 moves into the interwar years, to show that the WRNS was not maintained post World War I, as part of a wider policy to reassert traditional gender norms, showing the significance of the social position of women in the 1920s and 1930s in maintaining their exclusion from the military. It outlines the national security situation nearing the end of this period and the processes, again more political than social, which influenced the formation of the second WRNS in 1938 even before war broke out.

The remaining chapters address the service in World War II. Chapter 4 explores how the service grew up until 1941 and the significance of its dual identity as civilian with a militarised mandate. It shows that the service was afforded a great deal of independence, due to the lack of Admiralty management, which meant it was able to move beyond its remit, building strong relationships with individual Commanders-in-Chief.

Chapter 5 explains how the WRNS was meritocratic in its employment procedures, marking it out as different from the ATS, which was dogged by the image of it being the 'Cinderella' service.[59] It counters the commonly held belief that the service was socially selective, demonstrating that the service was, in fact, more interested in women with ability and integrity. Chapter 6 explores how the role of the WRNS became essential to the running of the Royal Navy as the war progressed, with their roles increasingly becoming combatant, although never front line, subverting the combat taboo in a discreet and often secret manner, such as with the Operation Outward Wrens. Finally, Chapter 7 indicates the nature of relationships in the WRNS and the lives of individuals in terms of their sexual relationships, friendships and working interactions with officers and male personnel, always acted out within the confines of the service's strict moral code of behaviour.

The WRNS proved themselves to be essential in supporting the Royal Navy in World War II. The roles and operations they undertook throughout the war were many and varied, including combative jobs. Their leadership and recruitment practices were distinct, having come from different origins to their equivalents in the army and air force. This little-known organisation was an important British military institution that helped lay the ground for the changes in gender roles that would come.

CHAPTER 1

The Creation of the
World War I WRNS

The only consideration which influences me toward an integrated women's service is that I think it will be more efficient in the end. No question of the advancement of the women's cause, or anything of that kind, affects me in the slightest.[1]

Sir Eric Geddes, 1917

Sir Eric Geddes, political creator and military instigator of the WRNS, indicates in this letter to Katharine Furse that the first Women's Royal Naval Service, created in November 1917, was not the result of women's emancipation. 1917 represented a cultural change in the Royal Navy, based on wider political, cultural and social structural shifts created in a Britain gripped by total war that saw its leadership and institutional practices transformed. Certain individuals recognised the expediency of using female labour in response to productivity shortages facing the British government by this point of World War I, coupled with an unwillingness by the War Office to form one united women's auxiliary corps (which Geddes favoured), having formed the Women's Auxiliary Army Corps (WAAC) independently from the Navy in March 1917. Eric Geddes, as the First Lord of the Admiralty, was integral to this. His background is important to establish how the WRNS developed differently to its counterparts and how the Royal Navy came to be able to accept women carrying out naval duties.

The national security situation in Britain had become so dire by 1917 that an unusual response was required. British cultural norms and values toward the role of women in society had shifted somewhat during the war, allowing women to aid the war effort. However, these roles were 'predominantly seen as that of helping and supporting the vital male "work" of combat'.[2] It was a long, political process to make the idea of women doing 'war work' acceptable. Noakes, in her study of the role of women in the army, demonstrated the significance of women not being employed unless they were directly replacing a man who could go and fight. Within the WAAC in particular, attempts were made by the leadership to present the organisation as female rather than military, holding a supportive role by referring to the homely nature of their barracks.[3] The result was that the cultural norms of the time were maintained. The WRNS did much the same, forming a militaristic institution that was governed by strict rules of propriety.

It has been assumed in the current literature that the idea for the WRNS was the responsibility of Sybil Rocksavage, later the Marchioness of Cholmondeley, who suggested it to Geddes at a social gathering.[4] Documentary evidence does not support this, with sources about the formation of the service in the National Maritime Museum and Geddes' personal documents about the WRNS in the National Archives showing the difficulty of supporting such a claim. In fact, the evidence has only served to establish how important Geddes himself was in setting up the conditions possible to form a women's auxiliary for the Royal Navy.

The introduction of the WRNS by the Admiralty was the ultimate culmination of the increased value placed upon female labour as part of the wider inclusion of women into traditionally male occupations such as munitions (which Geddes had been involved with as the head of the Gun Ammunition Department) and the formation of the WAAC. It went against a 100 years of naval tradition as part of a general introduction of women officially into the military, and as a major political and military restructuring of the administration of the Royal Navy, which was placed within the wider administrative reforms of the Lloyd George government due to his desire to place men in roles to improve productivity and bureaucracy.

As such, Lloyd George's role is significant, as he was the person to select men to transform unproductive departments. Geddes could simply be seen as a tool of Lloyd George's wider political goal to achieve widespread reforms, with the formation of the WRNS as an aspect of this. However, the latitude he afforded Geddes, due to his very hands-off approach, meant the latter had the most significant impact on the changes in the navy and the formation of the WRNS. Lloyd George may have placed Geddes in a position of responsibility, but Geddes made the decisions and drove the reform of the Admiralty. Despite the precedent of a women's corps within the army, Geddes would not have been able to establish the WRNS without the reorganisation of the wider structure of the navy.

The Social Structural and Cultural Characteristics of Women's Employment Prior to 1917

Prior to assessing the specific political and military conditions which prompted the change in the Admiralty's policy toward the participation of women in the Royal Navy, it is necessary to trace the cultural and social structural composition of gender roles in British society leading up to the war and throughout the conflict. This is because of the way in which the social construction of gender, in terms of the norms and values concerning womanhood, influences their presence within political and military policy. Iskra et al. (expanding Segal's model) argue:

> an analysis of the culture and social conditions in a society inform much of the relationship between women and their participation in military forces. Through this dimension the underlying values and concepts of social relations are created in a society.[5]

World War I, Marwick argued, 'revealed very starkly the assumptions and attitudes which were widely held about women, and the sorts of discrimination customarily practised against them'.[6] The characterisation of women by social thinker John Ruskin is still pertinent in this period:

> her intellect is not for invention or creation, but for sweet ordering, arrangement, and decision ... By her office, and place, she is protected from all danger and temptation. The man, in his rough work in the open world, must encounter all peril and trial.[7]

Ruskin, seeking to define the role of middle-class women in this industrial period, demonstrates the broad dichotomy between the roles of women and men that were still present at the beginning of World War I.[8] The roles portrayed are stereotypical; women are depicted as virtuous, whereas men are faced with the dangers of life. The two sexes are responsible for different areas of social life; women held the expressive roles and men the instrumental.[9] These social roles were deeply embedded within the elites of Edwardian society, particularly the middle and upper classes, despite the opposition of some women at this time.

The growth of scientific thought, alongside traditionally held views of gender roles, meant that by the mid-Victorian era, there was an assumption of a 'natural order' based upon 'the supposed naturalness of women's supposed mental inferiority to men', particularly in the upper and middle classes.[10] It was at this time that social commentators were questioning the reasoning behind this staunchly held set of cultural and scientific beliefs. During the middle of the nineteenth century, the initial debate about female enfranchisement was beginning to emerge, and individual women were beginning to openly contradict the scientific and social arguments about the mental inferiority of women. This rise of intellectually capable and socially active women began to demonstrate the ability of females to go beyond their recognised social position, contending that there was no 'natural order'.

Florence Nightingale rejected the confines of the attitudes shared by the likes of Ruskin and indeed her own mother and sister. The archetypal protagonist, Nightingale demonstrated the ability of women to advance their roles beyond the social expectations of the time. She found the position of women at this time 'painful', recognising the obvious difficulty women had in contradicting the role prescribed for them, which in many cases would have resulted in derision and ridicule.[11] She became a figurehead for the inclusion of women in the military sphere through her nursing role in the Crimean War. The Secretary of State for War had requested that she oversee the introduction of female nurses into the Turkish military hospitals in 1854. Nightingale transformed the profession of nursing into one that was respectable for women, and in 1860 established the first professional training school for nurses at St Thomas' Hospital.[12]

In terms of Segal's expanded model,[13] it would seem in the case of Britain in World War I that the cultural dimension was not the most significant factor in allowing women to assume pseudo military roles by 1917. Even a cursory survey of the situation suggests that despite some improvements this could not have played a big part, beyond maintaining expectations of women's behaviour when the corps were formed, as throughout the early years of the war traditional gender roles were maintained. Nursing clearly supports this argument as it was the one profession where it was acceptable for women to be included in military roles, simply because it still allowed them to maintain a link to their expressive role.

Jenny Gould describes how the inclusion of women's labour in a potential conflict had not been considered in military planning prior to August 1914, other than in regard to a nursing role. The First Aid Nursing Yeomanry (FANY) was formed in 1907, 'with the aim of training its members as nurses on horseback to ride out from field hospitals to the battlefield'. Three years later, the Voluntary Aid Detachment (VAD) was formed as a reserve of the Territorial Force Medical Service for mobilisation in case of invasion. They would provide voluntary aid to the sick and wounded.[14] These services in the early years of the war were small and respected. However, middle-class women who joined other forms of voluntary organisations other than nursing or first aid were often ridiculed with the schemes being regarded as a 'fashionable fad'.[15] Many women's organisations set up in order to help the war effort were scorned. Participating in knitting garments for soldiers, for example, a popular voluntary activity, was not always appreciated, especially when it was unclear what the objects were supposed to be.[16]

Shifts were occurring within gender roles during the Edwardian period, however. The 'sex war', which had been waged by the suffragist movement from 1897, had reached its peak by 1914, soon after its effectiveness fell into decline because of the claim that by continuing their 'war' the women were being unpatriotic. Although it had not yet reached the Royal Navy, the social construction of gender roles, particularly those of middle- and upper-class women, was beginning to undergo a process of change by the end of the Victorian period.

These changes should not be overstated. 'For all that was achieved, inequality between the sexes was as clearly defined in Edwardian society as inequality between the classes'.[17] Most of the women of Britain were working class. They had always worked and were subject to pitiable pay and poor conditions. British society by 1914 was still the bourgeois industrial society of the nineteenth century. Female enfranchisement, of any kind, had not been achieved. Social values of gender roles still regarded women as inferior, socially, economically and politically.

At the outbreak of war on 4 August 1914, hundreds of women enthusiastically volunteered to help in anyway they could. Gould argues that 'although women's support for the war effort was widely approved, the idea that women might play roles other than those of nurse, fundraiser, knitter or canteen organiser was not popular'. There were still strict conventions of women's roles 'expressed most vehemently by those who also opposed women's suffrage'.[18] At the beginning of the war, despite some cultural changes to the nature of women's social roles, traditionally held beliefs were still deeply entrenched. There was not the cultural will to allow women to take on military roles at this time. Hostility was shown toward women choosing to wear khaki or joining pseudo-military organisations such as the Women's Volunteer Reserve (RVS), whose object, according to its colonel-in-chief, the Marchioness of Londonderry, was to organise women to release men for active service. This negativity decreased in the last two years of the war, but there remained a conflict between those who felt that women should not work outside their accepted occupations of sewing, nursing or cooking, and those who argued women should be organised along military lines similar to that of their male counterparts.[19]

Martin Pugh argues that the Great War made gender divisions extra clear and overwhelmed the 'sex war'.[20] The early years of the war had a massive impact on the role of women. Working-class women experienced high levels of unemployment, due to the loss of textile work, whereas middle-class women had voluntarily taken up clothes making for the troops, affecting 50,000 women who were out of paid work by March 1915.[21] Roles of women and men were firmly placed within the confines of traditional gendered narratives in the early years of the conflict. This was a very different cultural environment from Britain in 1938, where it was seen as essential that women volunteer to join military auxiliary corps as soon as war broke out.

Female Labour Characteristics Before and During the War

It was the escalation of the conflict, rather than cultural changes that led to the wider inclusion of women in the labour market and subsequently the development of the women's auxiliaries. In 1914, there were fewer than 6 million women in paid employment in the UK and Ireland.[22] Arthur Marwick argues that there were three stages in the war which affected the role and participation of women. The first phase of the war he calls the period of 'war emergency' followed by that of 'business as usual', which lasted from August 1914 to the early summer of 1915. In this stage, there was very little involvement of women. The second phase began with the creation of the new Coalition Government, established in May 1915, that created a separate Ministry of Munitions, which, as will be shown, would employ around 607,000 more women by 1918 than in 1914. Marwick states 'the still more important, and indeed absolutely crucial, turning-point came with the introduction of universal military conscription for men in May 1916'.[23] The Act meant that men removed from the Home Front to fight would need to be replaced.

Noakes found the first sign of a change in the official attitudes towards female war work came in 1915, supporting Marwick's second phase, which included the National Registration Bill. Debate in the House of Commons shows there was a split based between those MPs who felt the role of women should be as homemakers and mothers, versus the demand by women's groups that they should be included and service should be organised more efficiently to ensure there was no wastage of labour. The Bill was passed and led to the National Registration Act, which required women and men aged between 16 and 65 to record their occupations. This would then be used by the National Service Department to place women in suitable roles.[24] However, in the end the NSD placed very few women in war-related employment and rather than form the necessary women's groups, as would be done at the beginning of World War II, led to the burgeoning of unofficial women's uniformed voluntary groups that were not favoured by a wide swathe of the public because they were led by middle- and upper-class women with no clear mandate.

Phase three was the most significant to the increase of female participation because of the need to replace men conscripted into service and because of the demands total war was putting on the country. This meant by the end of 1918 the number of women in paid employment had increased by over 1.5 million to between 7.25 and 7.5 million.[25] This increase was significant; Searle argues it was 22.5 per cent, with other historians putting the number as high as 25.5 per cent.[26] Yet five in six women continued to be employed in what could be termed to be 'women's work',[27] particularly domestic service, although the latter had faced a decline throughout the war; in 1914 there were one million six hundred and fifty-eight thousand female domestic servants, but in 1918 this had decreased to one million two hundred and fifty-eight thousand.[28]

The increase of women in employment by 1.25 million was made up of working-class women who had not been working before because of home commitments, but also by a growing number of middle-class women, women who entered the labour force in 1917 in organisations such as the WRNS and the WAAC. 1917 saw an overall increase in employment of women in all industries.[29] By the end of the war, if all the industries and auxiliary services of the war are included, over 1 million women had entered paid employment for the first time.[30] This represents a significant change in the social and economic circumstances for women.

It is apparent that the involvement of women in industry only really became widespread by 1917, despite the change of policy in 1915, which reinforces Marwick's phase three as being the most significant. Prior to this, such participation was not culturally acceptable. A shift in values had occurred in British society toward the role of women, which was not really due to the gains women had been making for emancipation leading up to the war. The crucial condition for the increase of women in industry and subsequently the creation of the WRNS was the national security situation and the associated political decision making process of 1916–17.

Sir Eric Geddes: The Creator of the WRNS

The Women's Royal Naval Service of World War I was born from the shrewd business mind of the Great War efficiency reformer and eventual First Lord of the Admiralty, Sir Eric Geddes. As part of Lloyd George's wider vision for managing the war, he prompted a subcultural ideological shift in this most traditional of military establishments, founding the conditions to form the first WRNS.[31]

Born in 1875, the son of a railway constructor, Geddes was not in the mould of a typical leader of the Royal Navy. He had become Deputy General Manager of the North East Railway in 1911, at the relatively young age of 36, after a meteoric rise to power having demonstrated extraordinary talent for organisation. The North East Railway was one of the most powerful companies in the country at the time; as such, Geddes' position shows him to be a leading businessman and innovator.

Even before 1914, he was renowned for his organisational and problem-solving ability. His General Manager, Alexander Butterworth said of Geddes, 'I can speak personally as to his quite exceptional ability . . . drive and organising faculty. He has plenty of tact and knowledge of the world and gets on well with military men, as well as politicians.'[32]

Geddes' obvious capability to make complex infrastructure work more efficiently in the private sector gained him recognition within government. In April 1915, he met with Lord Kitchener, who at the time was Secretary of State for War. Kitchener put forward the idea of appointing businessmen as supervisory officers in large private sector munitions factories. As it was, 'the Board of Ordnance did not welcome the suggestion that men with industrial or commercial experience were appropriate recruits to the organisation of munitions work'.[33] At the time, under the leadership of Prime Minister Herbert Asquith, businessmen were kept firmly separate from war industrialism. Until 1916, appointing civilians to positions of authority in military departments held no precedent. However, with the growing challenges of total war, it became more commonplace to entrust the large-scale organisation of labour and production to business-men of with recognised experience.

The attitude of the Board of Ordnance was challenged following the Great Shell Scandal. This was one of the most damaging moments in the war for the Asquith government.[34] Throughout early 1915 David Lloyd George had publicly and actively criticised the Board's 'existing methods' of shell production, as had the media, including *The Times*.[35] In response, April 1915 saw the creation of the Munitions of War Committee under the leadership of Lloyd George. This later became the Ministry of Munitions in May 1915 following the formation of the new Coalition government.[36] The aim of Lloyd George's new ministry, arguably the hardest job in politics at the time,[37] was to address poor levels of output and management and to provide 'a stronger approach to the procurement of munitions'.[38]

Lloyd George was increasingly drawn to 'go-ahead' men of industry rather than party loyalists or other MPs.[39] Under his ministry, civilians were no longer disengaged from warfare and separate from the military, as had been the case in previous wars. He believed that the War Office was not a flexible enough administrative unit to deal with the rapid equipping of armies on its own.[40] Only with the mass mobilisation of the country, both in terms of people who could set in place infrastructures of production for total war, and in the use of labour from all members of the country fit enough to work, would it be possible to maintain the manufacturing required to keep Britain in the war.

In line with Lloyd George's attitude, Geddes was seized upon almost instantaneously in May 1915 to assist in the creation of his new ministry. In an extract from Grieves's biography of Geddes, the process by which Lloyd George appointed him is outlined:

> Geddes found the experience of being interviewed by the Minister of Munitions somewhat bewildering. He described his 'hiring' by Lloyd George, to A. J. Sylvester in 1932, as a process similar to the treatment of casual labourers in docks. Lloyd George, he continued, 'asked me if I knew anything about munitions. I did not. He asked me what I could do. I said I had a faculty for getting things done. 'Very well' said he, 'I will make you head of the department.' He was one of over ninety men of business experience recruited to the Ministry of Munitions in the first three months.[41]

Lloyd George's determination to get competent men in place to address the shell crisis is evident in this extract. The interview also highlights Lloyd George's reputation for being 'unconventional'.[42] Dissatisfied by current working practices, he was willing to take an unorthodox approach in the aim of winning the war as quickly as possible with the least waste of materials and human life. Throughout the war, within his many roles, Lloyd George would continue to bring experienced civilians into government roles.[43]

On 28 December 1915, Geddes was appointed head of the Gun Ammunition Department, which included responsibility for the construction, equipping and staffing of the New Filling Factories.[44] In this role he helped bring female labour into the munitions industry during his time in the ministry.

Geddes' approach fitted within Lloyd George's vision of increased productivity. The latter had done much to boost the workforce levels, setting the precedent for the inclusion of women in war industries. Up until May 1915, very little had been done to include women.[45] In July 1915 there had been 256,000 women employed in the munitions industries and by 1916 this had doubled to 520,000. A year later, in part, arguably, due to the National

Service Scheme, this had tripled to 819,000[46] as men already in employment were signing up for war work in other locations.[47] Around 20,000 factories came under direct government control with the Munitions of War Act 1915. Government control over munitions meant it became possible for the Ministry to employ women outside the jurisdiction of the male-dominated trade unions, which had often created barriers against women workers.[48]

Alan Simmonds suggests that by the summer of 1915 'the terms of industrial employment had turned in women's favour. Opportunities had expanded.'[49] This was in part due to two factors. The first was the Munitions of War Act in July 1915, which allowed the government to reorganise wartime industrial production, simplifying processes that used to require skilled labour or by using greater automation. The other was an increased demand for women's work as a result of the boost in industrial activity.[50] At the end of 1918, 39 per cent of the Ministry of Munitions' staff were women.[51] Marwick notes how technological change, through the mechanisation of processes, helped to remove the significance of women's lesser physical strength, which had always been used as an argument to exclude women from industrial work.[52] This would continue to be an argument used to exclude women from sea service in the Royal Navy until 1990.

The use of state propaganda, such as posters for female munitions workers stating 'These Women are Doing Their Bit', spurred on the use of female labour, which saw the steady expansion of women working in the government controlled munitions factories. Propaganda became very significant to the recruitment of women, using heavily patriotic yet also reproachful messages. As social values were adjusted to fit new demands of the war, in this case the lack of workers in the munitions industry, it became more acceptable for women to undertake work of a dangerous and strenuous nature. Adaptations were made to the industry to ensure women would want to work, such as regulations created from 1916 onwards to protect women's working rights.

The type of propaganda employed allowed for a mass cultural shift in the discourse of acceptable gender roles. Feminists, such as Nancy Goldman, have argued, however, that these changes 'were imposed by men upon women who had no vote; wartime experiences enforced independence, they dealt out death to some, bereavement to many, suffering to most'.[53] Although women became a massive part of the war production industries increasing the freedom of many, it was an enforced role, one which few women were able to negotiate.

The Expansion of Geddes' Wartime Role

The Woolwich Arsenal, which filled over 90 per cent of all shells in the UK, came under the scrutiny of Lloyd George when the factories were transferred to Ministerial control on 19 August 1915. Woolwich, due to its ineffective management, was hampering the entire process of shell production across the country. The workforce in June 1915 only consisted of 34,000 people, 195 (0.57 per cent) of them women, and too few to deal with the output needed.[54] By May 1916, the workforce had increased to 60,000, including 10,000 (16.6 per cent) women.[55]

His work was challenging and difficult. At times, his relationship with Lloyd George was strained. In March 1916, Geddes' wife, Ruth Lee, described her husband as 'discouraged and utterly exhausted' because Lloyd George was constantly harrying his department. It seems he failed at the time to appreciate the magnitude of the task of shell production and he eventually turned on Geddes for a lack of productivity.[56] However, by July 1916 Lloyd George's attitude reversed. He rewarded Geddes with a knighthood (GCB) in 1916 for the successful implementation of a new working policy that produced enough shells to meet the deadline for the Somme offensive.[57]

When Lloyd George became Secretary of State for War in July 1916 it became a condition of his appointment that selected businessmen, including Geddes, would follow him to the War Office. Because of this, during the latter months of 1916 Geddes was appointed Director-General of Military Railways and a member of the Army Council, with the rank of Honorary Major-General.[58]

During this period, he developed a strong working relationship with Sir Douglas Haig (who at the time was heading the Somme offensive, and in January 1917 was made a Field Marshal). In this role Geddes was afforded far greater executive freedom.[59] It was his changing relationship with Lloyd George, alongside respect earned from military leaders such as Haig, which meant that Geddes became increasingly trusted to get the job done without constant oversight. This ultimately resulted in Geddes being offered more powerful and influential roles in the government, not least within the Royal Navy.

The subcultural ideological shift of the Royal Navy

The end of 1917 saw a very different Royal Navy emerge than had been in existence at the start of the year. The changes to the navy of both leadership and policy represent a subcultural ideological shift within the institution, which saw the traditional approach, represented in the leadership of First Sea Lord Admiral John Jellicoe, challenged and redressed by men like Geddes.[60] This would open the way for the male-dominated Royal Navy to officially grant access for the first time in its history.

Lloyd George had become increasingly anxious about the ineffectiveness with which the war was being waged by 1916. The coalition cabinet created in May 1915 was too large and subsequently unwieldy. It was doing little to address the political and domestic upheavals of the time, such as ensuring that there was fair conscription of fighting men. An article in the *Manchester Guardian* on 6 December 1916 denounced the Asquith cabinet, declaring: 'Nothing is foreseen, every decision is postponed. The war is not actually directed – it directs itself.'[61] This disorganisation, which had been evident in the munitions industry in 1915, had become a regular feature of the government. Lloyd George felt the position had become untenable and by December 1916 he offered an alternative war cabinet, which would have seen Asquith sidelined but still Prime Minister. Asquith's expected refusal of Lloyd George's proposal led in the end to his eventual resignation. On 7 December Lloyd George was invited by the King to form a ministry as Prime Minister. The establishment of this new government led to far greater direct state control of the war effort, replacing the mixture of government and voluntary action, which had characterised the first half of the conflict.[62]

The Admiralty, often called the 'state within a state', soon came under the scrutiny of the new Prime Minister with his visit to the Admiralty on 20 April.[63] Following this, Lloyd George began to rationalise the management of shipbuilding and the organisation of dockyards, which he saw as being in a 'chaotic condition'.[64] At this point in the war, with the unrestricted U-boat campaign being waged by the Imperial German Navy, Sir Walter Runciman (previously President of the Board of Trade) had warned that 'a complete breakdown in shipping would come before June 1917'.[65]

Lloyd George tackled the reform of the Royal Navy in much the same way as he had done with munitions production, radically, by creating a new ministry and by appointing civilians with proven records of accomplishment to take on its leadership and control. In 1917 he created the Ministry of Shipping. This was designed to address the mismanagement of resources at the Admiralty, particularly supply, much as the Ministry of Munitions had done. As a proven reorganiser, on 11 May 1917 Geddes was appointed Controller of the Navy. This post provided Geddes with a position on the Admiralty Board as a civilian with the rank of Vice Admiral. The aim of the role was for Geddes to develop a ship building programme. It was also part of Lloyd George's plan to impose change upon the navy. As a result, May 1917 marked the beginning of a rapid era of reform within naval affairs, both in terms of strategy and bureaucracy.[66] For example, Geddes' appointment as Controller led to the first investigation of the war into the relationship of construction rates to tons of shipping produced. This is not to say that Geddes had it easy. Lloyd George left him to resolve the bureaucratic hindrances in the Admiralty with little involvement on his part.

The reason Geddes was given a naval rank lay in the suspicions some of the Admiralty Board held towards the addition of a civilian. This opposition was voiced by Vice Admiral Sir Henry Oliver who was critical of the 'bright people full of new ideas from the north'.[67] What was regarded as an intrusion into naval traditions of leadership meant First Sea Lord John Jellicoe refused to give Geddes 'control of design and inspection' of shipping production, and First Lord Edward Carson did not reconcile the design and supply branches, which only resulted in a continued overlap of resources and a far lower rate of manufacture than Lloyd George desired.[68] Geddes was shocked by the Admiralty Board's inability to attain executive requirements of decision making. This led him to split it into two committees, one for operations and the other for maintenance, marking a significant shift in the organisation of the Royal Navy.[69]

The 'intricacies of naval convention' and Jellicoe's 'persistent reluctance or rather refusal to delegate authority' infuriated Geddes throughout the former's time in authority.[70] The Admiralty was burdened by the weight of its organisational structure, which loaded those working for it with too much paperwork and specificity. Including the First Sea Lord, who did not possess the will to change it. Jellicoe was regarded by Lloyd George as a pessimist and 'apt to get "cold feet" if things did not go quite right'. Haig had become convinced that the Admiralty was not safe in his hands. Following the War Cabinet meeting on 20 June 1917, he shared this view of Jellicoe's approach to leadership. Haig arranged a meeting with Geddes to determine the state of affairs.

The latter expressed his disquiet. He saw the First Sea Lord as 'feeble to a degree and vacillating' and the First Lord Sir Edward Carson was very tired, leaving everything to his admirals.[71] In response, Haig agreed to relay Geddes' concerns to Lloyd George and Lord Curzon (a member of the War Cabinet).

The next day Geddes, Haig and Lloyd George held a meeting at which the Prime Minister resolved that 'something must be done at once'. The consequence of which was the dismissal of Carson because of the obstruction he had formed to effective action in the Admiralty.[72] Surprisingly, to many, Lloyd George eventually took the decision to appoint Geddes as First Lord of the Admiralty, desiring a minister with 'greater reserve of vitality ... and greater mastery of detail'.[73] He offered him the post on 6 July 1917 (only 16 days after Geddes expressed his concerns), and he was eventually appointed on 17 July.

It is not evident from the archives whether Geddes was unaware of the possibility of receiving this appointment or whether it had been planned between the two men in June. However, in the years after his appointment, Geddes said that 'he did not want it'.[74] In March 1918, he wrote in a memo 'when the day comes to relinquish it, no one shall be better pleased than I'.[75] This was in part due to his dislike of the political side of his ministerial job and a desire to return to his passion for transportation systems.

In an interview with George Riddell of The Newspapers Proprietors Association, Limited on 13 August 1917, Geddes is reported to have said that his role at the Admiralty was to improve administrative organisation, to establish the Admiralty on a business-like footing, and to improve the Admiralty war staff's productivity.[76] These were the aspects that Lloyd George had found lacking at the Admiralty following his inspection in April 1917. It was clear that Geddes' intention was not to interfere with 'naval strategy'; instead, his focus was upon streamlining the Admiralty.[77]

In the eyes of some, including Beatrice Webb (Co-founder of the London School of Economics), Geddes' rise to the political head of the Admiralty was viewed as one of the 'most sensational' changes made in the Lloyd George reforms of 1917.[78] Within his new role, Geddes' latitude to implement change increased, flouting hundreds of years of naval tradition in the process, much as he would do by creating the WRNS.

However, owing to the Prime Minister's 'hands-off' approach, Geddes was left to try and negotiate the challenges of ministerial responsibility without knowing its procedures. He was also constrained in his action because, despite leading a fighting department, he was not a member of the War Cabinet, and Jellicoe was still causing obstructions to reform by pessimistically addressing the problems of the navy. Throughout his year as First Sea Lord, Jellicoe increasingly came to be associated with the deteriorating naval outlook, including the stalemate in the North Sea and the effect of the sustained U-boat offensive.[79]

The result of these various issues was Geddes' eventual dismissal of Jellicoe from his post on 24 December 1917. The tone of the letter he sent to Jellicoe informing him of his decision is cordial but direct, an approach for which he was sometimes criticised.[80] In it, he states:

> After very careful consideration I have come to the conclusion that a change is desirable in the post of First Sea Lord. I have not, I can assure you, arrived at this view hastily or without great personal regret and reluctance.[81]

Interestingly, Geddes does not provide an explanation for his dismissal of the First Sea Lord; instead, he merely explains that change is needed and that Jellicoe would receive a peerage 'in recognition of your past very distinguished services'. However, according to Patterson, Jellicoe's position had become more untenable by December 1917. Doubts about his ability to adequately fulfil his role dogged his year as First Sea Lord. He had come to be seen, in the eyes of many, such as Lloyd George, Geddes and Haig, as 'a tired and over-conscientious man who could not delegate business, constantly overworked himself and always saw the black side of things clearly'.[82]

Within the National Archives is a speech that Geddes wrote for the House of Commons on 6 March 1918, but which he never delivered. In it, he explains his reasons for removing Jellicoe:

> I knew that Lord Jellicoe had not impressed the Prime Minister, and also other members of the War Cabinet ... After close association with Lord Jellicoe for 5 months as First Lord, I arrived at the conclusion deliberately, and regretfully (I am sorry to have to say this but it has been rendered necessary by statements which have been made in this House and elsewhere) that Lord Jellicoe did not evidence progressive adaptability and effectiveness in decision. Therefore, entirely as a result of my own uninfluenced judgment, I thought the change should be made.[83]

Jellicoe had not been the man to make the navy more efficient with reform. The piece reflects Jellicoe as a 'relic', outdated and unadaptable. Even Admiral Beatty, who was careful not to assail

Jellicoe personally, attacked the Admiralty, stating in a letter to Carson in April 1917:

> The impression left on my mind was that there seemed to be a lack of concrete ideas and principals ... Cut and dried plans based on sound principles were lacking ... We are not using the brains and energy of the youth of the service.[84]

Ultimately, Geddes' decision to dismiss Jellicoe demonstrates his goal of greater efficiency and organisation within the Admiralty, which would later have so much to do with the establishment of the WRNS. The statement also serves to highlight his independence from Lloyd George. It is not apparent in their dealings that they had become friendly. Sir Rosslyn Wemyss (Jellicoe's successor as First Sea Lord) in his memoirs stated Geddes 'hated the job' of dismissing Jellicoe from his post.[85] Geddes even tried to return to transportation work thereafter; however, Lloyd George was disinclined to release him 'from a department where administrative reform was vital'.[86] Although unwilling, Geddes did achieve widespread improvements in the working practices of the Admiralty and contact with the Grand Fleet had become smoother.[87]

The change of leadership within the Admiralty in 1917 has been much debated in the literature and remains a controversial issue. Some have argued that Geddes could not have come to the decision to dismiss Jellicoe alone owing to this limited political experience. However, that Lloyd George remained aloof and the evidence of Geddes' abandoned House of Commons speech may demonstrate his independence in this decision.[88]

It is argued here, however, that the subcultural ideological shift the Royal Navy underwent during this period pushed it to reform its organisational structure.[89] These adaptations to the organisation and running of the navy laid the way for the creation of the WRNS because it became possible for the first time to see where men needed to be substituted for and where additional roles created. The dismissal of Jellicoe occurred at the same time as Geddes' formation of the women's auxiliary. The presence of the First Sea Lord would have proved a challenge in this endeavour because of, first, the lack of organisational structures within the Admiralty, which were necessary to make such a change, and, second, the values held by Jellicoe and Carson in relation to the Royal Navy. Carson had stated in the past that he would not let politicians interfere with the running of the Admiralty whilst he was in power and would let sailors have full scope.[90] And Jellicoe was not open to ideas voiced from inexperience and regarded the problems facing the Admiralty with a deep pessimism.

Geddes, on the other hand, represented the advent of new ideas and an alternative perspective on running large institutions, shaped by his previous experience within the transportation and munitions industries. In addition, he was pushed into the leadership by Lloyd George who swooped on opportunity like a hawk and who was intensely vital, indomitable and ruthless in his goal to make every gain he could in the aim of keeping Britain in the war.[91]

The conduct of the war over its five years was the catalyst for these changes. The great bastion of the Royal Navy was on rocky ground by 1917, compounded by problems of shipping shortages, unrestricted submarine warfare, a lack of staff and ineffective leadership. Had there not been a strong political leadership at this time, the navy might have faced greater decline and it would have been unlikely that it would have had the bureaucratic structure to enable the formation of the WRNS.

Geddes' 'Bombshell'

Turning now to the actual creation of the WRNS, it has been assumed within the literature that the idea for the Women's Royal Naval Service came from Sybil Rocksavage (later the Marchioness of Cholmondely), sister of Sir Philip Sassoon. Rocksavage was friends with Mona Chalmers Watson, Eric Geddes's sister and leader of the WAAC. In a biography of her life by Peter Stanksy, it is claimed:

> the dramatic event was her becoming fully involved in the war as, in effect the founder of the WRNS . . . or at the very least the originator

of the idea ... The idea for it originated in a conversation Sybil had with Eric Geddes. He was one of the businessmen whom Lloyd George had brought in to help with the war effort ... Sybil knew him socially and at one point she suggested there were many jobs women could do in the Navy that could free a man to go to sea.[92]

Mason suggests in her history of the WRNS that Lady Rocksavage had invited Geddes for drinks on St George's Day and had suggested using women for shore duties. Geddes 'looked stunned. I don't think it had occurred to him before.'[93] It is difficult to know whether this is true as Mason's lack of references for her sources makes corroboration difficult.

It may well have been that Geddes had not thought about it before. However, the sources suggest they met on St George's day, which would have been 23 April 1917, a month before Geddes was appointed Controller of the RN by Lloyd George. The evidence does not seem to fit the reality of what actually happened. Although Lady Rocksavage may have made such a suggestion, the impact this had on the creation of the WRNS is questionable. Geddes was in no position to make such a decision when the social event occurred, and in any event, the suggestion was merely that, as Stansky states, Lady Rocksavage had little experience of war administration; she was only 23 years old at the time. She had no real knowledge of women's organisations, with her life 'not all that different to what it might have been if there weren't a war on' up until that point.[94] What she could have contributed, other than the idea of having a women's naval service, like the army equivalent (formed in March 1917) is questionable. The precedent of an army auxiliary being run by his sister was a much more likely influence over Geddes' eventual decision to form the WRNS as was his use of female labour power in the munitions industry.

Coupled with this was the critical labour shortage that prompted the change in policy that allowed women to assume roles within the military structure of the navy. 1917 saw the emergence of an Admiralty with the subcultural values to see the potential in the use of substituting women for men, which had been shown in other industries and the army to be socially tolerable. Geddes appointed a committee to address the issue of labour shortage. His plan was to release almost 100,000 men for sea service by 1918. Most of these men would be non-substantive ratings (men trained but not yet in service), accounting for 71,319.[95] In all 7,000 WRNS served during and just after the war. Had the war continued past 1918 it is very likely far more women would have been employed in the service.

Wherever possible, men were replaced with female labour so that no man would be enlisted for work where a woman or a man categorised as physically unfit for military service was able to carry it out. In 1917 a limited amount of female labour was already being used in the Royal Navy, particularly as clerks. Geddes' approach to reorganisation indicates that a unified women's auxiliary corps, with its own rules and leadership, would be far more efficient in replacing men than a random assortment of women who were assisting departments here and there.

Without the use of female labour, it would have been impossible to free as many men for sea service as was achieved between 1917 and 1919. In a meeting which took place on 11 November 1917, Geddes explained to Katharine Furse how the War Office was reluctant to share the WAAC with the navy, as 'had been suggested and as he thought the best policy'. Instead, he proposed dropping a 'bombshell' by immediately setting up a competing service of women for the RN.[96] This reflects his desire for efficiency; debating with the War Office to form a united women's service would have got nowhere. Therefore, it was more expedient to get on and establish the navy's own corps.

The WAAC had been established along similar lines as the army, but maintained as a clearly separate organisation. The official announcement of its start was made in March 1917. The introduction of the Military Service Act, introducing conscription for men in January 1916, meant there had to be a reconsideration of the role of women in war work by 1917. Concerns were widespread about the need for more labour, but equally the potentially destabilising nature of having women behind the lines in France. 'The introduction of women into the army was to be managed in such a way as to not destabilise the existing "natural" linkage between masculinity and soldiering.'[97] Lieutenant-General H. M. Lawson had commissioned a study to assess which occupations could be carried out by women in France. One suggestion of his report, which helped to resolve fears was that women should not be integrated in the army, rather they 'must form part of definitive units provided with their own women officers and NCOs'.[98] Strict control was made of the WAAC early on, the intention was 'women's work with the armed forces was not to become an opportunity for women to prove they were the equals of men and thus claim equal citizenship'.[99]

The leadership of the army was not that interested in the opinions of women.[100] There was a very strong determination to keep the male and female spheres of war firmly separate, with women maintaining their traditional roles, rather than winning an opportunity for emancipation. Whilst this was the same within the WRNS, the very distinct difference was the independence afforded to Furse by Geddes in the formation of the service.

Initially, women in the WAAC were recruited to work in France, with the first draft sent on 31 March 1917. It was not until July that the Army Council Instruction 1069 authorised the employment of the WAAC for both home and overseas duties. The War Office oversaw the auxiliary, with the women's branch of the Adjutant General's department having been formed in January 1917. Its Chief Controller was Mona Chalmers Watson and Helen Gwynne-Vaughan was appointed Controller of the WAAC in France.[101] Both were upper-class professionals, Chalmers Watson a medical doctor and Gwynne-Vaughan a lecturer in botany at Birkbeck College. She would also become the Commandant of the Women's Royal Air Force (WRAF) in 1918 and later would become the first Chief Controller of the ATS, World War II's equivalent of the WAAC, from 1939 to 1941.

From Geddes' letters to Furse in November 1917, it is clear that for Geddes the creation of the WRNS was not based upon any liberal ideas of emancipating women, in much the same vein as had been stated by the Adjutant-General Leigh-Wood. In a letter to Furse (14 November 1917), Geddes asserted that he felt the creation of a women's service would be more efficient than the current situation. He did not take the decision out of a desire for female emancipation, merely what was the most logical step. To achieve a more efficient and effective navy, the use of female labour was a natural conclusion, based upon his experience of employing women in the munitions industries and the promising work demonstrated by women in the VAD and the WAAC. Although he desired a women's corps to assist both Armed Forces (the RAF was formed 1 April 1918), the still unwieldy nature of the War Office did not make this possible.

The WRNS may have been created without him but Geddes was the one who took the decision to create the service. In many respects, his decision to use female labour is an extension of his overall attitude to the organisation and running of the navy. He took a logical approach to a situation that was becoming untenable: the decline in available labour (by the end of the war 67,000 seamen were either dead or injured) and the need to increase shipping output.

CHAPTER 2

The World War I WRNS: 1917–19

If Geddes was the political and military instigator of the WRNS, Katharine Furse was its constructor, the individual tasked to build and shape the service. Her testimony and archived documents are very important in this chapter in helping form a picture of the service due to the lack of remaining evidence about World War I WRNS. The WRNS leadership was given far more latitude than the army auxiliary by the Admiralty, which in both wars left it to get on with the job. As such, Furse's character and experience directly shaped the WRNS in a way that did not occur in the WAAC (which became the Queen Mary's Army Auxiliary Corps in 1918).

Unlike the service of World War II, the first WRNS was more significantly delineated along class lines, as opposed to the egalitarian nature of its second inception. The first WRNS also had a much shorter time in which to develop (two years, as opposed to the seven of World War II, which would turn into 48 before the service was amalgamated with the Royal Navy in 1993). Despite its brief existence, the first WRNS did establish a foundation of tradition and expectation of behaviour, which would be carried into the future.

Katharine Furse

A formidable woman, known as a 'shover' by members of the other women's services, Furse held several positions of power throughout the war.[1] Early on she was a member of the VAD and rose to become Commander-in-Chief of the women's VAD. Throughout the war she showed herself committed to the idea of using women's labour efficiently by having it overseen by the National Service Department, which did not happen to the extent she wished. Her drive for efficiency gave her a similar outlook on the war to Geddes. She was motivated by a desire for effectiveness rather than being constrained by traditions of either the navy or the traditional sphere of women's work, much as he was.

Furse's upbringing and working life were unusual for women of the time. She describes her childhood as 'bohemian', and she states, 'ever since I can remember people having used the words "peculiar" and "original" and "eccentric" about us'. Her father, an author, was noted to have said at one point that he 'did not mind whether' she or her sisters were educated or not, which although seems odd reflects his attitude that they could make their own choices about their lives. Her home background, predominantly in Switzerland, consisted of an environment whereby exploration, choice and experimentation were encouraged. Furse, reflecting on her early life, writes: 'looking back, I realise what an unusual life I lived and with what individualists', quite at odds to a typical middle-class family in this period.[2]

Until her teens, she was the 'boy' of the family, the youngest of three sisters, allowed to bobsleigh and go off on hikes on her own. Later, even in her rather short married life to Charles Furse, the painter, the sense of the bohemian is present, with traditionally adopted roles giving way to shared opinions and decisions between husband and wife.

The socialisation of Furse in her early years, and the effects of her life experiences later on, is critical to knowing how she came to lead the first WRNS. A free spirit, Furse was strong willed. Her ability to provide for her family when her husband died of TB in October 1904, a day after the birth of their second child, is evidence of this.

When, in 1909, the first Voluntary Aid Detachments were formed, Furse saw 'an opportunity at last of doing Red Cross Work',[3] joining the 22nd VAD, London, in the Westminster Division. Her keen mind for detail and efficiency came out in her early VAD work. Between 1912 and 1914 she was asked to start a number of new divisions across London, and when the war broke out she was called upon to help interview new VAD members and organise their training in home nursing, hygiene and sanitation, and cookery. Following this, she led the first all-female VAD detachment sent to France, a challenging and difficult experience, which set the precedent for all future VADs despatched to France. In 1916, after heading the VAD department in London, she was appointed Commander-in-Chief. For her work, she was awarded the Royal Red Cross in February 1916 for services to nursing and in 1917 was made a Dame Grand Cross of the British Empire.

Furse had, by the end of 1916, become committed to the idea that a large number of women were not being usefully employed, 'that a considerable amount of overlap, confusion, and waste of effort' had been present.[4] Along with a number of other women who had risen to dominant positions within their respective fields,[5] during the war she called for a central committee to organise and control women's labour.[6] In January 1917 she had a meeting with Neville Chamberlain and Sandford Fawcett (civil servant for national service) where she explained that she felt all women's services, including the VAD, should draw their members from National Service Headquarters.[7] From a memo written to Fawcett on 22 January her reasoning for this seems to have been linked to a frustration with duplication and wastage.[8] At the time it was becoming clear that a women's army auxiliary corps was likely to be created very soon, to follow on from the increased use of female labour in the munitions industry and agriculture. Furse wanted a tight organisation that would ensure women were centrally selected for roles and given duties that fitted their level of experience rather than who they knew or who they were socially. When ideas for a women's auxiliary army were being proposed she desired a body of women, led by women, based and run on military lines with a uniform and a chain of command.

In December 1916 Furse wrote to Chamberlain requesting to run the WAAC. She said,

I have had two years experience organising and controlling the VAD work at Devonshire House. The work I should be best fitted for would be the organisation, selection and control of women working for and with the army.[9]

Her insistence in offering herself for this role is then repeated in a letter dated 15 January 1917 to Chamberlain, who at the time was Director-General of National Service, in which she again offers her services 'in any capacity in which you may require them' and states: 'please realise that I am prepared to leave the VADs if necessary'.[10] Furse was so committed to the idea of working in the women's army she was willing to give up her role within the VAD. It is not clear why her offer was not taken up, with the WAAC formed under different leadership. Perhaps she was too forthright for the more conservative army leadership.

In her role as Commander-in-Chief she had increasingly come to believe that VAD members were not being recognised for the role they were undertaking in France and inefficiency dogged the organisation. She writes that the conditions of her appointment meant that she 'in no way interfered with the County Directors'.

'The VAD department was to all intents and purposes a Registry Office and when once we had appointed members to military formations we had but little say with regard to their conditions'.[11] This was a key point of conflict in Furse's role in the VAD, which led to offering herself for other roles and calling for a central recruitment system for women workers. She was critical of the conditions of work for the volunteers and the undervaluing of the members by nursing staff.[12] The opposition Furse met in trying to gain consistency for the conditions of VADs meant that:

During the autumn [1917] several of my colleagues came to the same conclusion as I had, that we should no longer accept responsibility for conditions over which we had no control, nor consent to work a system which we believed to be wasteful, so we put in our resignations, mine taking effect officially from the 14th November, when Lady Ampthill took over the VAD Department.[13]

On 10 November the leaders of the VAD at Devonshire House who had handed in a petition and their resignations were called to a meeting with Lady Ampthill and Sir Arthur Stanley (chairman of the Central Joint VAD Committee). Mavis Carter, who had been working with Furse at the time, reports in her diary that 'insults were hurled at Dame Katharine'. Her close colleagues Edith Crowdy, Winifred Dakyns, Lucy Cane and Tilla Wallace, who were to become the first Assistant Directors and Principals of the WRNS, were told they would be turned out of the VAD on 16 November as Lady Ampthill saw them as 'an evil influence in Devonshire House'.[14] Carter herself ended up resigning and joined the WRNS, having held the same views as Furse and believing that there was a 'ridiculous waste of energy and duplicating' in the VAD.[15] In an outright criticism of Furse, Sir Arthur Stanley sent a letter to *The Times* on 16 November, stating:

> The Joint VAD Committee deeply regret the necessity for accepting the resignations of Dame Katharine Furse and those of the staff who think, like her, that they are at liberty to prevent any policy being carried out which they themselves do not approve.[16]

That so many women resigned with Furse demonstrates the concerns they had with the running of the women's section of the VAD. It also indicates a growing boldness, with some middle-class women being increasingly able to speak their minds publicly.

In the VAD Furse felt she was merely a figurehead, granted the control of administration but not the power to 'ensure the proper well-being and control of all VAD members wherever they may be working'.[17] The essential difference between the VAD and the WRNS was the power afforded to Furse. In the VAD she felt that women officers, not a committee consisting mainly of men, should run the women's VAD. She publicly denounced the service, which, in her eyes was failing the women working within it, and in doing this opened herself up to criticism. Some argued that she went exceeded her brief. However, that she was able to do so and with support demonstrates the power she held and the strength of her argument. Her ideas were integral to how the WRNS was organised with

Divisional Directors (called Superintendents in World War II) at the different ports responsible for looking after the Wrens under their care but also directly accountable to headquarters. During the process of her resignation, Furse was offered the job of Director WRNS by Geddes. Her leadership ability was also shown in her being offered the leadership of the women's auxiliary corps for the Royal Air Force, which was formed 1 April 1918.[18]

In a memo that Furse wrote on 11 November 1917, it is noted that she received a phone call from Mona Chalmers Watson, requesting she meet her brother, Eric Geddes, to discuss his wish for her to become the leader of 'a Naval Organisation of Women'. This meeting took place the same day. In it, Geddes explained to Furse how the War Office was reluctant to share the WAAC with the navy and that he intended on dropping his 'bombshell', as previously discussed.[19]

From the letters to and from Furse, Chalmers Watson and Geddes, it is clear that following Furse's meeting with the brother and sister on 11 November the WRNS very quickly took shape. In this early meeting it was evident that Geddes was more than willing to give Furse control of her staff and a free hand to make decisions, as Furse states in her memo of the meeting:

> I asked him whether I might choose my own staff and he said certainly and that no one would interfere and that he hoped I might bring with me a lot of Devonshire House staff which I said I would do with great pleasure.[20]

This extract also demonstrates the obvious value Geddes saw in the experienced senior VAD staff who had been working with Furse and who had resigned along with her. It also illustrates his continued desire to cut red tape that was restricting capable individuals from performing efficiently for the war effort because of perceived 'social acceptability'. Instead, Geddes took these types of individuals into his own service. It also shows that he thought women, perhaps influenced by his sister's role in the WAAC, should lead a women's naval corps. He was not one of the traditionalists who had shunned the assistance of women in the formation of the army auxiliary.

The War Office and Army Council, Noakes argues, 'focused on controlling women whom they believed to be motivated by a desire for excitement, higher rates of pay and the opportunity to mix with the male soldiers', rather than building an esprit-de-corps.[21] This was significantly different from the way in which the WRNS was organised (helping to instill its particular cultural values). Lord Derby, the then Secretary of State for War, firmly wanted the War Office in control of the formation and governance of women's involvement in the military. The Adjutant-General Neville Macready, who would eventually have oversight of the service, wrote to him stating that any women employed should be 'part and parcel of the army, and entirely distinct from any outside organisation', demonstrating his distrust of women who wanted to undertake service in the army, particularly those from women's suffrage organisations. Lord Derby wrote in response, 'I am entirely with you in resisting any outside interference whatsoever.'[22] In contrast, Geddes placed a woman in charge from the beginning, providing Furse with a great deal of autonomy, recognising her ethos and work ethic. Gould indicates that Derby and Macready 'did not afford much importance to the ideas and opinions of women they invited', it can be assumed because they did not want to give women a sense of power or privilege.[23]

Creation of the Service

On 12 November, Furse took up the offer in a meeting with the Second Sea Lord Herbert Heath and Rear Admiral Seymour, Director of Mobilisation, and Sir Oswyn Murray. Furse was offered the directorship of the naval women's corps, which at that time did not have a name. The title 'Director' was a naval term, which would effectively place Furse's rank as Rear Admiral, although the WRNS in this war would not have directly equivalent ranks to the navy. At this meeting she was instructed to 'put in place a scheme' along the same lines of the WAAC with the intention of substituting for up to 10,000 men in occupations such as cooks, clerks, writers and painters. The WRNS would have no involvement in the dockyards, although women would be needed for sail making and netting.

The memo of this meeting also highlights Furse's lack of knowledge of the navy and its procedures because she requested any books that Admiral Seymour might be able to provide her. As with Geddes, she was an individual with no naval background who had been set the task of leading and promoting change within the most traditionally male of military institutions. In the end, a copy of 'King's Regulations for the Navy', which she obtained in a bookshop after the meeting, was adopted to become the WRNS 'bible'.[24]

On 13 November, Furse wrote to Geddes expressing her wish to be part of his plan although she requested that he be patient with her slowly growing knowledge of the navy. In this letter she shows a deep respect toward Geddes, his brother Auckland and their sister Mona Chalmers Watson.[25] Furse believed the country was likely to be saved by the vision Geddes' typified, if his colleagues played fair. There was a recognition by her that they were both outliers, from untypical backgrounds, who could fall foul of petty or self-aggrandising individuals.

Furse reports that her Admiralty leaders were supportive of the WRNS. In a memo about a meeting Furse had with Admiral Seymour on 21 November, he indicated that 'there would be great reluctance on the part of all Commanding Officers to substitute women for men but the Admiralty wished these relieved'.[26] There was obviously great resolve on the part of Admiral Seymour and Second Sea Lord Herbert Heath to carry through the Geddes policy, and those who did not wish to conform would be reprimanded. Once the decision was taken to replace men with women it was swiftly acted on and further demonstrated the shift that had occurred within the Admiralty.

The central task Furse faced as Director would be to determine where women could replace men.[27] This would be the key role of the Divisional Directors and Principals of the Service who spent a great deal of their job travelling around the various offices and locations in their division talking to male officers. In effect, Furse was provided the license to be a 'shover', to be a nuisance to effect change within the Royal Navy, and the women working under her would also be expected to push for men to be replaced

Table 2.1 Options for the title of the service in World War I[28]

WANKS	Women's Auxiliary Naval Corps
WNS	Women's Naval Service
WANS	Women's Auxiliary Naval Service
RNWS	Royal Naval Women's Service

where necessary by Wrens. It is fair to say that in Furse, Geddes recognised a woman who could get things done and who was not afraid to speak her mind.

The name of the WRNS was adopted on 21 November. This was selected from a choice of:

Despite some offensive acronyms, which might be used, the eventual decision allowed the service to have a pleasant nickname for the women who served: Wrens.

Katharine Furse was appointed as Director on 23 November. Six days later, Charles Walker, Secretary to the Admiralty, issued office memorandum number 245, on behalf of the Board, announcing the establishment of the WRNS. In this memo he states:

> The Head of this Service will be Dame Katharine Furse, GBE, who will have the title and status of Director.
>
> The members of this service will wear a distinctive uniform, and the service will be confined to women employed on purely naval duties, and will not include those serving in the Admiralty Departments, or in the dockyards [. . .].
>
> The Director will be responsible to the Second Sea Lord for all matters connected with the WRNS.[29]

The draft scheme for the organisation of the WRNS was submitted on 29 November. In a memo attached to the draft, Furse states:

> The Director, WRNS begs to submit the attached detailed scheme for the Organisation of the Women's Royal Naval Service. This scheme is based on Army Council Instruction 1069/1917 and on subsequent A.C.I.s applying to the Women's Auxiliary Service.[30]

> It is pointed out that certain improvements and alterations in WAAC conditions have been added in the proposed scheme for the WRNS with a view to obtaining the most suitable women and to maintaining them in health and contentment.[31]

This reference to the alterations of the WAAC scheme of service is significant. Noakes points out that questions were being raised in the press about the behaviour of women in the army auxiliary and their motives for joining the service. The end of 1917 saw recruitment to the corps being possibly harmed by widespread rumours of sexual immorality. The reports were very damaging to the reputation of the WAAC and would leave a legacy for the ATS. Chalmers Watson wrote to Gwynne-Vaughan in France describing some of the claims that had been made about the women in France, including an incident in which 90 women from Rouen were sent back for misconduct, alongside a claim that 'another aristocratic bird asserts that the War Office is sending out professional prostitutes dressed in our uniforms', and assertions that women were being encouraged to have sex to gain a monetary bonus.[32]

The rumours, Noakes argues, 'reflected concurrent concerns regarding female behaviour in wartime. The widespread absence of men combined with higher wages for women produced a picture of female independence that threatened the established mores and values of pre-war society'. It was not uncommon for women who lived in the location of army bases and naval ports, or women working in the munitions industries, to be blamed for suffering from 'khaki fever' (lust for men in uniform), accused of extravagance, drunkenness and sexual promiscuity.[33] Grayzel argues that 'regardless of where it took place, wartime mobilisation upset traditional gender arrangements. This was partly because it was seen as removing "rational" male heads of households'.[34] The new independence of women, who had traditionally occupied a very specific role in society, threatened the dominant discourse of gender identity. The government, in shaping the women's auxiliaries, sought to temporarily adjust women's roles for the greater need, whilst still being careful to maintain traditional gender identity as closely as possible.

There is also an issue of class here. Members of the VAD, who tended to be middle class, were far less likely to be victims of the gossip that affected the WAAC. The VAD's role was seen as an extension of the domestic sphere of women, rather than an attempt to adopt masculine roles.[35] The VAD was also more likely to include middle- and upper-class women, mainly due to its voluntary nature.

Being middle or upper class and determined to participate in 'war work' did not always mean women were safe from disdain. The Women's Volunteer Reserve (WVR) was formed from a small group of upper-class women wearing khaki uniforms who wanted to defend the country in case of invasion. Indignation followed and they were regarded as Amazonian suffragettes.[36] The crucial aspect that may have affected the view of the WVR was that it was created by an elite group of self-appointed volunteers. Although the WAAC did receive negative press in the first year, at least it was officially authorised and regulated, which made it more palatable.[37] Its close control by the Army Office and Army Council helped reduce some of the negativity levelled at unsanctioned women in uniform.[38]

The WAAC suffered from a situation that none of the other women's services had to face. Some of their members were in France directly replacing men who had been working behind the front lines as postmen, orderlies, cooks and such like. Some men ended up resenting and mistrusting them because they were being perceived as pushing men who had not been in combat roles before to the front line.[39] The WRNS and WRAF did not suffer in this way because they were not visibly seen in the arena of war. In the case of the WRNS they were used to dilute, with several women replacing one man, or they would end up creating new roles as the need increased. As such, their role was not resented in the same way that members of the WAAC who were stationed in France were.

Some soldiers also regarded the WAAC as a bad influence. Noakes argues that some men saw them as 'parasitic, preying on vulnerable men who needed to conserve their energies for the male sphere of battle'.[40] It is the inclusion of women within the 'male sphere of battle', which is significant. Up until this point conflicts had been the preserve of men. Watson demonstrates that trench warfare in particular pushed the view of the war into an exclusively masculine realm.[41] To have women coming into the support lines would have been challenging for men who had faced horrors in the preceding three years. Some men would have certainly seen the presence of women as inappropriate, if not as a bad influence.

The class issue was significant for the WAAC because it directly affected the image of women who did war work. Watson makes the point that many working-class women joined the service because they found better pay and working conditions than they could in civilian work. One woman, Doron Lamm, argued, 'patriotism, remunerated work, and personal autonomy were inseparable'.[42] The women serving in the WAAC may well have been viewed with derision and scorn in France because they were moving beyond their very restricted lives. Most would have worked as domestic servants before joining up, a heavily constrained life with clear social conventions. Joining the auxiliary services allowed women greater freedoms than they would have had in the past. Conversely, however, women working in these organisations would come to be closely monitored because of the claims that had been made against the WAAC.[43]

The WRNS was not as challenged by class differences as the WAAC. In World War I this was because fewer women joined from the working classes than in the army corps. The WAAC's ranks were delineated on class lines, with the majority of women being working class and the leadership upper class. The WAAC received more focus because it was far larger than its contemporaries. At its height in January 1919, there were nearly 40,000 women in service, whereas the total of the WRNS only reached 7,000 throughout its short two-year existence.[44] It is obvious that more attention, which was not always positive, would be levelled at the WAAC for the very reason that it was more visible, with a much larger number of working-class women being in the public eye for the first time in history. The social class divisions in the women's auxiliaries reflected the social importance of class stratification in this period. Furse suggested in 1916 that if a women's corps was to be organised 'the urgent and immediate need is to select gentlewomen to act as officers',[45] mirroring attitudes of the time about social superiority.

What was also significant was the way World War I pushed middle- and working-class women together as had never happened before. Watson uses the recollection of Dorothy Pickford, an administrator (officer) in the WAAC. She found it difficult to know so much about the lives of the women serving under her because at home she would not have seen her servants when they were off duty, whereas in the army 'when they are not on duty they are as such at liberty to do as they please as anyone'.[46] The war threw differences between the classes into stark relief, forcing middle- and upper-class women to understand their working-class contemporaries in a way they had never been able to before.

Official efforts were used to 'redeem the reputation of the WAAC'.[47] In March 1918 the War Office also commissioned a report 'to assess the work and behaviour of the WAACs' which concluded that they had found 'a healthy, cheerful, self-respecting body of hardworking women, conscious of their position as links in the great chain of the Nation's purpose'.[48] In April 1918 Queen Mary gave her name to the corps, now called Queen Mary's Army Auxiliary Corps, in official recognition of their good service in France and at home. Marketing played a significant role in improving the image of the army auxiliary. Many of the women serving were resentful of the way society had portrayed them. The main issue was the differences in expectations of behaviour based on class background. On the whole, the behaviour in the service was good, it just may not have been to the same standards as some members of society. These issues with the WAAC, which were identified within its first year, had a direct impact on the scheme of service for the WRNS.

The Scheme of Service

The WRNS created its scheme of service with a clear statement of the type of behaviour it expected from its members, which it also released to the press, the aim being to make it appear superior to the WAAC. The general regulations specify that:

> Every member of the service will on all occasions strive to promote the welfare of the WRNS. [. . .] She will remember that persons in

uniform are always conspicuous and open to public criticism, and that members of the WRNS must, when representing the Service, avoid any behaviour which, though not incriminating in itself, may be undesirable from the point of view of the WRNS.

There were also rules that governed propriety and personal behaviour:

> Smoking on duty and in public places and thoroughfares is forbidden. [. . .]
> No member of the WRNS may consume intoxicating liquor at a public bar.
> Members of the WRNS will avoid the using of powder, paint or scent. These are very much out of place when in uniform, and do not lend the serious air so much to be desired if the best reputation of the Service is to be maintained.
> Members of the WRNS will behave discreetly in public places and will by their quiet bearing obtain a name for great sincerity of purpose. [. . .] They will invariably stand up and offer their seats in public carriages to those who appear to need them, will by their gentleness and kindness win a reputation for womanly sympathy and patience.[49]

The service established very high standards from the outset. Many of these slipped from usage in World War II. Wrens, for example, would regularly wear make-up, adding to the glamour the service presented at this time. Jean Rawson, who joined the World War II service at the age of 18, recalled being told by her Wren officer to wear make-up as it 'was in keeping with our appearance'.[50] She found this surprising at the time having not worn make-up before.

On the next page of the regulations are some interesting rules about going out with men:

> Association with persons outside the WRNS. As a general rule, association with Officers and men will not be forbidden, but will be controlled by such regulations as may seem necessary to insure discreet and dignified behaviour. Joint entertainments, such as concerts and dances, are permissible, but mixed theatricals are to be avoided.[51]

It is not clear what the problem with 'mixed theatricals' was, whether this was in regard to acting with a man, or in going to see a drama production; however, it serves as another example of the way in which the service sought to ensure the propriety of the women's behaviour, which is clearly demonstrated in this last comment:

> When off duty ratings must be discouraged from walking arm in arm with anyone and must be made to realise that loafing about with men causes a great deal of adverse criticism of the service and must not be indulged in.[52]

This could be regarded as a direct response to the rumours circulating at the time about the WAAC. Much of the scandal was mainly speculation. Dorothy Loveday, Watson details, was a member of the service who thought most of the issues arising out of a lack of supervision. The number actually sent back from France was eight, far from the rumoured 90.[53] It was the presence of working-class women going out at night after being on duty and being seen standing smoking in public places that had the biggest effect on the reputation of the army auxiliary. Working-class women previously constrained within domestic service were for the first time free to do as they wished, which meant they were more publicly visible.

The WRNS leaders could be regarded as more controlling, establishing a moral code that they expected all members to follow no matter their background. In one sense this could be seen as a reflection of middle-class values. Even so, it was as an attempt to build an esprit-de-corps that aimed to see all women within the service as Wrens, rather than women of a particular class. The smaller size of the service allowed it to afford such attention to creating a unified identity, which would have been a more challenging task in its sister auxiliary.

Katharine Furse recalled in her memoirs 'the fear of what might be looked on as unsuitable behaviour was always at the back of our minds but, so far as my experience went, there was very little cause for it'. She goes on to say how the VADs were nicknamed the 'starched brigade', having had a very 'clean sheet', whereas the Wrens were known as the 'Prigs and Prudes' or the 'Perfect Ladies'. She saw this as a massive compliment. The WRNS only had a couple of cases of pregnancy and venereal disease in World War I. The pregnant women were discharged on benevolent grounds and the women with diseases were treated. Furse felt that 'we should do more to maintain a moral code by humane treatment than by punishment'.[54] That the WRNS was willing to behave in such a manner reflects forward thinking attitudes in matters of sexuality that were only gently shifting in wider society.

Furse went on to explain the two reasons she believed there was a 'good moral tone' among the women in the WRNS. The first was due to the popularity of the navy, which allowed the service to select the best applicants from those who volunteered to join the services. This would also be the case for the second WRNS, which was small yet popular, allowing them to handpick from a range of women. The second was that many women worked in close proximity with men in their working day, which meant that they were not that interested in spending time with them in the evenings.[55] Whether the latter is a significant reason is questionable. It is much more likely to be due to the high expectations placed on Wrens and the careful selection procedure they went through that controlled behaviour.

Charles Walker wrote to Furse at the end of the war stating 'the way you have caught on to the true Navy spirit is one of the secrets of the extraordinary success of the WRNS'.[56] Geddes wrote more strongly, stating that out of the women's services 'there is none which in my opinion has attained the general high standard and the absolute reproach of any kind which the WRNS has maintained throughout'.[57] The first service built an excellent reputation. This identity was very significant in shaping the moral ethos of World War II WRNS, which was founded on similar values.

Organisation of the Service

Uniform was, of course, one of the key ways that identified women as belonging to a particular auxiliary. Women wearing military-style clothing had been very controversial at the beginning of the war. Many argued that, in doing so, they undermined 'images of manhood by diluting the associations between the uniform and risk of death'.[58] The WVR suffered from these criticisms. Social commentators writing letters at the time thought that the wearing of khaki degraded the nature of womanhood. Some felt that it made women behave in a masculine way at the very point when they should be performing their expressive role.[59]

This opposition was challenged when the women's military auxiliaries were introduced in 1917 because of the strict controls the War Office had over uniform. However, there were implications 'that female appropriation of military attire and attitudes, whilst tolerable in wartime, had to be just for the duration, acceptable only due to the rigours and demands of a society experiencing total war for the first time'.[60] The official sanction of uniform did not mean that problems were entirely solved. One new recruit to the WAAC thought the military uniform led to relaxed attitudes between the sexes in the army. 'She was irritated that "once we are in uniform any Tommy thinks he can make advances".'[61]

Furse had pretended, early on when being appointed Director, not to be interested in the uniform servicewomen would eventually wear, 'because we were very anxious that the usual remarks should not be made that women only think of dress'. Of course they were thinking about it and 'wanted to copy naval uniform in all essentials'.[62] The uniform did not have the gold lace that the men's did, being replaced with royal blue lace with a curl in the shape of a diamond. Officers had a three-cornered velour hat, known as a tricorne, whereas ratings wore a 'pudding basin' hat. The officers wore a double-breasted hip length jacket, with a shirt and tie, and long ankle-length skirt, whereas ratings had a mid-calf length dress with sailor collar. The uniform conformed to contemporary ideas of respectability, with little glamour or elegance attached, which would change in World War II.

In November 1917 the following ranks with their signifying stripes and diamonds were authorised for the uniform:

Table 2.2   Ranks and badges of World War I WRNS[63]

Appointment	Employment	Badges of rank
Director	HQ WRNS	Broad and narrow stripe with diamond
Deputy Director	HQ WRNS	Broad stripe with diamond
Assistant Director	HQ WRNS	Four stripes with diamond
Deputy Assistant Director	HQ WRNS	Three stripes with diamond
Divisional director	Attached to HQ of commands and to certain areas and base ports at home and overseas	
Deputy Divisional director		Two stripes with diamond
Principal	In charge of hostels or units	Three stripes
Deputy Principal		Two stripes
Assistant Principal		One stripe
Quarters Supervisor		Patch on collar
Subordinate appointments		
Chief Section Leader	1–50 women	Anchor with 3 rings on left fore-arm
Section Leader	1–25 women	Anchor with 2 rings on left fore-arm
Leader (Acting rating)	1–10 women	Anchor with one ring on left fore-arm

The following equivalents to the navy (if not necessarily official) were added in December:

The women worked in ten divisions across the UK, having been trained in the Crystal Palace Training depot, gradually taking on a range of roles in over 75 different locations. Later in the war, divisions would be established in the Mediterranean and Ireland.[65] A division was made up of 20 or more sub-divisions under a Principal. Sub-divisions included two or more companies under Principals, Deputy or Assistant Principals.[66]

Table 2.3   Equivalent ranks of WRNS to Royal Navy, World War I[64]

Director WRNS	Rear Admiral
Deputy Director	Commodore 2nd class
Assistant Director	Captain
Medical Assistant Director	Captain
Deputy Assistant Director	Commander
Divisional Director	Commander
Deputy Divisional Director	Lieut Commander
Principal	Lieut Commander
Deputy Principal	Lieutenant
Assistant Principal	Sub Lieutenant
Quarters Supervisor	Sub Lieutenant
Subordinate officers	
Chief Section Leader	Chief Petty Officer
Section Leader	Petty Officer
Leader	Leading Hand

There were eight different categories (denoted with a letter from A to H), as they were called in World War I WRNS, that women could be employed in, whereas in World War II categories referred to the actual job a person did, with these being grouped into wider branches.[67] Category A comprised the clerical and accounting branch, including typists, shorthand typists and clerical workers. Category B was the household branch of stewards, cooks and laundresses. There was even a steward role of wine waitress, a job that would not exist in World War II, reflecting the culture of the time.

Garage workers formed category C, another role that would not exist in the future, coming under the role of motor transport driver instead. Category D included general unskilled roles such as orderlies, messengers, porters and store women. Similarly, category F included miscellaneous jobs such as bakers, gardeners, pigeon women and net mine workers. Category E involved any roles related to the postal service, which at the time included telephone operators and telegraphists. The category G covered the technical branch, which included the largest number of roles under the broad headings of engineers, electricians, aircraft hands, photographers and storekeepers. The final category, H, was the signals branch of wireless telegraphists.[68] Additional roles would be added on 30 August 1918, including gas mask inspectors and depth charge workers within category G.[69]

As in the case of naval ratings, Wrens were given badges that indicated both their rank and category. Chief Section Leaders had a cap badge of blue with a gold anchor. Section Leaders crossed anchors and crown and Leaders an anchor. Below this was their small badge that indicated their category,[70] which were:

A.   Clerical and accountant branch – Crossed quills
B.   Household branch – Shells
C.   Garage workers – Wheel
D.   General unskilled branch – Crossed keys
E.   Postal branch – Letter
F.   Miscellaneous branch – Star
G.   Technical branch – Crossed hammers
H.   Signal branch – Arrows and lightening

Uniforms and placing women in naval categories established their military status, so whilst not being *in* the navy, they were symbolically tied to its ethos. The WRNS uniform could have been a simple smock dress; instead, it reflected an inclusivity with the RN. This suggests the Royal Navy was trying to project an image that had prestige and appeal. Such an image has been part and parcel of the modern British navy, still encapsulated in its late-twentieth century document *Ethos, Values and Standards* which highlights the expectation of 'the demonstration of high personal standards; whether it is immaculate uniform, smart civilian attire or excellent behaviour at all times'.[71] In the 1913 *King's Regulations and Admiralty Instructions*, under the 'Discipline' section the instructions for Captains notes; '[t]he Captain will at all times and in all circumstances show an example of respect and obedience to his superiors, of unremitting attention to his duty and of cheerful alacrity in performing it'.[72] The emphasis is on responsibility and hard work, which was then reiterated in the WRNS regulations. The creation of the WRNS by the Admiralty, rather than the War Office, enabled its first leader to reflect the values and expectations of its Royal Navy brother in its scheme of service. The presence of blue braid on the uniform of WRNS officers signified this relationship, integrally tied but different. The women's service was afforded a great deal of respect in its two short years, not least in having ranks that were equivalent to the RN. Whilst its existence would be short-lived, it managed to establish a much clearer identity than the army auxiliary was able to, dogged as it was by its unfounded poor reputation.

The End of the World War I WRNS

The announcement of the end of the service came on 19 February 1919 in an Admiralty Fleet Order, stating:

> The Board desire to take this opportunity of placing on record their high appreciation of the war work which this corps has accomplished. The WRNS was brought into being at a time of national emergency when it was necessary to release every man that could be spared for the active fighting forces.
>
> The rapidity with which the corps was organised to that end and brought to a high state of efficiency constitutes a remarkable achievement and one that reflects the greatest possible credit on the Director and her officers and ratings.
>
> All who have come into contact with the WRNS have been impressed by their discipline, zeal and esprit de corps.[73]

The positivity of many senior officers from the Admiralty toward the WRNS, which had gone through so much change during the war, was publicly demonstrated in the 19 July Peace Parade when they clapped the marching Wrens who were passing. The then Second Sea Lord, Montagu Browning, wrote officially to say the service had earned the right to be represented at such a historic event.[74] Despite this positivity toward the service and calls from Furse (having received many appeals from Wrens) to maintain a uniformed reserve, the service was finally disbanded on 1 October 1919. From this point there was no involvement of women in the navy, and Mason suggests that the Admiralty found the few WRNS headquarters staff still there at the end 'uncomfortable company and wished them gone'. She describes a file opened in December 1919 relating to the possible reorganisation of the service. It had an illegible signature and was dated 15 August 1922 and had boldly written across the front 'Dead. Scheme dropped by Board Order'.[75] This would be the end of the service for the next 19 years.

Katharine was instrumental in forming the identity of the service, which would create an important legacy for the future. She would not have been able to do this without the independence afforded her by Geddes and the Admiralty who, given the view of women at the time, were more accepting of giving them positions of responsibility than the army was. A precedent had been created that made the establishing of the next WRNS far more reasonable. The foundation for giving strong, independent women control of this naval institution was established and would continue in the next war.

CHAPTER 3

The Re-Creation of the WRNS

The following two chapters are related to each other, weaving the many strands that came to form the distinctive identity of the WRNS by 1941. This chapter identifies the conditions under which the auxiliary was re-formed. It will assert that the position of women in the 1920s and 1930s had returned to 'business as usual', with women expected to take up their pre-war roles. The disbanding of the service in 1919 was therefore consistent with wider policies of the postwar government.

The intention to recreate the women's auxiliaries in 1938, which led to the ATS being officially re-formed on 27 September 1938 and the WRNS 12 April 1939, represented the careful decision making of the armed forces and politicians. It was not the result of a significant change in gender roles in the interwar period, although the legacy of female involvement in the first war was very significant. Full enfranchisement by 1928, and the increase of middle-class women in paid employment, such as the legal profession and accountancy, was not reflected in female involvement in political decision making surrounding the military. They had been totally excluded from this sphere at the end of the first total war. Instead, it was the planning by the male-led inter-Departmental Committee, who recognised the need to rely on the mobilisation of members of the public far earlier than in World War I, which formed the conditions under which women would become involved in the British military again.

The Position of Women in the 1920s and 1930s

There was a large backlash against the victories women had achieved in the war. Separate sphere ideology became the dominant discourse, fuelled in part by psychiatry and the work of Freud in the 1920s with health and happiness for women relying on them becoming mothers, with equality within marriage seen as abnormal.[1] The legal acts passed in the early 1920s aimed at improving gender equality had virtually stopped by the end of the decade.[2] Susan Kingsley Kent argues that World War I slowed female social development and feminist ideas, and that it took a second war to restore the progress feminists had made prior to the war.[3] In doing so, British society made it virtually impossible for women to have any significant involvement in the military in a time of 'peace'.

A number of legal acts following the end of the war appeared emancipatory. However, all they did was prevent any feminist militancy. They did not provide a reward for the work women had done in the war. The 1918 Representation of the People Act allowed women over the age of 30, who were either a member of, or married to a member of the Local Government Register, the right to vote. In addition, the Sex Disqualification (Removal) Act 1919 opened up professions to women. For example, between 1911 and 1928 the number of female doctors increased from 477 to 2580.[4] Yet, there was no immediate need for women to maintain the typically male roles they had taken on in the latter years of World War I.

Feminist organisations had a negative public image in the interwar period. They were often portrayed as 'radical, even revolutionary groups of women who wished to transform society and break up the family'.[5] Vera Brittain remarked in the *Manchester Guardian* (13 December 1928) that feminists were perceived as 'spectacled, embittered women, disappointed, childless, dowdy and generally unloved'.[6] This was a dramatic move away from the image of the bold and daring suffragettes of the early twentieth century.

The emancipatory policies of the early 1920s were limited; 'the opportunities opened up for women by the war were largely

closed down'.[7] In part because of the Restoration of Pre-War
Practices Bill 1919, that meant,

> all pre-war customs which were given up during the war, and in
> connection with the purposes of the war, shall be restored by every
> employer throughout the country within two months of the passing
> of the Act.[8]

The consequence of the Act was that women who had replaced men
in war industries stood down so that returning male service
personnel could regain their jobs. There was much debate in the
House of Commons as to whether this Act was ethical, with women
having just gained the vote and the ability to stand as Members of
Parliament. Major E Wood, argued the Bill could have a
detrimental effect on working-class women by 'establish[ing] a
sex bar debarring them from engaging in industry at the very
moment when the doors of other professions are being opened to
their richer sisters'.[9] The consensus view held that, overall, the Act
was necessary to prevent competition between women and men in
the workplace.

The participation of women in paid work, which had reached
between 7.25 and 7.5 million at the height of World War I, had by
1921 returned to the levels of 1914 (around six million), despite the
large loss of men in the first war.[10] This number stayed relatively
constant in the 1920s and 1930s. Population drift occurred postwar,
with some men moving from declining industrial locations to
London and the south-east, leading to a redistribution of labour
power.[11] The main employer of working-class women changed in
the interwar period from domestic service to the textile and
clothing industry, which employed about 1.2 million women
in 1931.[12]

Professional women, with secondary school qualifications, were
either teachers or nurses, of which there were 134,000 and 154,000
in 1938. One large growth area in the two decades was in office
work. There were 124,843 women clerks in 1911 and 565,005 in
1931.[13] This may explain why the decision to reform the women's
auxiliaries came earlier than in the 1914–18 war. A precedent of

women working in offices had been firmly established as acceptable, particularly for young and older unmarried women. The main categories, early on in the services, particularly the WRNS, were office based and as such could have been viewed as an extension of 'women's work' rather than a military role.

The rate of women in employment only increased significantly from December 1941, when women were legally required to register at Labour Exchanges, following the introduction of the National Service Act (No.2). 1943 saw 46 per cent of all women aged 14–59 undertaking paid work for the war effort.[14] This was over 7.75 million[15] and many more were undertaking voluntary work.

World War I did little to change the employment of women, but on the other hand, it provided women with a sense of self-worth.[16] Domestic service saw the largest change in the attitudes of women toward work. Following the war it came to be seen as servitude. A survey of women outside a Labour Exchange by the journal *Women Worker* in 1919 found 65 per cent of women questioned would not take domestic work in any circumstances.[17] However, women faced a double-edged sword; they had to make way for men at work whilst avoiding becoming 'scroungers on the state'. Women who refused domestic work were popularly ridiculed for 'taking a holiday at the public expense'.[18]

Self-worth had to be put aside in the face of the practicalities of existing in a male-dominated society where status was rarely gained from work. For many women marriage was an attractive alternative to low-paid, unskilled jobs, or the prospect of being on the dole.[19] In addition, the social values of women as 'wife and mother' firmly took hold again in the early 1920s as a way of realigning the employment patterns postwar.[20] Women were encouraged to resume these roles, in the aim of readjusting the 'confusion of values', which 'has led women astray' during the course of the war, as expressed in Catherine Hartley's *Women's Wild Oats*.[21] By 1931, 90 per cent of married women were not in full-time employment. For many women, 'the convention that marriage was a woman's normal fulltime occupation was still very strong' and having working mothers within society was still not the norm.[22]

The opportunities women had taken in the war had opened some new possibilities. Yet, as Noakes argues, British government policy and public opinion were both determined to push women back into 'pre-war patterns of employment and behaviour', despite changes in employment that the war had brought.[23] Some women, such as Vera Brittain, found the lack of social change following World War I disappointing, as many doors that had opened closed sharply following the end of the conflict.[24]

Alongside the contraction of women's employment more generally postwar, a negative view was increasingly held toward maintaining the women's auxiliary services. The Women's Reserve Sub-Committee, which included Katharine Furse, Helen Gwynne-Vaughan (representing the WRAF) and Florence Leach (representing the QMAAC), met at the War Office in 1920 to consider the establishment of a women's auxiliary military service on a permanent peacetime basis. Their report recommended that a Women's Reserve be established with the support of the Territorial Army, consisting of 100,000 members in local branches. However, by the time the report was published, public and political opinion had changed. This was in part due to a general desire to move away from the traumas of the war years. The creation of the League of Nations reflected the desire of the populace to avoid warfare, and the first Ten Year Rule created by the government in 1919 reinforced this. There was also the growing backlash toward women taking paid work at this time.[25] As a result, a country now committed to peace would have looked unkindly on such an organisation and the plan for a Women's Reserve was 'quietly dropped'.[26]

There were changes within women's lives in the interwar period, however, for example with the growth of powerful women's organisations in the 1930s. These were important in shaping the identity of women such as Vera Laughton Mathews who would become the World War II WRNS Director. However, the labour force's characteristics and public discourse regarding gender had not changed to the extent where women would have been accepted into military roles without the threat of war. The anti-war sentiment within Britain was very significant as it was unpalatable. It made the making of any moves to appear as though the country was rearming or planning for conflict in the 1930s. Consequently, the planning for any future military campaign and the inclusion of female labour into this was done surreptitiously.

This was critical to the inclusion of female labour in another potential European and possibly global war. Rather than being created as a reaction to a labour shortage situation during the course of the war, the decision to reform the women's auxiliary services was made in April 1937 by the inter-Departmental Committee on the Emergency Powers (Defence) Bill well before the public awareness of the threat of war. Crang argues that the involvement of women in a military capacity had come as early as 1936 with the establishment of the Emergency Service led by Helen Gwynne-Vaughan. This organisation was sanctioned by the Committee of Imperial Defence, with the aim of training potential female officers if the auxiliaries were re-formed. The recruits were very much upper middle class, personally invited by Belinda Boyle (the daughter of the organisation's vice-chair Viscount Trenchard) who simply leafed through her address book for suitable candidates. Training was given in the evenings, with the War Office and Air Ministry providing lectures – the Admiralty did not see what role women would play in the navy if conflict broke out again and so distanced themselves from this group.[27] The Emergency Service can be seen as a precursor to the ATS and WAAF, having no connection to the re-formed WRNS. It established an informal, and arguably, tokenistic, relationship between women and the military.

Throughout the 1920s and 1930s the former women's auxiliary corps maintained the bonds built during the conflict and became associations of members, based upon common interests, comradeship and collective activities, rather than official women's reserves. The Association of Wrens included ex-service members, who began their own magazine, *The Wren*,[28] and held events within branches, including camps and swimming galas.[29] Many of the members also became the leaders of the new Sea Ranger units within Girl Guiding, when the two associations affiliated in 1922. The two Directors of the First and Second World War WRNS were both active guiders. Katharine Furse was the director of the World Association of Girl Guides and Girl Scouts from 1928 to 1938, whereas Vera Laughton Mathews ran various units and was appointed as commissioner to several districts and divisions. These associations are significant, because unlike World War I, they created a voice for women in a way that had not existed to the same degree before. They included women who had worked during the war and promoted the future involvement of women in any future conflict. The emphasis of the organisations was to build skills and strength of character in their membership, whilst being run as an exclusively female environment. This is clearly shown in the copies of *The Wren* for the period.[30]

The nature of male and female relationships, despite this return to domesticity, did experience change. During the 1930s there were increasing opportunities for the British public to engage in leisure activities. There was a massive increase in women and men socialising together in dance halls and cinemas.[31] 1939 saw 19 million people a week attending the latter.[32] This resulted in an increasing number of women having a more mixed circle of friends. Strict chaperonage and rules about males and females interacting together declined somewhat. The primary data indicates this was more likely if women were attending clubs and organisations (such as church groups) or were working in an occupation with a mix of genders. Gender segregation, whilst still present, was not as prominent by 1939 as it had been in 1914. Many of the women interviewed for this research talked about their mixed groups of friends, particularly if they had been to university, where many organisations included members from both genders, such as the archaeological society Kathy Baker joined when she was at Oxford.[33]

Not all women in the interwar years returned to the status quo of the Edwardian era. Hall argues that 'many of the rigid rules which had circumscribed women and courtship before the war were receding if not wholly overthrown'.[34] Although the feminist movement had diminished, there were a number of large and powerful women's organisations, across the working and middle classes that campaigned for the social and economic rights of women.[35]

Vera Laughton Mathews is an example of a woman who was part of this shift in gendered values. Having served as WRNS Unit

Officer of HMS *Victory VI* in World War I, she would become World War II Director of the WRNS. Providing a backdrop for the status of women in British society by the late 1930s places her in context and shows the significance of this environment in shaping the WRNS, both for how she developed as an individual and in how she dealt with other people, particularly men who were not in favour of the service.

Daughter of the naval instructor and later famous naval historian, Professor Sir John Laughton, she describes her family as a 'rather wild lot', given to an independence of thought (reminiscent of the childhood Katharine Furse experienced). In her early twenties, she became the sub-editor of the *Suffragette* (when the previous staff had been put in prison), having been 'caught up in the Women Suffrage movement'. However, she argues in her autobiography that her confidence only really developed when she joined the WRNS in 1918 and discusses the far-reaching effects the service had on the lives of the women who were Wrens. She states, 'they went back to ordinary life imbued with a romance of the service'.[36] Many accounts of wartime Wrens (from both world wars) reflect this particular sense of identity, that the WRNS was both special and had an impact on their later lives, providing many with a self-worth and range of interests that women who had not been in the services might not have had access to. Laughton Mathews argues that the first service 'established the WRNS tradition for high standards and devotion to duty, which the future service was proud to build on'.[37]

After the war, Laughton Mathews's life could be seen to have charted a different course from many other middle-class women of her age. Unlike the countless women who were moving from the world of war work back to domesticity, she held a full-time professional job as a journalist, editing the women's paper, *Time and Tide*. She did a lot of voluntary work with the Girl Guide Association and Association of Wrens. Her path only converged with many of her contemporaries when she married Gordon Mathews in 1924 and spent many years travelling with his work, although she still maintained her voluntary roles.

By 1928 she had two small children and spent the next ten years, before her appointment as Director, busily with her Guiding, as editor of *The Wren* magazine (from 1930), and speaker for the Women's Movement among other prominent women's organisations. As she got older, she became convinced of the need for the equal partnership of women and men in society in all spheres, a view she maintained when Director.[38] In interview, Kathy Baker, a Second Officer in World War II, stated that she held a great admiration for Laughton Mathews because 'she believed that women could do any job the men could do within their physical capacity'.[39]

Women like Laughton Mathews helped drive changes in attitudes toward women in the interwar period. Despite the broadly conservative stance of the government in regard to women's roles, changes were happening. The birth rate decreased over the two decades. Women chose to have fewer children, in part helped by the underground birth control advice of the 1920s (from women like Marie Stopes who opened her first clinic in 1921) and legal guidance from 1930 onward. Women's organisations grew throughout the period, including the Women's Movement and Association for Moral and Social Hygiene (Vera Laughton Mathews was a member of both). The latter campaigned for the 'equal responsibility of both sexes in matters of sex morality',[40] an issue that was translated into WRNS policy. Laughton Mathews writes, 'in the event of Wrens contracting venereal disease they should receive medical treatment in the service, unless there were additional disciplinary reasons for making discharge desirable'.[41]

It is evident that Laughton Mathews represented a new group of forward-thinking and more open-minded women of the 1930s. She held very high moral principles, both for herself and those serving under her, promoting the education of Wrens in maintaining standards of behaviour. This policy reflects a pragmatic view that women who were suitable to carry out their duties should not be dismissed, especially when it was so hard to recruit good people. It moved away from the idea that the blame lay with the woman who caught sexually transmitted diseases, rather than the man.

British society changed for some women in the interwar period. Women had begun to be seen as citizens in their own right with a political voice and an ability to do 'men's work' to an extent, particularly in regard to office work. However, women were still excluded from the male dominated military, bar the 600 upper-middle-class women in the Emergency Service who can be regarded as tokenistic. Neither had there been a massive shift in the cultural values associated with gender roles. The numbers of married women not in full-time work demonstrates this. It was other factors, beyond the cultural, that saw the reformation of the women's auxiliaries take place.

The Impact of Disarmament on the Exclusion of Women from the Royal Navy

What may be more significant than the role of women in society to the reformation of the WRNS is the economic and military situation in the interwar period that saw senior civil servants, politicians and the military by 1935 predicting a future conflict with a range of potential protagonists. In terms of the circumstances under which the WRNS was re-formed the national security situation was very important. Disarmament and a society that was against female military participation at the end of World War I had a lasting impact on the involvement of women in the Royal Navy until rearmament in the late 1930s. 1937 became a turning point that shifted the rhetoric that had excluded women from the military. The nature and scale of the decline of the Royal Navy in the 1920s and rise of the naval arms race in the mid 1930s has been widely documented in historical accounts, so a brief explanation will be made here to place the reformation of the WRNS within its historical context.[42]

Gibbs argues that the disarmament of the Royal Navy after World War I was the most striking of the three armed forces. It had been the largest navy, yet within three years it had relinquished this title as part of the Washington Naval Treaty.[43] The Royal Navy of the 1920s and early 1930s was curtailed as part of a plan to 'halt the naval spiral' of a global naval race.[44] Economically, it was not considered possible to sustain the Royal Navy's size hegemony, particularly when national spending had to be reduced sharply to deal with the national deficit, although the service tried hard to maintain its stocks of cruisers in the 1920s.[45] Two thousand officers were dismissed as part of what has been termed 'Geddes' Axe' from 1922, following the decision of the Committee on National Expenditure as part of wider national spending cuts.[46] Eric Geddes' role as chair of the committee could be viewed initially as sitting uneasily with his reputation as a grandiose reconstructionist. However, the focus lay in reducing waste, a not too dissimilar role to that of his tenure as First Lord of the Admiralty. In fact, the term 'Geddes' Axe' is misleading, as Geddes took no part in the Cabinet decisions that formed the final policy that cut the Royal Navy by over £65 million.[47]

Throughout the interwar period, increasing public anti-war sentiment became entrenched in the many treaties brokered in the first five years of peace (although these treaties were not necessarily influenced by such sentiment, but rather by practical considerations of cost). Those which had the greatest influence on the navy were the Washington Naval Treaty of 1922 and the revisions made to it in the London Naval Treaty 1930. These limited the construction of aircraft carriers, battleships and battle cruisers, and placed a maximum tonnage of 10,000 for other categories of warship, the aim being that by limiting the naval construction of Britain, the USA, France, Italy and Japan an arms race would be avoided, making it unlikely that war would be used to resolve international tensions. Instead, the League of Nations would act as arbiter for disputes with countries using political measures.

Maiolo argues that by 1926 it became apparent that the cost per ton of warships was increasing hugely. Orders for warships tailed off after this point, as did orders for merchant ships. The result was many 'ship makers went bust or gave up the arms trade altogether ... By 1935 Britain's naval building capacity had shrunk by about half'. However, he states that 'the situation was bad but not irreversible ... Britain's building capacity was still the largest in the world' in 1933. The problem would come if there were another naval arms race because Britain's shipyards were too busy modernising old ships to 'out-build the whole world'.[48]

At the same time as the League of Nations was being formed in 1919, Britain's political leaders were reassessing the country's defence requirements. On 15 August 1919, the War Cabinet put in place the Ten Year Rule. This based defence planning on the assumption that there would be no great war in the next ten years. In one form or another, the rule was the guiding principle for Britain's defence policy until it was rescinded in 1932,[49] having been annually re-endorsed from 1928.[50] The rule limited Admiralty spending and stated that no new construction was to be undertaken. No real consideration was given to rule's impact upon the timeframe of its existence, particularly with regard to military modernisation.[51] Despite its obvious benefits, economically and politically, it had a significant impact on the Royal Navy's ability to rearm when the time came.

Therefore, the decision to disband the WRNS was consistent with the wider economic and social policies of the interwar government and pervading social sentiment. This was in opposition to a small group of former female military leaders who wanted a permanent women's auxiliary maintained postwar, as previously discussed.

Rearmament: The Changing Fortune of the WRNS

It was a distinct set of circumstances, not seen to the same extent in other European countries, which led to the recreation of the women's auxiliaries before the outbreak of World War II. Their reformation is fundamentally linked to the government and armed force's military policies in the 1930s. Britain, by this decade, faced three major issues. The first was the economic position of the country following the 1929 stock market crash in the United States and Britain's exit from the Gold Standard in 1931, which had led to mass unemployment across the country and weakened economic prospects for years to come. Secondly, the Axis Powers were becoming increasingly more menacing, leading to the decline and destruction of the 1920s peace policies and arms limiting treaties. The third issue was the public anti-war sentiment that limited the state's ability to rearm and operate beyond policies of appeasement. However, from 1935 onward there was recognition that war with Germany, Italy, Japan or all three together was a distinct possibility.

As such, rearmament began in earnest and plans for total war were much discussed. Many committees were set up to assess the future needs of a country at war and possible measures for the worst-case scenario. This is where the issue of female military participation came back into the policy debate having been dropped in 1919.

Throughout the 1920s, the combination of anti-war policies that limited the size of the Royal Navy and economic policies that hampered its reach resulted in a service by 1932 that was unable to honour its obligations under the League of Nations or help maintain the borders established in the Locarno treaty.[52] In March 1932 the Cabinet, following the call of the Chiefs of Staff, Sir Maurice Hankey,[53] and Sir Robert Vansittart of the Foreign Office, allowed the Ten Year Rule to lapse. First Sea Lord Sir Ernle Chatfield argued that 'it was impossible to see three years ahead, far less ten'.[54] The lapse of the rule was 'Britain's first halting step towards rearmament', allowing for the restoration of the armed forces.[55]

In 1933, the Chiefs of Staff recommended 'new and clear instructions' as to how the government would defend Britain and the empire. Their response was to form the Defence Requirements Committee, composed of the three Chiefs of Staff, Vansittart, Hankey and Sir Warren Fisher representing the treasury.[56] The committee's remit was to explore in more detail the deficiencies of the military, propose plans for rearmament and establish strategic defence needs. It was decided in the first report of 28 February 1934 to put in place a five-year programme of rearmament. It was not clear at this time what capability Germany held, but it was assumed that five years would be necessary before the country 'became a definite menace'.[57]

The committee was constrained in its ability to amend the nation's military deficiencies, particularly those of the navy, due to the political decisions made by President Hoover and Prime Minister MacDonald at the London Naval Treaty, which restricted shipbuilding for another three years. The navy was limited to modernising its warships, the building up of essential stores and developing naval bases between 1932 and 1935. Although in terms of tonnage the Royal Navy was still the most dominant globally,

Britain had the largest merchant fleet and a worldwide network of bases, so the situation was not as dire as it could have been.[58]

More significantly, public anti-war feeling was still high in the mid 1930s; the Geneva Disarmament Conference 1932–3 was evidence of this, as was the defeat of a Conservative MP with a large majority, in the East Fulham by-election in October 1933, by a Labour candidate who fought for a programme of disarmament. Consequently, the government did not announce its 'deficiency programme' until March 1935 when a White Paper was unavoidable.[59]

At this stage the Axis Powers were growing increasingly hostile. Germany had built three new battleships between 1931 and 1934, which circumvented the naval treaties; Hitler had withdrawn Germany from the Disarmament Conference and the League of Nations on 14 October 1933 and was increasing a massive rearmament programme. Japan did not renew the restrictions of the London Naval Treaty after the second London Naval Conference on 15 January 1936; and Italy looked intent on invading Abyssinia and was being hostile in the Mediterranean. The result was the replacement of the Defence Requirements Committee by the Defence Priorities and Requirements Committee in July 1935, which, unlike its predecessor, was not so financially constrained.[60]

From then until the outbreak of war, rearmament increased but continued to be slow because of concerns about the state of Britain's economy. Britain had a favourable balance of trade for only one year of the decade. As a result, the governments of the 1930s consistently minimised defence expenditure.[61] In the late 1930s, the navy, as part of the rearmament policy, received new escort vessels, minesweepers, harbour maintenance and an airbase at Scapa Flow.[62] It also modernised older ships and naval bases and began production on new battleships and submarines. 1939 saw defence spending finally increase dramatically. It doubled to £1 billion and the Territorial Army doubled to allow Britain to support France on the continent, in case Chamberlain's appeasement policy did not succeed.[63]

In October 1935, as part of the review of military deficiency, a Special Sub-Committee of Imperial Defence was set up to consider the establishment of a women's reserve corps. In May 1936, the committee reported: 'Women's Reserve deemed not desirable',[64] the reason being that any female labour needed could be obtained through Labour Exchanges if war broke out.[65] The conclusions drawn by Mason indicate that women were not being discounted from war service, far from it. There was an expectation that female labour would need to be used, but the creation of women's auxiliary services when the country was at peace were seen as unnecessary and politically challenging, given national sentiment. The only female pseudo-military organisation, the Emergency Service, was given a title 'designed to avoid any overtly warlike connotations'.[66] In doing so it looked much like any other women's group with self-styled connections to the military, such as the Association of Wrens.

The Association was calling in early 1938 for news of the possibility of the service being re-formed. Dame Katharine Furse wrote to members in *The Wren* in April 1938 that she had been in touch with the Admiralty:

> [I] understand that if women were again needed to replace men in the Navy the WRNS would be again brought into being. But there are, as yet, no plans for this, and only a real emergency would make it necessary. So far as I can ascertain, the Government is not at present much concerned with the possibility of using women for war service.[67]

The article serves to highlight the desire of many women within the Association to take on military roles if the need arose, a common theme in the magazine during this period. It also demonstrates that, to all intents and purposes, there was a desire, but not a lot of belief, that women would be required in the near future.

According to Braybon and Summerfield 'the summer of 1938 was ... a turning point in the government's acceptance of the need to prepare for war', altering the status quo Furse had written of in April. 'Women figured in its plans, in acknowledgement both of their usefulness in World War I and the extensive devastation' expected from the looming war.[68] The decision of the Special Sub-Committee of Imperial Defence changed in April 1937 when the inter-Departmental Committee on the Emergency Powers (Defence) Bill stated that the War Office intended to create women's corps for all three services early in the event of war.[69] The latter months of 1938, which had followed increasing instability in Europe with the German invasion of Austria in March and the Munich Conference in September, saw the British government forming policies for mobilising the country in the event of war, including the recreation of the Women's Royal Naval Service.

Maiolo argues that the 'buzzwords of the total war systematisers entered the vocabulary of everyday politics' from 1936 onward as Hitler's expansionist policies became more apparent with the occupation of the demilitarised Rhineland. The belief that any impending war would be a total war galvanised state ability to be 'total', society 'regimented' and the economy 'planned'. 'Planning, whether military or economic – with the distinction between them becoming more blurred all the time – was invoked as the way to make the future certain'.[70] 1938 was the point at which women finally became a necessary element in the regimenting of society and the planning of the economy to prepare for total war. Lessons had been learnt from World War I: female labour was necessary and desirable. This change in policy was one of the shifts Segal et al. see as a part of the process of altering the inclusion of women in the armed forces. Precedent no doubt helped it come about far earlier in this war than the creation of the women's auxiliaries in World War I.

Provisions for organising 'national service' began at this point. The Man-Power Sub-Committee had on 29 September 1938 published its final report considering the 'measures to be taken, both on the outbreak of a major war and in making preparations for it, to secure the most effective use of labour of the country'.[71] The action of this plan is outlined in a memorandum by the Lord Privy Seal Sir John Anderson MP to the Cabinet, dated 18 November 1938, where the objective to 'find people for jobs, not to find jobs for people' was proposed.[72] It was expected that there would be two main needs for labour, firstly defence in the early stages of the war against an intensive air attack, the second, for the long-term effect of conflict on the country. It was felt that 'all preparations for the first stage needed to be completed beforehand in every detail'.[73]

Volunteers were recruited using a *Handbook for National Service* (published January 1939), which was delivered to every house in the country. All volunteers were listed at Divisional Offices of the Ministry of Labour and Employment Exchanges with local National Service Committees. In the event of war, these bodies would all come under the Ministry of National Service, which was set up by the Emergency Appointments Act.[74]

The *Handbook for National Service* provided 'a guide to the ways in which the people of this country may give service'.[75] It was addressed to both the countrymen and countrywomen of the UK. The aim of the guide was to provide people with information to help them judge what service they could best give. For women there were 15 occupations they could choose from, including: air raid wardens, first aiders, ambulance drivers, auxiliary fire service, St John's Ambulance, British Red Cross, Auxiliary Territorial Service (ATS – the new name for the WAAC, QMAAC), Royal Air Force Companies, Civil Air Guard, WRNS, help in evacuating children and trained nurses. The terms of the Women's Service in the Royal Navy (as the handbook called it at the time) stated:

> It has been decided to employ in time of war or emergency a limited number of women (initially about 1,500) to take the place of naval and marine ranks and ratings in naval establishments upon secretarial, clerical, accounting, shorthand and typewriting duties; and domestic duties as cooks, stewardesses, waitresses and messengers.[76]

This passage indicates expectations that only a few women would be needed to be Wrens throughout the war. On 13 October 1938 C. M. Bruce (secretary to the head of Civil Establishment [CE]) placed the requirement at 1194.[77] The Board of the Admiralty in July of the same year estimated the total number to be around 3,000 women.[78] These estimates were all proved unrealistic. By its peak in June 1944, 74,620 women were serving as Wrens.[79] In total, over 100,000 women served throughout the war. In 1938, there was no sense of how big the service would eventually become. The way that all of the women's services grew beyond their 1938 expectations reflected the totality of the war on the UK's resources and the changes in thinking this required.

The listed duties for Wrens in the handbook are characteristically very feminine, with jobs such as secretaries, typists and cooks reflecting social conventions of the time. In the initial plans for the service, there was no departure from the traditional spheres of women's work. However, these nine (or so) roles grew to around 125 by the end of the war.[80] Wrens undertook all manner of jobs in the navy, bar those specifically related to front line fighting.

The documents also serve to highlight the government's recognition of the need to be firmly in control of the procurement of people to fill roles early on in the war, the aim being, that there would be far less disorganisation and inefficiency than in the first war. Ensuring that labour was controlled at the centre by the Ministry of National Service would mean people would be placed where there were vacancies in jobs and hopefully those with the skills to do a job would be matched with a suitable occupation.

Differences in the Formation of Women's Auxiliaries Internationally

In comparison, the origin of the women's auxiliaries in the UK was very different from its counterparts in other countries. The Canadian WRNCS, Australian WRANS and New Zealand WRNZNS were later formed in 1942, developing along similar lines as Britain. In the United States, plans were put in place from 1939 to form a women's army auxiliary corps. However, the navy was far more reluctant and restricted enlistment to 'male citizens'.[81] Intriguingly, 13,000 women had served with the US Navy in World War I, so it was not as though there was not a precedent. Yet, the navy was generally apathetic to including women, not deeming the establishment of an auxiliary service as 'desirable'.[82] This only changed in July 1942 when President Roosevelt signed new legislation to adjust the preceding policy, creating the Women Accepted for Volunteer Emergency Services (WAVES).[83] Between 1943 and 1945 the number of WAVES grew from 27,000 to 86,000.

In Germany, the creation of women's auxiliaries occurred from 1 October 1940. Had the needs of total war not required the employment of women in industry and uniformed services, it is likely Hitler would not have agreed to their use. In 1929, Germany had the largest number of women in Parliament. Within four years, there were none and all women's organisations had been wiped out. In Hitler's phraseology, women were 'mothers of soldiers and relaxation for the tired warrior'.[84] The Mother's Cross was introduced to reward women for having as many babies as possible. However, compulsory service for women aged 18 to 40 years was introduced in December 1941. Unlike the equivalent policy in Britain, it was not robustly enforced, possibly due to the negative view of women as workers. In addition, uniform was only worn by serving women outside of the borders of the Third Reich. Women serving in Germany were only issued with a protective smock or overall.[85]

Throughout the war, women in the German military services were not held in the same esteem as those in Britain. In contrast, the Soviet Union was the only state that actively encouraged women into military roles, allowing them to serve in combat alongside men, as snipers, tank drivers and pilots.[86] However, the policy of women being non-combatant would be actively upheld in the UK during the conflict. As an example, the ATS in 1941 employed women in anti-aircraft sites, replacing the majority of men.[87] However, unlike the Soviet Union which allowed 300,000 women to run these stations completely, in the UK women were not allowed to operate the guns. Women were also banned from firing the pilotless V1 and V2 rockets in 1944 and 1945 although they did help staff the anti-aircraft artillery batteries.[88]

The Formation of the Second WRNS

As we have already seen, the WRNS in World War I came into being following Eric Geddes' decision to form the service in response to a declining labour supply situation in the navy and because the army had set a precedent in forming its own women's auxiliary. The actual shaping of the service was left to Katharine Furse upon her appointment as Director. However, plans to recreate the second WRNS, which occurred in 1938, arose in conjunction with the wider policies of national service being shaped by the cabinet and the soon to be published *Handbook for National Service*. The Board asked Commanders-in-Chief at port to provide specific requirements for the replacement of men by women should war break out in the aim of then deciding what role the women's auxiliary service would adopt.

Rather than appointing a Director to work on a scheme of service for the re-formed women's auxiliary naval corps, a retired civil servant C. M. Bruce was appointed to begin the task following the decision of the Man-Power Subcommittee and the plans to create the national handbook.[89] Bruce's notes suggest that the reason the scheme was written by men was because no suitable woman had been appointed to head the service at that point.[90] There is no indication that women were being actively excluded, as the Army Office had done with its own auxiliary in the first war. An initial discussion of the nature of the service, dated 12 October 1938, also shows that the Civil Establishment (which would have responsibility for the WRNS until 1941 and had Bruce write the scheme of service) wished to work through some of the reputational issues the WAAC had experienced in the previous war, before forming the actual WRNS and appointing individuals to service.[91]

In the histories of the WRNS, it is emphasised that Katharine Furse had in the autumn of 1937 and again in spring 1938 written to the Admiralty offering the help of ex-Wrens should the need arise. Many ex-Wrens also wrote to offer their services.[92] In a letter from Furse on 25 September 1938, three days before the reformation of the ATS and its RAF companies was announced, she re-emphasised the impatience some of the association members were feeling in regard to the lack of information about whether a women's service for the navy would once again be needed. She felt 'there is first class material and it would be wasteful to lose it if there is even a remote chance of the navy requiring women for replacements on shore'.[93] The lack of information from the Admiralty drove this impatience by Furse and other women in the association. There is a sense that they knew preparations were being made for the possibility of war but that they were being left on the outside. This is evident in this letter in which she said:

> Please give me the chance to talk to someone at the Admiralty this week. I have tried hard not to force myself upon busy people but I think the time has come when the women who want to help the navy should be allowed to have some idea of whether the Navy is likely to accept their help or not. Then they will know where they are and be able to take on other forms of work or not as the case may be.[94]

The Wren magazines of 1938 indicate the impatience of members to know if the service was being re-formed following Furse's approach to the navy in September. In an article dated October 1938, Furse asks the members:

> To be content and go slow so far as wanting to work with the Navy is concerned. Having been through 1914 and having experienced the fatuity due to small groups of women being formed and the waste of valuable energy . . . I am determined, personally, to wait till I know what the Government is planning and wanting of us before I take any hand in producing the same wastage.

The article reflects her prudence and suggests that she had no involvement in the plans for reforming the service, as she had very little knowledge of this. Interestingly, she also states: 'it was not till 1917, after more than three years of war, that the WRNS was formed. The navy must, for obvious reasons, be the last service to use women.'[95]

Furse was not even aware at this point that the Man-Power Sub Committee had decided to reestablish the women's auxiliaries. There is a certain expectation that the WRNS might not be re-formed until much later in the war. What is interesting is that the navy is viewed as the service least requiring women, owing, it can be assumed, to the dominance of sea service, from which women were barred. This sentiment could reflect why it would not be until April 1939 that the reestablishment of the WRNS was announced, months after the ATS. This time difference may also have something to do with the WRNS being administered by the Civil Establishment which, as will be seen in the next chapter, reflects the lack of interest it held towards the women's auxiliary, making the need to reform it less immediate.

The importance of Furse's letters to the Admiralty in September is questionable, in the light of her article in *The Wren*. The re-founding lay in the hands of the Secretary of the Admiralty Sir Archibald Carter, Deputy Director of Personnel Services Captain M. H. A. Kelsey and the Head of Civil Establishment Branch A. S. Le Maistre and the Secretary to the Civil Establishment C. M. Bruce. The necessity of female labour had already been decided. Evidence of the government and Labour Sub-Committee's approach to the use of labour in the event of war points toward the steadfast acceptance of this. Vera Laughton Mathews also states in her memoirs that the Home Ports Commanders had pushed for the employment of women, recognising the need to replace male office staff at the outbreak of war.[96] The archive evidence indicates Furse was merely an adviser. Sir Archibald Carter, in response to Furse's letter, wrote to her on 29 September 1938 requesting she meet with Second Sea Lord Charles Little and Bruce on 30 September.[97]

Where Furse did have some influence was in the promotion of 'a suitable woman to organize the service'. The two women were Beatrice Wyatt and Vera Laughton Mathews. She had also kept all of her 1917–1919 papers and gave these to the Admiralty to make use of. Following this meeting Bruce set about writing the new scheme of the service. Mason argues that the re-formed Women's Royal Naval Service could be said to date from 22 November 1938 as this was when the paper 'a Corps to be known as the Women's Royal Naval Service' was started by Bruce. This was the result of discussions between himself, Carter, Kelsey and Le Maistre.[98]

CHAPTER 4

April 1939–41: Management and Growth of the 'Civilian' Service

Although always non-combatant and a separate entity under civilian law, the nature of the WRNS changed significantly between 1939 and 1941, becoming an integral part of the Royal Navy's war effort. It was re-formed, unexpectedly by its new leadership, as a civilian service, managed through the Civil Establishment (CE) branch of the Admiralty. As a result, it experienced a dual identity in the first two years of World War II. On the one hand, it was formed as a uniformed women's auxiliary with an organisational structure based on similar lines to the RN and became increasingly militarised by 1941. On the other, its CE managers did not see it as comparable to its male counterpart, for example, stalling the requisitioning of uniforms and blocking the equivalence of ranks.

This initial dichotomy, which was overturned in April 1941, was highly significant to the creation of the nature of the World War II WRNS. This chapter argues that this discrepancy, unlike its army and air force equivalents, allowed the service to create its own distinct character, framed by the ideas of Vera Laughton Mathews who was instrumental to this. Her memoirs are integral to this chapter, providing an insight into the first two years of the service, which is little documented. The movement of the WRNS into the Naval Personnel Division of the Admiralty in 1941 saw all shore-based naval roles that did not need sea experience or great physical strength filled entirely by Wrens and the massive expansion in categories.[1] Having to forge its own course in the early part of the war, because of the lack of naval knowledge of its leaders and the lack of interest on the part of its CE managers, the WRNS extensively expanded its remit and the roles of women within the service beyond its initial scheme of service.

The Service is Re-Formed

The Commanders-in-Chief and Lord Commissioners of the Admiralty approved the scheme of service for the WRNS in early February 1939. Vera Laughton Mathews and Beatrice Wyatt were invited to discuss the scheme on 17 February with Sir Archibald Carter (Secretary of the Admiralty), C. M. Bruce, A. S. Le Maistre (Head of Civil Establishment Branch) and Charles Little (Second Sea Lord).[2] Minutes dated 22 February outline the discussions between the women and officials. The name of the service was agreed by all those present believing 'it was impossible to improve on the old name of Women's Royal Naval Service, which would, moreover emphasize the traditions established twenty years before'.[3] The uniform was discussed and it was suggested that members of different branches should wear badges modelled on those of the navy; it was assumed to place it alongside its male equivalent.[4] The name 'Wren' was also made official at the meeting, becoming the suffix to ranks, such as Wren, Leading Wren, Chief Wren and later Chief Petty Officer Wren.[5]

Interestingly, these ranks did not necessarily equate to Royal Navy ranks in terms of 'stripes' (the bands worn on the arm to indicate rank). Early on in the war, Wrens with greater responsibilities had fewer stripes than their male counterparts. This became an issue in 1940 when it became clear that Second and Third Officers had the same one stripe despite Second Officers being in charge of a unit of around 100 Wrens and several Third Officers. It was considered that their status should be shown to be higher than a Sub-Lieutenant (equivalent to the WRNS Third Officer) because of this.[6]

What was made apparent at this meeting was that the WRNS would be under the responsibility of the Second Sea Lord in name only. This was different from how it had been in World War I, and different from what Laughton Mathews and Wyatt had expected. Instead, the service was regarded as civilian and it came under the control of the Civil Establishment Branch. The significance of this is understated in the contemporary literature. The only acknowledgment is the passing comment Mason makes with respect to the meeting, that 'they had not realised the significance of the involvement of the CE branch. The new service would be regarded as civilian, not as part of the Navy.'[7] This significance, however, is neither described nor indeed even further mentioned. The assumption appears to be that this early duality did not affect the identity of the service. It is argued here, however, that this was, in fact, extremely significant of the ability of the WRNS to shape its identity in the way that they did.

The Admiralty was split into a number of branches, including the Military Branch, Naval Branch, Legal and Civil Branch. The Military branch was responsible for the distribution of the fleet 'and in wartime acting as the channel of communication for operational orders'.[8] The Naval Branch was responsible for deploying personnel and acted as the main channel of communication for the Second Sea Lord. The Civil dealt with civilian establishments within the RN. This branch was a part of the Secretary of the Admiralty, Sir Archibald Carter's department. Headed by the Permanent Secretary, Le Maistre, the department was responsible for the general administration and coordination of the Admiralty.[9]

Laughton Mathews' autobiography provides the most detailed account of the impact of the service being a part of the CE. She was of the opinion that the service would be under the direct control of the Second Sea Lord, taking it for granted that this would be the case due to the precedent of World War I. In her meeting of 22 February when she first saw Admiral Charles Little, the Second Sea Lord, she expected him to be 'future lord and master of the new service'. In fact he would have very little to do with the service in 'many a long and weary month'.[10]

In regard to the WRNS command and control, it was clearly stated in First Lord of the Admiralty Lord Stanhope's letter to the King (requesting approval for the WRNS), dated 3 April 1939 that, the Director was 'responsible, under the Second Sea Lord, for administration and organization of the service'.[11] The service was firmly connected to the Admiralty, as the Director was 'responsible to the Board of Admiralty for the recruitment, efficiency, welfare and discipline of the Women's Royal Naval Service'.[12] However, in the early years of the war, decisions made by the service had to be approved via the Civil Establishment, rather than through the Naval Branch, which would have been more logical as the WRNS was directly replacing (male) naval personnel. The decision to make the service civilian might have been due to the initial 'categories' developed in the scheme of service not being directly related to combat operations, despite this changing from August 1939 when it was decided that cypher officers would be trained. It included two branches and around nine categories.

These branches and categories would already start to give way by 1940 with the addition of further roles. This tiny number of categories would grow to 129 by the end of the war, taking the service far beyond its initial civilian status.[13]

The Director found dealing with the Civil Establishment challenging owing to their lack of knowledge of naval affairs, their area of responsibility being administrative rather than military. Laughton Mathews recalls the 'CE had no sympathy with [the] WRNS naval aspirations'.[14] The CE was very clear that the WRNS was civilian. This distinction led to a number of problems and battles for the service; one included the issue of uniform. It had been agreed by the King, following the letter by Stanhope, that the

Table 4.1   Early World War II Categories[15]

(a) Clerical	(b) Domestic
Writer	Waiters
Supply	Cooks
Motor Driver	
Signalman	
Telephone Operator	
Clerical Staff	
Confidential clerk etc.	

WRNS would wear a distinctive uniform, which had some similarities to the naval uniform, in terms of style and the nature of branch badges.[16] However, several months into the war the WRNS still had no uniform. It became increasingly clear that the reason why none had been made related to the CE and the Director of Victualling, believing that because the service was civilian, no uniform was required. The victualling department was not responsible for clothing civilians. In fact, the Director of this department felt that if women should wear uniform it should be khaki. It was only when the Fourth Sea Lord, who was responsible for uniform, became aware of the situation that he ordered the Director of Victualing to provide uniforms for the WRNS, whether they were naval personnel or not.[17]

Laughton Mathews' tenacity had a formative influence on the identity of the WRNS. The Director's two battles were to create a distinctive uniform and to have officer's ranks match similar positions in the other women's auxiliaries and to men within the Royal Navy. Involving the Second Sea Lord Admiral Little was essential for this.[18]

Le Maistre, head of the CE, wrote a letter to Laughton Mathews dated 3 September 1940, arguing that 'nobody can seriously maintain that there is a real connection between the "ranks" of the WRNS and those of the Navy' and 'the WRNS officers [should match] properly with ATS officers'.[19] This discussion clearly demarcates the difference in opinion between the leadership of CE and the WRNS about the nature of the service. The WRNS saw itself as having a naval identity whereas the tone of Le Maistre's letter is sneering about this request, particularly shown by the term 'ranks' being in inverted commas. His focus seems to be far more on issues of pay and similarities between the other women's services. Admiral Little replied, 'I am not impressed with the arguments of the Head of CE. The object is to obtain for the WRNS the best working conditions possible vis-à-vis naval personnel and not be a comparison with the ATS.'[20]

His support may, in part, demonstrate why Laughton Mathews managed to keep her job despite frequently challenging the CE.

Its lack of interest in the WRNS could have also played a role, in that most of the time it ignored this new service that had been put under its management, viewing it, perhaps, as a small annoyance.

The issue was about how effectively women could work alongside their male naval counterparts if their ranks were not equivalent, reflecting a need for parity between the two services. WRNS Superintendents noticed the difficulties of the differences most acutely. Muriel Mackenzie-Grieve, the Superintendent at Rosyth, wrote to Laughton Mathews on 20 May 1940, five months before the CE began discussing the issue, arguing that the problem was that WRNS officers who were in charge of units of 80 women and over, ranked below a Lieutenant Royal Naval Officer.[21] This both defied the authority of women in such a position but also meant the challenges of their job were not recognised in their rank.

When the issue came up for discussion in October 1940 many of the Commanders-in-Chief of the Royal Navy concurred with the argument made by the WRNS and Admiral Little, returning letters to the Secretary of the Admiralty in support of the change to stripes on WRNS's officers uniform.[23] Finally, after various small changes to the officers' stripes, the WRNS ranks finally became comparable to naval officers' ranks on 24 September 1941 as shown below.

Table 4.2   Equivalent WRNS and RN ranks in World War II[22]

WRNS Officers	RN Equivalent	WRNS Ratings	RN Equivalent
Director	Rear-Admiral	Chief Petty Officer	Chief Petty Officer
Deputy Director	Captain	Petty Officer	Petty Officer
Port- Superintendent	Commander	Leading Wren	Leading Seaman
Chief Officer	Lieutenant Commander	Wren	Able Seaman
First Officer	Lieutenant	Ordinary Wren	Ordinary Seaman
Second Officer	Sub-lieutenant		
Third Officer			

It was these 'battles' that served to strengthen the position of the Director, bringing legitimacy to her role, but also forming a distinct militarised identity for the service.

Vera Laughton Mathews becomes Director

Carter wrote to Laughton Mathews on 31 March 1939 on behalf of the Lord Commissioners of the Admiralty asking her to become the new Director of the WRNS. She was later told that her previous meeting with the Secretary of the Admiralty on 22 February had effectively been her interview.[24] She found the date very memorable as it represents 'Thinking Day' in Girl Guiding, celebrating the birthdays of the founders of scouting and guiding. Her name had been 'brought before their Lordships as a person who could fittingly carry out the duties of Director'.[25] She was told that if she accepted she would be given full details of her responsibilities in due course. On 1 April, she replied expressing her 'deep sense of honour'.[26] At a similar point in time, the King approved the re-formation of the service following a submission of the scheme of service and details of the new director.[27]

Laughton Mathews' appointment officially began on 11 April. Carter wrote to her again listing her responsibilities, including, 'entry, promotion, accommodation, medical attendance, pay, allowances, travelling expenses, leave of absence, and retirement or discharge of members of the service'.[28] This letter, and the scheme put in place by Bruce, was '[her] only terms of reference for three-and-a-half years'.[29] The WRNS was 'largely left to work out their own salvation', as Laughton Mathews put it.[30] The Admiralty, she states, had been looking for someone 'on whom they could dump the whole thing and leave her to get on with it'.[31] Despite having a clear scheme of service the new Director had to build it from the ground. No support structures or administrative organisation existed when she was appointed. Contrastingly, when her equivalent in the ATS, Helen Gwynne-Vaughan, was appointed in the summer of 1939, the army auxiliary had already appointed county commandants. These appointments were made by the presidents of the Territorial Army associations, tending 'to approach

the local "great lady" to fill this role'.[32] This difference meant
Laughton Mathews had much greater control of selection
procedures that helped foster the WRNS independence.

The challenges of being part of the CE became apparent as soon
as Laughton Mathews was appointed. Fifteen thousand women had
applied to be Wrens following the publication of the *Handbook for
National Service*.[33] These letters went unanswered for months as
there was no WRNS to deal with them, and no one had been
assigned to sort the problem out at the Admiralty, with more
letters coming from applicants every day in early 1939.[34] Nearby
members of the Association of Wrens offered to volunteer to help
sort through the mail.[35] The WRNS office staff consisted of these
volunteers in the early months, as only the Director and Deputy
had been appointed.

Laughton Mathews had to start her service immediately. She
initially visited the large naval ports to ascertain their need for
Wrens should war break out. She undertook these visits with her
Deputy, Angela E M Goodenough, who was the only member of the
service who was appointed before the Director, since she had
previously been Chief Woman Officer for the Admiralty. This was a
civilian role that entailed looking after the welfare of female
employees. Laughton Mathews initially found their relationship a
challenge because Goodenough knew everyone at the
Admiralty, which meant it was hard to forge new relationships.
However, Laughton Mathews contends, 'in spite of differences
in general outlook, I think we had a fundamental respect for
each other ... [s]he was one of the most honest people I have ever
met.'[36]

Laughton Mathews and Goodenough set up their offices in a back
room of the Admiralty. The new Director read through all of the
papers Katharine Furse had compiled in case a women's service was
re-formed. Her reflection upon these documents was that, if
anything, the new service had regressed, as it was now administered
through civilian channels. In her memoirs, she later stated, 'I had no
idea at the time what a handicap this would be; I merely knew it was
a wrong status.'[37] The problem was that, especially in the early
months, she was 'dealing with people who were not concerned with

the detailed manning problems of the Navy, and had no idea of how urgently and how soon the WRNS would be needed'. Because the service was not under the direct control of the Admiralty, it was difficult to get help as 'everyone ... was weighed down with work and responsibility'.[38] During the five month build-up to the outbreak of war, she and Goodenough had very little help or involvement from the CE. She notes, 'I never knew if I was doing what was required of me, though I have no doubt now that I should have heard if I had not',[39] reflecting her feeling that the service was left to its own salvation, as she called it.

These documents also opened her eyes to her ignorance of Admiralty protocol and the task ahead of her. Yet, from the personal accounts of the women who served under her, Vera Laughton Mathews was viewed as tenacious and a very good organiser. Jean Atkins, when interviewed, felt that the Director was a domineering personality (she notes not unpleasant), who was able to get her point across.[40]

They had to travel around all of the naval ports in the early months to ascertain where women could substitute men, or where there would be immediate need of workers in the future. The Director and her deputy met a mixed reception at the different naval ports. At Chatham they were given a real welcome by the Commander-in-Chief. Each head of department had compiled a list of what help could be given by the service and the number of Wrens required.

At Portsmouth, however, the Commander-in-Chief and the Commodore of the Barracks did not meet them. Laughton Mathews believes the possible attitude 'of the premier naval port savoured a little of "when we get the Wrens we shall know what to do with them without the Admiralty poking its noses in"'.[41] In the early days of the war, she received a number of patronising and 'extremely rude' letters from various officers. 'More than once I was told that I flouted the opinion of an Admiral of thirty-five years' experience.' In time, she came to regard these letters with a form of sympathy, thinking, 'dear, dear he doesn't know what he's talking about' as she became more confident about her position and the role of the WRNS in the navy.[42]

In the early years, some RN members were not hostile, merely unreceptive. However, there was not the same sense of inertia in the WRNS' dealings with naval officers as there was in the Director's communications with the CE. In the interviews and archive sources, women note that generally naval personnel had a very favourable view of the WRNS, or if they did not to begin with, they soon changed.

In the same month in which Laughton Mathews was appointed Director, advertisements were placed in national newspapers calling for applicants for the posts of Port Superintendent in Portsmouth, Plymouth, Chatham and Rosyth. These women would form the managerial level under the Director and had responsibility for the recruitment, efficiency and discipline of the Wrens serving in their localities.[43] The advert resulted in 700 applications for the posts, indicating the obvious draw of the service for many women. However, most were unsuitable as they lacked qualifications. It was made clear in the initial scheme of service that a 'drawing-room committee composed of well-meaning ladies who have no qualifications whatsoever for organizing a big body of women should be avoided at all costs'.[44] From early on it was established at all levels that women's selection would be based upon their educational and personal qualities rather than upon their status or class in society. This was in contrast to the ATS under the leadership of Gwynne-Vaughan, which was re-formed along the same lines as in the first war, replicating what were becoming outdated views of class and gender, with older women selected from the middle class who had led the WAAC.[45]

After an intensive selection interview by a board that included the Director, her deputy, Myra Curtis from the Treasury (who would become Principal of Newnham College, Cambridge later in the war) and Nancy Nettleford, the Managing Director of Nettleford and Sons and a member of the Equal Pay Commission, four women were appointed following interviews with a great many 'pleasant amateurs'.[46] Joan Carpenter was sent to Chatham, Muriel Mackenzie-Grieve to Rosyth, Effie Welby to Plymouth and later, once the war had started, Amy Curtis to Portsmouth. A Chief

Officer was also appointed for Portland and recruiting officers selected for Bristol, Cardiff, Dover, Deal and Liverpool.[47]

Carpenter had been Secretary of the Women's Club before applying to be Superintendent and had served as a Wren in World War I as a motor driver in Dover; Mackenzie-Grieve was also another ex-service woman who had served in Malta as an officer in the department of the senior naval officer. After the war, she had trained as a social worker at the London School of Economics and worked for London County Council. Laughton Mathews felt that she was one of the most experienced of the early Superintendents. Welby had carried out much voluntary work, including being a division commissioner within Girl Guiding, and Laughton Mathews viewed her as a 'born leader' with an inbuilt knowledge of the navy owing to being the daughter and wife of naval officers.[48] Curtis had been in the WAAC during World War I and had been a Conservative Agent prior to joining the WRNS. Laughton Mathews recalls her as having been a dynamic personality, somewhat of an individualist, but a 'stickler for committee procedure'.[49] Having appointed the Superintendents to get on with peace-time recruiting and training, Laughton Mathews and Goodenough pursued their work in the headquarters, creating enrolment forms, forms for references, plans for the Officers' Training Course and designs for uniforms.[50]

They worked past 8 o'clock every night and between them staffed the office seven days a week.[51] Mason argues that at the outbreak of war 'there were no WRNS Headquarters staff, no trained Unit Officers but there were about 1,000 immobile Wrens, and immediate cries for Wrens across the country'.[52] The outbreak of war saw the service's head office swamped with applications from women wishing to become Wrens, both by letter and in person. In early September, the Treasury and Admiralty finally gave permission for 12 officers as Headquarters staff.[53] In the first month, the service had to undertake two office moves, eventually settling in the Board of Education offices on Kingsway, off the Aldwych, where Laughton Mathews and Goodenough had their own offices. The WRNS would eventually make a final move to offices in Queen Anne's Mansions in St James' Park when the Admiralty decided to take over the buildings for the operations of the Second Sea Lord in

1942, finally bringing the WRNS back within the Admiralty itself. Laughton Mathews felt this final move marked the WRNS as having 'arrived' within the navy and that it had comfortably taken up its position.[54]

At Kingsway there was an office for half a dozen clerks presided over by the Director's secretary, N. K. Kellard, who had been transferred from her job in the Admiralty earlier in the year, and a large room for the 12 HQ officers. The officers had responsibility for registry, recruitment, applications, interviews, officers' appointments, drafting and clothing.[55]

The first two years of the war were extremely challenging for the Director and senior officers in the service. They faced a great deal of pessimism from the 'back room in the Admiralty, when everyone was saying, "Wrens can't do this, can't do that; can't go here, can't go there".'[56] Such negativity made it very difficult for them to meet the growing needs of the service. This is not surprising given the position of women prior to the outbreak of war. Being able to stand up against the negativity of some officers and the CE was fundamental to the growth of the service.

The increasing demands of the war meant that the WRNS was called on to do a great deal more by the navy, prompted by individual requests by Commanders, which was not always reported to its CE leaders. In 1940 there was a huge need for a training centre. Laughton Mathews went to the Second Sea Lord in desperation to try and get his backing. Amusingly, she states, 'he kindly but firmly took me more or less by the ear and trotted me along to the Secretary's room, explaining as we went that the WRNS did not come under him because it was non-combatant'.[57] The senior people in the CE were overburdened and decisions were not being made; this meant that every decision made about the WRNS had to be fought for.

The Build-Up to War: Laughton Mathews' Defiance of the Civil Establishment

One of Laughton Mathews' most rebellious acts when still governed by the CE came before the war even broke out. In the early part of

1939, the Director felt great demands would be soon placed upon the service, which was constrained in its ability to appoint valuable individuals in peacetime. The scheme of service amendments in 1939 stated:

> In peacetime 'immobile' members of the Office Duties Branch only will be enrolled and trained. They will be enrolled for four years and will be required to attend twenty-four drills a year ... No pay will be given in peacetime but each member who completes her twenty-four drills will receive ten shillings to cover any expenses.[58]

This meant that any women enrolled as Wrens in peacetime would not be paid, receiving only expenses. In fact, only the Director, her Deputy and the Superintendents were paid. For branches other than office duties, including cooks, general duties and motor transport, women could apply for a role and if accepted would have to wait until notified to begin their job, most starting at the outbreak of war. It was also believed that all Wrens would initially be 'immobile'. This meant that only women who were resident in the immediate area could apply. It was estimated that around 6,000 women would be enrolled and trained in the areas of Portsmouth, Plymouth and Chatham.[59]

The problem for Laughton Mathews was that the restriction on only having 'immobiles' apply meant that 'mobiles' with high qualifications could have applied for paid work elsewhere in peacetime, believing there was no point in applying to the WRNS. Consequently, she began 'secretly and guiltily interviewing mobile applicants and compiling a "Mobile list" of people who were informed in rather vague terms that they would be accepted in certain events'. She says in her autobiography, 'this got to the ears of my CE mentors and my action was queried; I was asked whether I realized that I was preventing these women joining some other organisation. I argued that was precisely my object.'[60]

Three days after the declaration of war, approval to admit mobiles was granted, leaving the Director in a position to instantly appoint the best candidates. This meant that she had prospective local officers ready to start recruiting in Bristol, Cardiff, Dover, Deal and Liverpool when the war started.[61] In defying her management, Laughton Mathews developed the service in the way in which she felt it would best serve the country. This was a daring move that further helped to cement her role.

The administrative endeavours undertaken by the Director and Deputy Director in the lead-up to the declaration of war resulted in Wrens starting work in the naval establishments as soon as war broke out. Consequently, there were about 1,000 Wrens working during the first week of the war. Unlike the ATS and WAAF, there was no general mobilisation of the WRNS. Instead, women who had been accepted were called up as and when they were needed, 'and in the case of mobiles when accommodation was ready'.[62]

The Expansion of Roles: The WRNS Becomes Part of the Armed Forces

1941 was hugely significant in the mobilisation of women for war work and marked a turning point in the fortunes of the WRNS. 350,000 women had become unemployed since the beginning of the war because of the decline of consumer industries. Unlike World War I, the government decided it could no longer wait for 'women to be employed spontaneously on the scale required'.[63] Under the influence of Ernest Bevin, former trade union leader and then Minister of Labour, the wartime coalition assumed control of women's labour by introducing the Registration for Employment Order in March 1941. As a result of this, all women aged 19 to 40 were required to register at employment exchanges so that the Ministry of Labour had a record of what work they were doing and could direct those considered suitable into 'essential war work'.[64]

Braybon and Summerfield highlight the impact National Service had upon female employment. 'Most of the 350,000 women who were unemployed in January 1941 had found jobs by the end of the year. By October 1943 only 24,000 women were registered unemployed.'[65] The National Service (No.2) Act in December saw a further advancement of the need for female labour. Britain became the first country to conscript women aged 20 to 30 for national service.[66] Later, the age range was expanded to 19 and 43 and included all women who were available of serving, being women without dependents under the age of 14. Conscription required women to choose either to work in one of the women's auxiliaries, in farming or in industry. The choice to undertake a particular form of work was left open to women as a condition of the Act, as it was felt by members of the government, including Churchill, that women should not be compelled to do certain work, such as being stationed on anti-aircraft sites.[67]

Theoretically, women conscripted 'had a choice between the services, Civil Defence, the Land Army and industry. But in practice the usual destinations were the ATS and munitions where shortages were most acute.'[68] Marwick argues that national service only played a minor role in the changes in women's employment in wartime, as women not living apart from their husbands were exempt. In reality, only unmarried women in the age group 19–24 were, in practice, called up.[69]

Concerns and objections were raised about the conscription of women by many MPs. Noakes argues that these concerns were focused on the extent to which the state was undermining the private sphere of the home. Chapter 3 noted that in the 1930s family and marriage had resumed their conservative nature, with women, although more firmly in charge of their own home, pushed back into domesticated social roles. Agnes Hardie of the Labour party argued that 'war is not a woman's job ... women share the bearing and rearing of children and should be exempt from war'. There were also opinions that removing young women from the 'moral guidance' of their homes could result in the undermining of their characters.[70] The sentiment reflected the conservative view of the role of women present in the interwar period.

Laughton Mathews took a dim view of the arguments opposing married women taking on war work. She herself was married with two young children when she decided to take on the role of Director. In her memoirs, she discusses First Officer Thomas who was an immobile Wren at the Royal Naval Barracks, Chatham. Thomas was able to combine running her family home, looking after her husband, shopping and cooking with no domestic help, alongside her WRNS duties. 'She was one of the many who vindicated the policy of having married women as immobiles.'[71] Early objections to the conscription of women gave way to a national sentiment that was overwhelmingly positive. Images of female participation was concentrated on young single women, who overwhelmingly became the main 'conscripts' of the National Service Act.

Summerfield says, 'the woman war worker was presented as performing tasks which were exceptional for women ... she wore a distinctive dress, the uniforms of the three auxiliary military services or the land army.... [H]er heroism resided in her public service, undertaken not for personal gain but for the greater good.'[72] Women who entered the women's services were far from derided; instead, they were congratulated for doing so. The opportunistically patriotic advertising of the time, such as Bovril doffing its cap 'to the splendid women of Britain',[73] linked with the National Service Act, combined to make joining the services very attractive to young women required to do some form of war work. Patriotism had a great impact upon all of the women's services, which began to grow rapidly after 1941. Numbers of Wrens doubled between 1941 and 1942.

This expansion can be partly explained by Vera Laughton Mathews's insistence that women take on any job they could, to allow men to be freed for combat duties and to meet the new demands of total war the navy was facing. As Mason argues, and many interviewees noted, including Kathy Baker, 'from the beginning the Director had held the view that, given training, women were perfectly capable of undertaking most shore duties in place of

Table 4.3   Numbers of Wrens throughout World War II[74]

September 1939	1601
January 1941	10653
January 1942	22898
January 1943	41415
January 1944	66500
June 1944	74620
August 1945	63395
December 1945	48866

men'.[75] The growing need to release men for service at sea and the requirement for further shore-based support roles meant Laughton Mathews' vision was realised through the massive expansion of categories and roles for Wrens throughout the war. This expansion up until 1941 also had the consequence of undermining the role of the CE and allowing the WRNS to flourish.

1939

The initial categories for Wrens were gender-determined, linked fundamentally to the domestic sphere or office duties. However, an Admiralty letter sent to all home naval authorities on 20 September 1939 demonstrates that the nine initial categories in the scheme of service had already begun to be expanded in the months between the service being re-formed and the start of the war.

> I am to acquaint you that the requests for WRNS personnel to fill vacancies and release naval personnel wherever practicable, to the maximum extent, for the employment as cyphers, coders, writers, supply ratings, telephone operators, signallers, motor drivers, messengers and orderlies.[76]

At this early stage, plans were put in place to employ women in code breaking and cypher work. 'Before the end of 1939 WRNS ratings were enrolled for intelligence duties as linguists and special writers' for confidential work.[77] Documents in the Portsmouth archives suggest that the employment of WRNS officers on cypher duties had been discussed in a secret Admiralty letter dated 19 August 1938. This letter outlined general proposals for the replacement of men by women.[78] The various commanders-in-chief discussed the merits of such a plan, deciding by April 1939 that the WRNS remit would be to train cypher officers and coders during wartime. The role would be included in the Office Duty Branch. That such a discussion was occurring in August 1938 indicates how early the use of Wrens to replace men was figuring in the Royal Navy's pre-war planning.

Coder and cypher officers dealt with codes or encrypted data being communicated from ships to bases and vice versa. The early cypher officers were nearly all daughters or wives of naval officers.[79] Nancy Jennings was one such officer, and her story allows us to see the nature of the work involved in the role. Her first posting was to Southend where the officers dealt with the secret signals and the Wren ratings with confidential papers. Her second posting was to Plymouth, which at the time was still the base of the Western Approaches Command. She did not really like working in Plymouth because the Wrens' quarters were 'horrible' and the work was increasingly being moved to Liverpool and as such was limited. However, when the base of the Western Approaches finally moved to Liverpool, Nancy was reposted there too.

She recalled that she found the work very satisfying because of its direct involvement in the activities of the war. Her job entailed sending signals to ships in the Atlantic with details of their route and any U-boat activity in the area.[80] Cypher officers, such as Nancy, often commented on the important role they felt they had in the conflict, seeing their job as having an immediate impact. Clearly it was very early on that women had a role in combat operations, despite not being on the front line.

The status of cypher officers proved problematic for Laughton Mathews in the early stages of the war. Many, as stated, were the daughters or wives of naval officers who were locally employed. In the initial years of the service, these women were officers in name only, as they had not attended the Officers Training Course (OTC). This put new First Officers in a difficult position as they were now in charge of Third Officer Mrs Captain or Miss Commander-in-Chief.[81] The desire of Laughton Mathews to exclude a class-based officer system was evident in her wish to overturn the initial recruitment processes for cypher officers. The unusual status of these officers took several years to resolve, with many either becoming trained officers or others choosing to leave the service.

Cypher officers were some of the first WRNS sent abroad. On 19 August 1941, the small merchant ship SS *Aguila* had the first international draft of WRNS aboard, including 12 cypher officers. During an attack on the convoy by a pack of U-boat submarines and Focke Wulfes (the first time 'packs' had been used in the war), the ship received a direct torpedo hit, causing the death of all Wrens, including the cypher officers, ten Chief Wren special operators and a naval nursing sister. The loss was a hard blow for the Director who had interviewed the draft before they left.[82] A consequence of the incident was that all future WRNS drafts travelled on HM Ships.[83] In October 1941 eight cypher officers were deployed to Gibraltar on the HMS *Malaya* to replace those Wrens who had originally been in the first draft. Despite the danger posed by travelling in convoy, new volunteers were very forthcoming and opting to go overseas became a very popular option for some Wrens. Overseas service also expanded the remit of the WRNS, making it solely a support service to the Royal Navy in all its international activities.

Other categories formed in 1939 included Motor Transport (MT) drivers, who formed a large group within the service. Initially, only women who could drive were accepted, but as the war went on training courses were developed to teach new recruits. Women took over most branches of motor transport, driving lorries and cars. They 'delivered anything from mail to blood plasma, picked up anyone from top brass to survivors of bombing raids. They drove in all weathers, for hours on end, often in pitch darkness with only their masked headlights to see by.'[84]

Pamela Bates began her service as a P5 (Special Duties X) Wren in November 1944 when she was stationed at Stanmore. At the end of the war, she was re-mustered into another category, as she was still only 18. She decided to become an MT driver. Training was provided in London by a motoring school, which instructed Wrens in how to drive various vehicles and do basic maintenance. After completing her training, she was eventually sent to the Signals School in Petersfield where she drove the older officers around. On one occasion she accidentally put her car in reverse on the quay and drove it into the harbour:

> I thought oh well I'll go forward, but I didn't go forward, I went into the water and out to sea I went flying, missed the pontoon, which was about six foot down [...] down into the water I went, glug. And I luckily got up through the sunshine roof.

Fortunately, Pamela did not face an enquiry; 'they knew, wartime things happen [...] and you just get on'.[85] It did not affect her standing as an MT driver either. As a group, they tended to be from the higher middle classes, with most having attended boarding school. Pamela claimed that to be an MT driver you 'had to be a certain calibre' and that most gave off a certain 'aura', as they were well spoken and smartly dressed. These were seen as necessary qualities for women who could be requested to drive high-ranking officials to functions. Pamela argued it was because 'they trusted us not to do any argy bargy' as she called it.[86]

These women were selected more for this job because they fitted the social expectations of many of the male officers, some of whom would have been from the older generation more accustomed to dealing with women from a similar background to themselves. Women from wealthier backgrounds would also have been more likely to learn to drive before the war, as their parents would have been more likely to own a motor car.

Motor transport drivers were in great demand during the war. In May 1944, a shortage meant the WAAF loaned 150 drivers for three months.[87] Janet Dodds took up a call for drivers.[88] She had come into the WRNS – from a working-class background in London – as a steward, catering for around 200 service personnel at the Fleet Air Arm base Worthy Down. She had been looking for a change and thought driving would be a lot easier than washing up and scrubbing floors. She recalls an air force song along the lines of: 'I'm sick of washing dishes [...] hear my plea and change my category.' She was trained at Westfield College, Hampstead where she learnt to drive a two-ton lorry:

> we did our hill starts in Camden Gardens, which is off the Marylebone Road; you would have to be able to do it proficiently enough so that if they put a matchbox behind your wheel you wouldn't squash it.

Her test involved driving down various roads in London and then coming back to the start where she had to reverse the truck into a very tight mews.

This gateway was just wide enough for the lorry and then it has these granite [blocks], it's to stop the wheels of carriages knocking the wall to bits, cos it's only [...] they had them, so you got to hit the hole absolutely spot on [...] I couldn't have done it again if he'd paid me, I really couldn't [laugh].[89]

Janet claimed that the training school had to pass you whether they wanted to or not because they were so desperate for drivers. Despite one mishap when she was posted to Chatham, Janet became a proficient lorry driver. She notes she was one of the first working-class girls to 'penetrate' the ranks of the MT drivers. It did not really bother her, but she did indicate a class divide within the category. Yet, in her case the issue of needing more MT drivers overcame any sort of bias within the category.

1940

The spring of 1940 saw a wider range of roles that were not typically feminine begin to emerge. Wren Dispatch Riders (who carried letters and memos via motorbike) took over completely from the naval dispatch riders and the first Wren Degaussing Recorders were employed (they controlled the processes of range instrumentation for ships to prevent triggering mines). In the summer, training started for Stores Wrens and Special Operator Coders and the first Plotters were employed. In December, there were 561 officers and 9,439 ratings.[90]

Daphne Coyne, whose memoirs are held in the Imperial War Museum, was one of the first Wrens in 1940 to be trained as a radar plotter at HMS *Skirmisher* (Milford Haven), having joined the WRNS in October 1940. She was trained on the job, as many of the early Wrens were, by a male officer who had just learnt about radar. Her role involved plotting signals recorded via radar sent in by the RAF on a map.[91] She found the work interesting and not too demanding. In summer 1943, she was recommended for a commission and became a Plotting Officer serving in Newcastle and later Fort Southwick in Portsmouth.

Claire James joined the WRNS in 1943 and after a short time as a radio mechanic was transferred in April 1944 to Dover as a Plotter when the role was expanded in the build-up to D-Day. She worked eight-hour watches [shifts] in the casements of Dover Castle. Her job was to draw plots on a large map on the wall based on the information received. As she described it, the map would show 'the convoys, going up and down the Channel ... which as you can imagine at that time was a lot!'[92] She plotted all of the activity in the build-up to D-Day as part of a watch of six Wrens.

Plotters were always at the heart of what was going on at sea and by 1941 had replaced most of the Sub-Lieutenants in the commands. Some of the Plotting Officers became Duty Staff Officers and later were in complete charge of the plotting room on their base, responsible only to the Staff Officer Operations. 'It was stated that Wren Plotters had undoubtedly saved hundreds of ships and thousands of men's lives by their accuracy and swiftness in directing and reporting enemy movements.'[93] The nautical knowledge of Wrens within such jobs came to be as detailed as any man within the navy. The Royal Naval Plotters saw the utility of using Wrens to replace male personnel successfully. The category clearly demonstrates how from small beginnings (there were only four Wren plotters in the summer of 1940)[94] the WRNS expanded throughout the conflict. Wren Plotters became present in all operations rooms across the UK.

Early on, women were being actively encouraged to take on traditionally 'masculine' roles. Dispatch riding on motorbikes was one such role. The job was extremely physically demanding and required women to work to tight deadlines. They had to ride very heavy 500cc motorbikes that many could not pick up alone. Women selected for this category were regarded as real 'characters'.[95] Most of the women who took on this job had never ridden a motorbike in their life. They were chosen because of their interest in being in the motor transport division but also for their sense of humour and willingness to work long hours.

Bunty Marshall, wishing to 'fight for [her] country', had applied for all the women's auxiliaries in 1940 at 18 years of age. She was accepted by the WRNS, having applied to be a driver, and on 1 July 1941 left home to join the service. Within a few days, she was told that she was going to become a motorcycle dispatch rider, which 'was a big surprise because we knew nothing about these strange machines'. She talks of her initial training, saying:

> After the unit officer in charge of the motor transport unit had recovered from the shock of the arrival of three young ladies wearing short pretty summer frocks ... (nothing to change into) [we] were told to mount the bikes. Thank goodness we had all ridden horses, so at least we knew how to sit on a saddle! The news got round that three young ladies were showing their legs and struggling to get off and on the awesome bikes. Soldiers arrived from everywhere and lined the paddock for a free show.[96]

After being trained to ride a bike in a week, she was posted to Rosyth, Scotland where she served for four years. Bunty recalls the trials and tribulations of being a dispatch rider. On one occasion she crashed into a truck, a not uncommon incident for dispatch riders who had to deal with other traffic, with no lights, in areas of bomb devastation. She broke her nose, ending her dispatch days (she was reassigned as a driver for the Admiralty in London until being demobbed in 1946):

> I was taking some important documents up to the C-in-C in Edinburgh and I was on the ferry going from North to South Queensferry. There was a crowd of army DRs on the boat, and I went on ahead of them and said see you on the way back. But a light armoured vehicle was overtaking a lorry on the brow of a hill and went slap bang into me. I went through his windscreen and landed up in hospital, luckily with not more than a broken nose and a few scratches, but my dispatch-bag never turned up.[97]

Laughton Mathews recalls a similar story of Wren Pamela McGeorge who was thrown from her motorbike by a bomb when on duty. She abandoned the bike, ran the rest of the way with her dispatch, and offered to go out again once she delivered it.[98] McGeorge was rewarded with a British Empire Medal in 1941 for meritorious civil or military action (the only one awarded to a Wren that year) for her service to the WRNS. The dispatch riders were a small but highly acclaimed category. Their work was dangerous and heavy, with eight-hour shifts as the norm. Admiral W. M. James in the Portsmouth General Orders issued a Special Order of the Day on 22 August 1942, showing the type of fortitude required for this category:

> Ten dispatch riders have, during the last fortnight, covered 10,000 miles and delivered several imminent and important dispatches without a hitch [...] Wren Steel completed a 200-mile journey to Plymouth in 5½ hours, and Wren Marsden the same trip in 10½ hours, at night, despite a puncture and having to use a torch for 20 miles after her lights failed. To both these Wrens the road was strange and included crossing Dartmoor.[99]

Soon after this statement, recruitment to the category was discontinued in October 1942.[100] Women who were already dispatch riders continued in their role, for the most part, but 'because the work was found so heavy and dangerous for women [...] recruiting was stopped'.[101] That such a category was created very early in the war demonstrates the WRNS was in no way going to be confined to the archetypal female military jobs of writer, cook and steward.

1941

October 1941 saw the most popular and symbolic of the WRNS categories open: Boats Crew. It was decided at this point that women would staff all harbour craft. This job became the most iconic and sought after job in the service. Laughton Mathews claimed, 'Petty Officers gave up their buttons to start again as unspecialized boats crew.' Stories about the Boats Crew Wrens were 'legion'.[102]

For some women the chance to be a Boats Crew Wren was the reason they joined up. Rozelle Raynes had grown up wanting to crew a boat in a busy port. At the age of 17, she got her chance after various options had been offered and rejected by her WRNS interviewer. Her poor eyesight meant she could not become a radio mechanic and a claim of claustrophobia managed to get her out of becoming Special Duties X. Because of her age, she was not old enough to be conscripted. This meant she got some choice; otherwise, she would have been assigned to the first available category. Finally, she was offered a job as a deckhand and posted to Portsmouth.[103]

Members of boats crews were given around two weeks' training for roles including deck hand, coxswain and stoker. Their job could include acting as a 'liberty boat' between the ships in harbour and the dock, crewing 75 foot diesel harbour launches, survey work and carrying stores and mail.[104] The coxswain managed the boat; the deckhand would carry out any job required; and stokers would have to manage the diesel engines, keeping them running and carrying out maintenance on board. Martha Rose looked after the engines of the boats she helped crew in Plymouth and later Holy Loch in Scotland. Martha talked of how the job of Boats Crew Wren was envied.[105]

Laughton Mathews had been struck in her pre-war visit to Portsmouth that 'there's no reason on earth why women should not run those boats'.[106] She quietly kept this thought to herself until 1941 when boats crews in Plymouth were pioneered. To begin with, this was trialled as an experiment but Portsmouth soon followed suit. It became increasingly apparent that women could run the small harbour boats, and eventually their role was taken for granted in the larger ports. These sorts of 'experiments' were common within the service, with RN officers trialling using Wrens to carry out typically male jobs in one location and this then being picked up elsewhere.

At the peak of the war, there were only 573 Wrens in this role.[107] The work was hard and demanding, with watches normally being 24 hours on, 24 hours off. The category was only abandoned on 31 December 1945 and those Wrens who still had some of their three-year service left were re-mustered into other categories.[108] Martha, for example, ended up being a writer by the end of the war, when the boats were returned to the sailors coming back from overseas. The Boats Crew Wrens have ended up being one of the most enduring aspects of the nature of the World War II WRNS. Photos of Wrens regularly include those of the boats crews jumping from boat to boat, or maintaining their craft in their iconic bell-bottomed trousers.[109]

1941: The Decision for the WRNS to be Managed by the Civil Establishment is Overturned

In numerous respects, the WRNS should never have been called 'civilian' unless the previous identity of the service had been overturned in the scheme of service, although this was a status it would legally retain until coming under the Naval Discipline Act in 1977. Instead, it meant Laughton Mathews had to reconcile the needs of her military service with the bureaucratic nature of the Civil Establishment. As the auxiliary grew, it became increasingly clear that it could not be governed through civilian channels.

This must have become increasingly evident because in April 1941, the control of the CE over the service was overturned and the WRNS became part of Naval Personnel Services under the control of the Second Sea Lord. This was in part due to the size to which the service had grown.[110] It was impractical for the CE to deal with the lodging and provisioning of such a large group of personnel. Laughton Mathews argued that the 'authorities', by which she could only have meant the CE, did not envisage or cater for the expansion of the service and that theirs was not a 'short-sighted policy, it was blind'. Whilst she states it was not the CE's fault that the WRNS was 'dumped on' it. She felt no doubts that it 'relinquished the unrewarding task with the utmost joy when the time came.'[111]

In some ways, Laughton Mathews' inexperience could have played in her favour. The way in which the service was also somewhat ignored and disdained by the CE allowed it to form a distinct identity. Laughton Mathews, and later her super-intendents, developed individual relationships with naval officers at the various port locations. It made their job far harder, which, although it may not have been recognised by them at the time, enabled the service to develop independently. One of the early ATS Commandants, Justina Collins, was against their service having a female chief because of the independence it would permit the ATS, undermining the relationship with the army.[112] Rather than doing this, the necessary independence of the WRNS developed its bond with the RN. Suggestions for widening the scope of the service, Laughton Mathews argues, always came from the navy, as in 1941 when a letter from the Commander-in-Chief, Nore, one of their best supporters, suggested Wrens had up to that point only been employed in 'duties conventionally applicable to women'. He suggested in view of the labour situation and efficiency of the WRNS that there were a number of roles women could take on. This led to an investigation and eventually to the training and employment of women on all duties ashore that did not require sea experience or great physical strength.[113]

These new categories included Signal Exercise Corrector and Automatic Morse Transcriber within the Communications category, Parachute Packers, Bomb Range Markers, Meteorologists, Aircraft Checkers and Fabric Workers, Teleprinter and Switchboard Operators, Vision Testers, Personnel Selection, Welfare and Amenities, Experimental Gunnery, Special Duties X, Cinema Operator, Qualified Ordinance, Boats Crew, Torpedo Attack Assessors, Photographic Assistants, Submarine Attack Teacher Ratings and Tailoresses. Other categories included Topographical Duties, Boom Defence, Minewatchers, Torpedo Wrens, Radio Mechanics, Maintenance (Air) and Gunnery Control.[114]

The replacement of male personnel with Wrens was most complete in the category of Submarine Attack Teachers. The Portsmouth archives include an account by Admiral Creasy of the work carried out by these Wrens throughout the war. In December 1941, the first teachers were stationed to Fort Blockhouse where they worked in conjunction with a male crew. By April 1942, the teaching team was led entirely by Wrens, including one Leading Wren and four Wrens. Teams served in various locations throughout the war, including Dundee, Rothesay and HMS *Forth*. Their job included training Commanding Officers in how to make periscope observations so that they could manoeuvre their submarines in such a way as to get into a favourable position to fire torpedoes. They also instructed members of the 'Submarine Attack Team' in how to plot the enemy's course using data supplied from periscope observations. The Admiral notes how effectively the Wrens carried out their role, with many becoming extremely proficient attack coordinators, even if they never managed to use their skills in a real life situation.[115]

The creation of such jobs firmly entrenched the WRNS within the Royal Navy, although it was technically *of* the navy rather than *in* it.[116] With women undertaking roles such as crewing harbour vessels, instructing male personnel in the strategic use of torpedoes, boom defence, gunnery control and mine watching, there was no sense by this point that the service was not militarised. Although women could not directly serve on front line ships and fire weapons, they had begun to undertake work that was firmly connected to the more overtly combative efforts of the war.

The civilian administration of the service in the first two years of the war had little effect on how the majority of Wrens viewed the service. Most of the interviewees, who had joined the service after 1941, were unaware that the WRNS had ever been civilian (despite this difference remaining until 1977). However, the effect of this distinction in the early years of the war had a huge impact on the later nature of the WRNS; it made Laughton Mathews push harder to create a distinctive service with a strong identity within the military.

Laughton Mathews' tenacity in getting regulations passed by the CE demonstrates the significance of her role. She was crucial to creating the identity of the WRNS. It was possible because of her strength of character but also the relative independence afforded her by the Admiralty. A less persistent leader could have resulted in the WRNS becoming another part of the CE, sidelined to traditional feminine roles or anachronistically governed as a civilian service. However, 1941 saw those leading the WRNS reach the point where they were able to organise their own accommodation, resources, recruitment and training along meritocratic lines, with equivalent military ranks.

CHAPTER 5

Becoming a Wren: Meritocracy Over Social Position

Braybon and Summerfield argue, 'there were well-recognised distinctions between the three women's services, the WRNS being seen as the most socially selective and the ATS the least'.[1] The prevailing idea was that this social selection was based on class, particularly social status, which has become a common belief about the service. This was not the case, with the reality being more interesting. In part, this misconstruing could be the result of a 1941 survey that showed middle-class women preferred the WRNS.[2] Whilst the naval auxiliary was far more selective than the ATS, this was based on the skills and abilities of the applicants, rather than their family backgrounds or social contacts.

The WAAF was also meritocratic but structured in a very different way to the WRNS. Stone has identified this being due to the WAAF being fully integrated within the RAF's organisational and administration practices. Women served in commands alongside their male colleagues and could just as likely be posted to a station requiring someone in their category as a man.[3] The emphasis of the RAF was on technical skills, which Martin Francis argues was always part of the ethos of the air force. Even with its pilots, who, like the WRNS, have been assumed to be predominantly middle class, the RAF presented itself as 'open to all those who were able to master the technological competence necessary to fly an aircraft in combat'.[4] Despite the dominance of middle-class pilots who possessed the right accents and engaged in the 'old school tie' networks, early on in the war this soon gave way to an armed force that provided greater possibilities for rising up through the ranks than did the army and navy.[5] The WRNS was similar, although its officers were never dominated by the upper-middle-class women the ATS would be, yet it provided a great deal of opportunity for social mobility. What is different is that its meritocratic nature was self-made and not commonly known. Instead, the service has been memorialised as being the 'best', with obvious connotations of class.

The scheme of service started in 1938 helped form the WRNS' distinct identity, built upon from World War I. It clearly separated the auxiliary from its counterparts, who were seen as lacking 'the best type', helping to perpetuate the belief it was the 'superior service'[6] a perception built upon its naval ties, its ability to select its own members and its capacity to set high standards for these individuals.

Comments made in interviews and archive documents indicate that the WRNS was the most admired. Daphne Coyne, for example, was discouraged from going to the WAAF recruiting office by her mother because the WRNS was seen as 'THE service'.[7] A husband to a WRNS officer noted, 'without being snobby the WRNS was a better class of girl, on the whole, having been in the army for seventeen years myself I know the sort of people that were in the ATS and WAAF'. Whereas Amanda Davies who worked as a P5 coder stated, 'I think there was definitely a glamour attached to the WRNS ... and the WRNS were always very popular ... you know we were ... not quite elite but there was that nice feeling that we were the senior service, the most popular service'.[8]

The Scheme of Service

The scheme of service was very important in establishing the ethos of World War II WRNS. In October 1938, the outline of the formation of the service began to be put together. An early document from this time, written by the Civil Establishment, drew together the broad expectations and requirements of a new women's auxiliary naval corps. The first page of the report states:

> Glaring mistakes in organization and administration of the WAAC during the last war can be remembered and it seems very necessary that the navy should not undertake a slavish adherence to the present army proposals [...] merely to produce a uniformity between the various women['s] auxiliary services.[9]

In World War I, Eric Geddes would have ideally liked to have had the women's auxiliary corps work alongside each other for greater efficiency. Yet this idea was clearly abandoned early on because the WAAC was perceived as lacking 'the best type' and women with 'social status':

> As is well known the WAAC suffered from this most severely in the last war. Young women having a pleasant 'outlook' on life and accustomed to conduct themselves in a reasonably reserved manner took the greatest exception to finding themselves forced to eat, sleep and work in company with some girls, however few, who were the roughest type.[10]

The khaki-clad appearance of the WAAC had led them to be seen by some members of society in the interwar period as masculine, 'abnormal' and 'unnatural'. The reputation of the corps was also called into question in 1917 'when it was widely believed that recruitment into the corps was being harmed by widespread rumours of sexual immorality'.[11] As discussed in Chapter 2, the truth of these rumours was limited, with many WAAC serving in France suffering by association.[12] The WAAC were mainly working class and more visible because it was a large corps. Some were regarded as 'lacking duty', being seen as deficient of a high work ethic and standards. This reputation had a lasting effect on the WAAC and the subsequent ATS. Hazel Williams, a member of the WRNS in World War II, said 'that the Wrens were the tops, WAAF a reasonable second, but the ATS – Yuk! We were a snobbish lot, I regret to say.'[13]

The sense that the WRNS should be kept separate from the 'not altogether savoury reputation' of army women in both wars is present in these early plans. This could be a reflection of the Royal Navy's perception of itself as the 'superior service'. This idea of not being elite, but 'senior' reflected the image the leadership of the WRNS sought to perpetuate.

In the early document, the WRNS is presented as a 'high-class' service with the emphasis placed upon the 'social status' of applicants. The CE was careful to state that this idea of 'social status' was not linked to class or 'snobbery', but rather to the personal behaviour of potential Wrens. It was argued: 'to present the WRNS with due regard to social scales [...] will present itself to the right applicants as a reasonable and sensible forethought on the part of the navy'.[14]

Early on it was suggested that a division between the clerical and domestic branches (the only two branches that were believed to be required at the time) should be made. This was because the type of women needed for each would have dissimilar 'social status', with one relying on 'educational achievement' and the other on 'physical strength'. It was seen as necessary to keep the two branches separate, and arrange that neither would have to work or live together.

Despite the appearance of clear social class divisions between the branches, the service was not shaped along these lines. The Director, from very early on, insisted that the service would be developed as a meritocracy, with the best women filling roles based on their skills rather than on their social contacts or status. Divisions between women of different backgrounds were somewhat overcome with an intensive two-week training for all new recruits.

The domestic and clerical branches did not always mix or live together, but that had more to do with having different jobs and watches than class divisions. The key in this document is the way the service was set up to have the 'right sort'.[15] This emphasis is revealed again and again in the documentary records and the interviews conducted for this study. The women recall that the WRNS was the one that most women would want to enter because they had 'a better class' of girls. There is also the view that the service was more 'feminine'. The uniform helped foster this view with its smart skirt, jacket, hat and the opportunity to wear silk stockings. In doing so, it demarcated itself by its standards of good behaviour and hard work, which it was successful in marketing from the very start of the war.

The WRNS did not bar women from the lower classes getting jobs beyond those of the domestic branch, as the earliest version of the scheme of service may have assumed. Daphne Coyne, whose memoirs are held in the Imperial War Museum, came from a single parent family and had been working in a nursing home as a cook before joining the WRNS in 1940. Her expectation when going for interview was that she would become a cook or steward, as these were the only categories open at the time and mirrored her work experience. However, after beginning work as a messenger in a cypher/signals office she became one of the first Wrens trained to interpret radar signals.[16] Clearly, the WRNS was more concerned about the ability of the people it employed than their social background.

The Importance of the Director in the Creation of the WRNS' Distinct Identity

What might have fuelled some of the difference in reputation between the naval and army auxiliary was that the former had a Director, who, although she had served as a Wren in World War I, had not been in charge of the service at that time. The ATS on the other hand was led by Helen Gwynne-Vaughan who had been Chief Controller of the WAAC and Commandant of the WRAF in the first war. Edith Summerskill, Labour MP for Fulham, laid the poor reputation of the ATS at the door of the War Office in 1941. Their unwillingness to form a women's auxiliary early on resulted in leaving its management to Gwynne-Vaughan and other members of World War I service who created an outdated organisational structure based on social class divisions.[17] The early organisation of the services definitely had an impact on forming their long-term reputation.

This is in contrast to the Admiralty whose instruction to the Civil Establishment to draw up a scheme of service meant the

WRNS had a clear structure of leadership and sense of purpose from the beginning of the war, despite it taking longer to announce the re-formation of the service. Noakes argues that the widespread unpopularity of the ATS in the early years of the war was due to the 'perception' that only women of 'wealth or influence' were able to reach 'higher positions' in the corps.[18]

Laughton Mathews fundamentally disagreed with this approach and would later introduce the policy that meant promotion to officer rank in the WRNS came from the 'lower deck', unlike the ATS who tended to appoint officers with social status in the early years of the war, rather than women with specific skills.[19] With the exception of some early direct entry officers, all future WRNS officers had to be ratings before they could be considered for promotion. This provided a boost in morale, not present in the ATS.[20] It also served to build good relationships between the officers and ratings because the former understood the position of those working under them, having been in the same position for at least six months. Kathy Baker felt that her experience of having served on the 'lower deck' gave her perspective, allowing her to introduce improvements for the working lives of her Wrens when promoted to a Third Officer at Great Baddow (where she had served as a rating earlier in the war).[21]

Gwynne-Vaughan was anachronistic throughout her tenure as Director of the ATS from 1939 to 1941. ATS officers were largely drawn from the aristocracy and upper classes, which, as Noakes argues, was out of step with the idea of the levelling 'people's war'. This helped contribute to the service's unpopularity, which saw far fewer women joining the ATS as a percentage of the army than the WRNS as a percentage of the navy.[22] In 1940, the 10,000 Wrens made up 2.92 per cent of the navy, whereas the 36,400 ATS of the time made up only 1.72 per cent of the army.[23] Between September 1939 and December 1940, 40 per cent of the 31,960 ATS intake left the service.[24] Lesley Whateley, Director of the ATS from October 1943, believed the nature of Gwynne-Vaughan in part held the service back and affected people's perception of it. She argues, 'our Director was so imbued with military spirit that she was quite unable to see that women could not be treated like men'[25] and that the class and gender divides that had existed prior to the war could no longer be used to inform the entrance criteria.

Most members of the WRNS and WAAF were volunteers rather than conscripts. To get in, it was important to apply as a volunteer well before being called up and assigned a job. The ATS on the other hand was dogged with the image of being the 'Cinderella service',[26] as in the early days its occupations centred on the typically female jobs of cooks, clerks, store women and orderlies, with the only exception being drivers. 'Gwynne-Vaughan herself argued that women were particularly suited to these duties'. Noakes argues that this helped foster the perception that the ATS 'were little more than general handmaids to officers'.[27]

Laughton Mathews on the other hand was beginning afresh, with ideas that had been shaped by engagement in the social transformations of attitudes toward class, gender and morality that had been occurring in 1930s Britain. This was a real difference between her and Gwynne-Vaughan, as the latter based much of her decision making upon her experiences of leading a women's corps 20 years previously rather than re-forming the service anew. Laughton Mathews, as a new entrant to the ways of the Admiralty, questioned her own temerity but decided she could only do her best and could not hark back to the past. She notes, 'conditions were so changed that there was nothing in the old papers to build on that was not already in my own knowledge of the service'.[28]

Yet, she was the more inexperienced of the two early auxiliary leaders. Logically, Gwynne-Vaughan would be seen as a better candidate, given her experience. Laughton Mathews did not represent the policy of selection she developed for the WRNS as she did not have the experience of managing a large organisation and was selected because of her social background. Unbeknown to her, the first discussion she had at the Admiralty was effectively her interview.[29] She had been responsible for large numbers of women in her voluntary work and had been a career woman in the years before marrying her husband. However, whether she would have seen herself as having the necessary skills and experience to be Director is not known. She was definitely very concerned about doing a good job and had experience of being a Wren in World War I, which would have stood her in good stead. The Admiralty must have recognised that although inexperienced she had the sort of character that would get the service off the ground.

Different organisational structures of the two smaller services also made them more attractive than the army auxiliary. Noakes argues that the WAAF benefited from a democratic and technocratic structure and leadership, 'prizing technical expertise above class background, and thus offering greater opportunity for progression to the majority of its members'.[30] The WRNS was similar, and as such, both services provided some women with greater prospects than they would have had in the much larger ATS.

The Army was additionally far more influenced by changes in the global conflict than any of the other armed forces and by 1942 had been stretched over a wider arena of war than at any other point previously. This had a huge impact on the ATS. The War Office revised the numbers of women it needed upward to be able to release more men for overseas service. From March 1942, around 3,500 women were being conscripted into the service each week.[31] The WRNS was never required to become this large; instead, it grew more steadily during the course of the war when increased need for female naval workers became necessary in bases in the UK and abroad. The gradual growth of the WRNS also allowed its Director to grow into her role.

The contrast between the way the women's services developed in their early years led to comparisons at a state level. On 20 March 1941 Irene Ward, MP for Wallsend, argued that the ATS was in fact not run by its women officers because the Treasury had control:

> I will give just one example. During the more difficult period of the organisation of the ATS it was felt that its administration in the War Office needed strengthening by the addition, to assist the Director, of experienced women, to deal with health, welfare and training. [...] The answer was that the Treasury would not give power to appoint senior officers. Only the other day I received a letter from the War Office pointing out that the Treasury had now refused

to allow the creation of further senior officers in the ATS. I do not propose to go into the whole of the organisation, but I want to suggest that to have one major-general to be responsible for inspection and organisation, and to set her up against the whole of the generals of the War Office, does not necessarily make for a really efficient service.[32]

Early in the war, the ATS lacked the strong leadership present in the WRNS. A combination of a lack of independence from the Treasury and a dogmatic leadership style by Gwynne-Vaughan, until July 1941, resulted in a service that was led by junior officers who had no oversight over the whole service. It also had to contend later with the strain of sudden expansion.[33]

This was in contrast to Laughton Mathews who had been left 'to get on with it',[34] developing a distinctive leadership style that was steered by her own sense of purpose, rather than bureaucrats in the Treasury. Unlike the ATS, Laughton Mathews was never undermined in her ability to maintain oversight of the whole service, being neglected by her Civil Establishment managers. The RN, having selected a woman with a no-nonsense approach who would get on with the job in wartime, afforded her a great deal of freedom.

Other significant differences between the services included that the WRNS not being brought under the Naval Discipline Act (and would not be until 1977). This made it responsible for its own discipline and meant its status was civilian despite the change in its management. This was unlike the ATS and WAAF who came under Military Law in April 1941 when they expanded their semi-combatant duties. Laughton Mathews had favoured the WRNS coming under the Act because it would have secured them with a military status. However, all of the Commanders-in-Chief, bar one, opposed any change. Arguments against included wanting to maintain the status quo because it had worked so far, wishing to see what happened with the other women's services, and preferring not to upset good team spirit.[35]

This was one of the only times where her leadership was overridden by the Admiralty. Laughton Mathews saw it as a 'major battle' of policy that was returned to over the years. In her eyes, not being under the Act meant the service was not legally recognised for its military status, which she saw as more significant than the disciplinary measures.[36] Despite this, the decision of the Commanders-in-Chief helped foster the positive image of the service, as many women commented that the lack of the Naval Discipline Act made the service more attractive when compared to the others because it provided women with choice. Vera Boyce, for example, claimed that one of her main reasons for joining the WRNS was that she could leave if she wanted to, although she did not in the end.[37]

Under its own code, Wrens could be discharged, disrated, suspended from duty, have pay deducted, given extra work, have leave stopped or privileges restricted. The WRNS could not imprison or detain members under their own disciplinary code, these being the only parts of the Naval Discipline Act not applied to the service. Mason argues it was because some members of the Admiralty regarded these aspects of the code as 'repugnant' to women. She states, 'the spirit of the service was considered sufficient to ensure a high standard of behaviour, and as the nature of the contract was civilian it was not considered right that naval regulations should be imposed'.[38] The discussion as to whether the service should be brought under the Naval Discipline Act was occurring at the same time as the service ceased to be managed by the Civil Establishment. It shows how the dual identity had a legacy that went beyond 1941, with the legal status of the service still civilian. Whereas members of the WRNS believed it was part and parcel of the Royal Navy.

The decision to not include the service in the Naval Discipline Act played into the perception of the WRNS being the 'superior service'. In reality, the inclusion of the ATS under the Army Act (Military Law) had more to do with retention and the changing nature of the auxiliary as a militarised service, than courts martial. Although it meant that ATS and WAAF officers received the King's commission, whereas WRNS officers received an Admiralty Board Commission. It helped the ATS stabilise some of the variability of its appointment procedures under its new leadership and removed the status of women employed within the ATS as 'camp followers', a problematic definition of the women's roles that did not help their relationship with the wider army in the first years of the war.[39] For the WRNS, its exclusion from the Naval Discipline Act assisted partly in promoting its image of having the 'right sort' of girls who did not need to be controlled in such a way. Whilst this was not an official view, it was a perception commonly held by its members. Betty Calderara recalled that some of her friends were 'jealous' that she had got into the WRNS.[40]

However, not coming under the Act did not always help the reputation of members of the WRNS. Sherit notes that service-women in the other auxiliaries would taunt Wrens for being 'mere civilians'.[41] This reflects inter-service rivalry as it was an ideal way to bring the 'superior service' down a notch. In her work on the maintaining of the women's military services postwar, Sherit makes the point that the distinction of the service as civilian appeared to be more problematic at the end of the war when its status provided issues with how it was portrayed publicly and with the discharge of Wrens who could just leave because there was no legal comeback (although it is unclear how extensive this was).[42]

Initial Training of WRNS Ratings

Following an Admiralty decision in 1941, the WRNS took on all shore-based jobs from the RN that did not require great physical strength or sea experience. This change, and parallel shifts in wider society, such as the National Service Act, had a huge impact on the nature of the WRNS. The organisation of the service had to adapt from training 90 new recruits every two weeks in January 1940, to 900 in March 1942.[43] There was also the need for officers to train and lead the new ratings. This training started a month after the war and expanded throughout. Whilst many of the officers were middle class, they were perceived as the hard working 'ordinary woman',[44] not the idle rich placed in a position of authority. This was unlike the early ATS who appointed the local 'great lady' as county commandant.[45]

An aura of exclusivity provided the leadership of the WRNS with the ability to maintain a high level of discipline and standards that had more to do with female capability than social hierarchy. Summerfield explains how discipline was used to ensure that a levelling process took place in an upward direction, whereby middle-class women were required to share their duties and live with working-class women, based on an ethos of pulling together for the war effort.[46]

There were no bars set on what type of woman could apply to join the WRNS, other than their age. The emphasis was on education, skills, conduct, personality and a desire by applicants to participate fully in the ethos of the service. Given its popularity throughout the war, Laughton Mathews argues that the service could have been double the size it was.[47] It was limited by the labour situation that needed more women in other industries and women's auxiliaries. WRNS applicants came from a wide cross section of society. However, women from more educated backgrounds always figured highly in the service owing to the large range of technical jobs that grew after 1941.

Expectations for applications were made in a pamphlet titled, 'Join the Wrens and Free a Man for the Fleet', clearly specifying that there were high standards for new entrants and emphasising real life skills:

> All recruits are required to be persons of the highest integrity and character. They should supply the names of three persons (not relatives) to whom reference can be made: one of these should be an employer or a person with knowledge of the candidate's ability for the work for which she applies.[48]

Before joining up, prospective Wrens would write a letter to either the National Headquarters of the WRNS or their local recruitment office. The pamphlet discussed above included details of how to apply and entry requirements. Second Officer Janet Swete-Evans's scrapbook of her WT experiences contains a copy of the pamphlet, produced after 1941.[49] At the end of the leaflet is an application form that could be sent to one of the regional recruiting offices. In 1938, when the scheme of service was written the age limits were set between 19 and 45.[50] In 1941, the age limits were changed to between 17½ and up to 49 years of age for women with special qualifications. For women aged less than 18, written consent had to be obtained from a parent.

The WRNS were looking for people with suitable skills, experience and knowledge to fill particular roles. For the more specialised categories, those that required Wrens to have the ability to absorb a lot of new information in a short period of time and learn complex skills, women were recruited from backgrounds where they had achieved a certain level of education or had relevant work experience. Many Wrens were not from educated backgrounds, but their character and experience in work before joining up made them suitable candidates for other non-specialised occupations. Seventy per cent of the women interviewed for this research had been in some form of work before being called up, such as Helen Clarke who had been in the Land Army before joining the WRNS. Twenty-five per cent had just finished education or training.

Nina Adams thought the Wrens were 'a nice type of person [...] they weren't rough, they knew how to behave'.[51] She herself had come from a modest background, leaving school at 15 to work as a secretary for the Stewart and Lloyds steel company. She did not have a school certificate (the equivalent to GCSEs) but her experience in work would have played in her favour, allowing her to become a coder.

Many respondents thought they had to have a school certificate to be able to join the service. Joyce Tapp recalls in her memoirs how there was a legend among the sailors 'that in order to approach a Wren you had to have your bank book in one hand and your school certificate in the other, since very few categories of work accepted girls without it'.[52]

The bank book aside, in some respects this was the case for certain categories where qualifications in mathematics or typing speed were required. Nancy Jennings was required to demonstrate her typing speed.[53] However, for various Wrens the lack of a school certificate did not restrict them to being assigned solely to the domestic branch. What seemed more important in some cases was work experience. Jeanette Wakeford had left school at 14 with no qualifications, but attending secretarial school and working as holiday cover in various secretarial jobs gave her enough experience to become a writer in the WRNS.[54]

Educationally, the respondents did not reflect the wider social trends of the 1930s. In this decade only 15 per cent of girls aged 11 to 17 went to secondary school; the norm was to stay in school until the leaving age of 14.[55] If this statistic is compared to the 21 interviewees included in the study who were at school in this period, only three left at aged 15 or below. Of those women who stayed in school, around half gained their school certificate and four gained a higher school certificate or matriculation (the equivalent to A levels). As a sample of the service, which admittedly is not representative of the whole, it does provide an insight into the educational background many of the Wrens had.

The need for educational qualifications to join the WRNS depended on the job applied for. A school certificate was not needed to join the domestic branch, for example, and whilst experience was preferable it was not always an advantage as new cooks were given training after being enrolled.[56] For specialised categories, such as coding, educational achievement did figure heavily in the interview process where it was one way of distinguishing between applicants. Jean Matthews recalls most of her initial interview being about her educational background. She had a school certificate and a place at the Birmingham College of Art, which she had started several months before joining the WRNS. She was selected to be a coder and was sent to Gayhurst Manor, Bletchley Park. At school Jean saw herself as 'run of the mill'. She thinks it might have been her quiet nature that led the selecting officer to choose her for Special Duties X (those people whose jobs were connected to the work at Bletchley Park).[57] In line with educational qualifications then, the character of the individual was also a key to deciding the category to which a Wren was assigned.

Laughton Mathews argues that alongside the preconception that women needed a school certificate to join the service, (leading to the assumption applicants were predominately middle class) was a misunderstanding that a close tie with the navy, such as a relative, was required. This error arose because when women's work was most needed, the Ministry of Labour laid down seven conditions in June

1942 to limit the numbers of applicants to the WRNS. One of the seven included a close relationship with the navy.[58] George Hall, Under Secretary of State 1940 to 42 and Financial Secretary to the Admiralty 1942 to 43, stated in a House of Commons Debate on 14 October 1942 that these seven restrictions for entry only applied to women born between 1 January 1918 and 30 June 1922. At the time, this meant women aged 19 to 23 were unable to apply unless they met one of the following conditions:

1. Past service in the WRNS or Admiralty; or in the Sea Transport Office of the Ministry of War Transport or G.P.O. Fleet Mail Office.
2. Practical experience of boat work, e.g., Sea Rangers or ex-members of the River Emergency Service.
3. Previous experience of domestic work and desire to enter as a cook or steward.
4. If written application to join the Women's Royal Naval Service was made before becoming liable for call-up under the National Service Acts.
5. Father or brother in the Navy or sister or mother in the WRNS.
6. Ability to speak and translate German fluently.
7. School certificate standard in mathematics and/or physics.[59]

It was made clear in the House of Commons debate that a lack of family connections did not mean applicants had no hope of acceptance. Henry Brooke MP made it clear that entry to the service 'depends on personal merit and suitability, not on family connections,'[60]

Although these conditions were temporary, they left lasting ideas about who were appropriate applicants. Kathy Baker held this view:

When I joined, which was the 24 July 1942, straight from Oxford with a degree in English, which was of no interest to anybody, you could be a Wren if you had a close relative i.e. father, brother, husband, even I think fiancé would count, in the navy, [...] otherwise, it was very difficult to get in because it was a small service.[61]

The specification of a close tie to the navy, which was only in place for a short time, was brought in place because Laughton Mathews felt it would have been more of a 'hardship for the daughter of a sailor to be refused than for someone without naval ties'.[62] In this sense, it was not so much about social capital (who you knew), for as she went on to point out, naval relatives could include RN stokers as much as admirals.

Kathy Baker had only tenuous connections to the navy. She says that the reason she got into the service was because in the middle of 1942 the WRNS were looking for better educated applicants to work in Special Duties X and to fill the widening range of technical jobs. Having matriculation and higher-level maths, Kathy argues, made her a suitable candidate to be trained for a technical role, in her case as a classifier, listening to Morse signals and measuring the reflecting power of the ionosphere to send forecasts of weather to operational units.

The application form did not commit the women applying in any way but did provide them with the opportunity to state the categories they would like to apply for. In some cases, new recruits were rejected at this stage because there were no openings in the categories they favoured or because they did not have the skills needed for roles that were open. Once the National Service Act 1941 came in during December this meant some women could not join the WRNS and they had to serve somewhere else. Janet Swete-Evans was informed when she applied to the WRNS in 1940 that there were no vacancies to be a coder (her chosen category). Luckily, because she had applied before the National Service requirements had come into effect she was able to wait to see if opportunities changed. The Superintendent of Rosyth (to whom Janet applied) expected there to be openings in the near future so she kept her record on file and forwarded it to HQ in London on 29 April 1940 recommending she should train as a wireless telegraphist.[63]

An officer from one of the regional offices would interview new recruits following the successful application stage. They would then decide if the applicant was suitable to go on the two-week initial training. E. Ridley provides a rich account of the process she underwent to join the WRNS in 1945. She went to the recruiting office in Birmingham, on Navigation Street. The petty officer who interviewed her asked her why she wanted to join, whether she had any relatives in the service, her school background, qualifications and interests. As she was still under 18 she had to have written permission from her father to join, which she duly delivered the next day. Ridley was informed she would hear in a week or so about attending a medical. Following her successful medical, she was told to report to Mill Hill on 7 November.[64]

The first organised training for WRNS ratings began in January 1940 when part of King's College of Household and Social Science, Campden Hill, London was taken over for the purpose.[65] The college could accommodate 90 new recruits at any one time. In June 1940, training ceased at Campden Hill and was established in the Queen Anne block at Greenwich (the same place as the Officers Training Course). This location provided accommodation for 230 trainees. By the end of the year, it was decided that entrants would serve a two-week probation before enrolment and being given uniform.[66] This allowed recruits to change their mind or for the service to ask them to leave if they did not think the candidate was suitable. From March 1941, all recruits were entered as Probationary Wrens and their category of work was decided at the end of their initial training. This came about following an interview with a senior officer such as the training centre's Superintendent or Chief Officer. Many would have had a good idea of their eventual category, having been selected because of particular skills.[67] Ridley, for example, was aware she was likely to become a Wren steward.

Once Probationary Wrens had completed their two weeks' training they were either sent for further training for their category, were drafted to a base to begin work, or were sent to a holding depot where they would wait for an opening in the category they had been selected for. Further training varied in length and was only provided for specific roles. In the service's *Regulations and Instructions* handbook issued annually to officers, details about the length of training for different categories were provided. In the handbook for 1943, the radio mechanics were given 30 weeks' training, the longest training period, followed by air mechanics who took 24 weeks. Both of these courses were held in the Royal Naval barracks at Lee-on-Solent. Other categories that took as long included boom defence. This length of training reflected the range of knowledge and skills required for these roles. Shorter training courses included six weeks to become a cook and two to three for stewards, whereas motor transport drivers had two to four weeks training.[68]

Westfield College, Hampstead, opened in April 1941 as an additional location for ratings' training. Other locations for training included depots at Devonport, Chatham, Portsmouth and Liverpool. Sheila Hamnett, for example, was trained in Dundee, reporting there on 7 April 1942. A possible reason why she was sent there, rather than one of the larger initial training centres, was she was selected at interview to go on a wireless operators' course, having trained herself to be proficient in reading semaphore, and this was the location of the training.[69] In March 1942 the central training depot in Greenwich closed and New College, Hampstead, took over.

The National Institute of Medical Research, Mill Hill (HMS *Pembroke III*) was also requisitioned in March 1942 as the WRNS ratings' training location, becoming the Central Training Depot.[70] It was a timely move because in the same month the National Service Act came into force, enabling the WRNS to increase in size. The Ministry of Labour would not allow National Service candidates to be put on a waiting list for entry and there were growing demands from Combined Operations bases for Wrens. Mill Hill, with a capacity of 900, was large enough to deal with the demand.[71] This massive expansion in the training for ratings demonstrates both the widening remit of the service and its increased organisational ability to manage and train nearly 1,000 recruits every two weeks. All mobile ratings after February 1943 (bar a few in 1944 when flying bombs were at their worst) had their probationary period at Mill Hill when the centralisation of general training was achieved.[72] Most of the Wrens interviewed who joined post-1942 were trained there.

Each new entrant would receive a letter sometime after her draft interview giving her details about when to attend initial training. These letters immediately set out strict standards of behaviour and compliance. A range of instructions, the letters set out how to travel, by whom they would be met, the need to be at the training depot for two weeks and the expectation that following enrolment new Wrens would be drafted straight to their ports. They may have been used as part of the process of trying to discourage the less committed by giving the impression that much was required.

Included with the letter was a list of items to bring for the two weeks, which included necessary clothing, a rug or blanket in case of air raids, the woman's identity card, ration card, unemployment and National Health Insurance cards, respirator and a torch.[73]

Civilian clothing was rather disregarded, in order to accustom newcomers to being in a uniformed service. New recruits received blue overalls, E. Ridley recalls on her arrival at Mill Hill,

> The following day we were issued with long sleeved navy blue dresses. After looking at each other we had a fit of giggles as we thought we looked like prisoners. We had to pack the civilian clothes we'd gone down in, into our suitcases and just keep our underwear out and keep our suitcases on our lockers but suitcases were later sent home.[74]

The WRNS was the only women's auxiliary that did not provide uniforms straight away. The issuing of a uniform at the end of two weeks' initial training was seen both as a reward and achievement for many women. This protocol reinforced the perception that only the hardest working and most suitable would make it into the service.

When Ridley took the train to London from Birmingham it was the furthest she had ever been on her own, a common experience for many of the younger Wrens. On arriving at Mill Hill she was put in Howe Division and slept on Swordfish Deck with the other prospective cooks and stewards. She was given a little pin with a white flag on it, which they had to wear all the time signifying they were probationary Wrens.

Initial training involved a mixture of cleaning, drill, lectures on navy life and what to expect when they joined the service. Ridley discusses learning navy language, something that came up as a common theme within many of the other interviews and personal documents. Rather than talking about floors, kitchens, bedrooms and time off, Wrens came to use terms such as deck, galley, cabin and stand easy.[75]

S. Carman recalled her initial two-week training at HMS *Pembroke III*, Mill Hill:

> We spent hours practicing marching, and to this day, I can march forwards, about turn and right and left incline. Our heads were examined for nits and our nether regions for goodness knows what, and eventually we were issued with uniforms.[76]

Views of initial training at Mill Hill were mixed. Joyce Wheatley recollects: 'memories are of marching, being trained by a Royal Marine and being in trouble for appearing outside the building hatless'.[77] M. Pratt, on the other hand, states:

> my most vivid recollections of this period is of scrubbing endless flights of stone stairs with cold water and carbolic, while others were assigned to kitchen chores. It was hardly surprising that many girls threw in the towel during that fortnight![78]

Margaret Boothroyd managed to avoid doing any 'working and scrubbing' as her job was polishing a very long corridor, 'which was already very highly polished!'[79]

Much was done in the first two weeks to put off those new recruits not cut out for a life in the WRNS. Amanda Davies remembered spending hours scrubbing and polishing floors. When they were allowed out, the probationary Wrens had to report back every hour, which meant you could not go very far. 'Some girls just couldn't stand it and left, which is what they wanted, to get the ones who were tenacious to stay.'[80]

Attitudes toward initial training were influenced greatly by the background of the individuals. Jean Atkins found her experience at Mill Hill an 'eye opener', having just left school in the summer of 1942 at the age of 18:

> [It was the] first time I'd slept on a double bunk, though quite a few of the women in the dormitory were older than myself and more

sophisticated. I'd never seen anybody pin their hair up or take so long to pin their hair up![81]

Jean had been to an all-girls private school. However, she had never lived with women who were older than her. Many of the respondents who were in their late teens when they joined the service commented on their initial naivety.

Martha Rose found her experience at Mill Hill 'terrifying', having joined at the age of 17. She had always been to boarding school, so was used to being away from home but she found the initial training intimidating because there were so many people and everything was done in such a rush. She would have gone home, except her father had been critical of her joining the service and wanted Martha to go to a domestic science college, which she did not want to do and so she stayed to prove him wrong.[82]

Kathy Baker was in the first group of probationary Wrens sent to Mill Hill on 29 July 1942. On her first night, there was an air raid at three in the morning. The behaviour of the officers in the situation gave Kathy a very good impression of the service:

> A Petty Officer with a torch grabbed us out of our cabin and walked us hand in hand, in the dark [...] to the basement where we sat in our pyjamas [...] and I looked up. We could hear the planes and bombs falling and so on [...] All the pipes for the gas and electricity and water were above us, and well I thought, 'if anything falls on this we've had it, that's my war service in a day'. However, after a time the all clear went and we were duly mustered back to our various cabins. We'd hardly got ourselves all sorted, round came a young Third Officer quarters with a rating and a trolley of tea, cups of tea were handed out [...] and I thought, 'if that's the Navy, that's for me'. It was a simple gesture but of enormous impact. We were nervous, frightened by then, I thought 'gosh if London's like this'.[83]

This might have been the first experience of bombing for the women. Many of the interviewees recalled only living through bombing in their service careers, as before they had either lived outside of the locations most likely to be targeted, or had been evacuated as children.

Prior to the end of 1940, when it was decided entrants would have a two-week probationary period before enrolment, training of ratings often happened on the job or within smaller training centres around the country rather than at the later large training depots. Daphne Coyne had her initial interview at WRNS Headquarters Bristol Channel area, Whiteladies Road, Bristol. In 1940 she recalls her mum coming into the interview with her. Daphne was shocked! 'Surely in the whole wartime history of the royal navy no officer has interviewed a potential rating "to fight the foe" with a "mum" sitting in on it to see if the service was to her liking.'

The rather large Mrs Bell, Chief Officer Bristol Channel Area, who was sister to 'the equally large Director of the WRNS', as Daphne describes her, interviewed Daphne and her mother. Bell even asked her mother, who was of a similar size, whether she would like to apply to be a Wren. Her mother replied 'Good gracious, at my size, what would I look like in the uniform?'[84]

Daphne's experience was common for early Wrens who, after interview, would be asked to report to a base where they began work straight away. In Daphne's case, she was told to report to Milford Haven on 8 October 1940 as a messenger. She recalls Milford Haven being called 'Mrs Bell's finishing school' as she recruited a large number of 'suitable girls'. The social life was still of pre-war standards with 'strict observance of officers' ranks' in the seating arrangements at dinner parties. Daphne's experience supports the argument that the WRNS would promote people based on their conduct and skills rather than class background as she came from a modest working-class background. She seems to have benefited from her time at Milford Haven and her later posting to Liverpool, as she was recommended for a commission in summer 1943. She reported to Greenwich in June and was appointed to Third Officer, having displayed 'Officer Like Qualities'. These qualities, Laughton Mathews indicated, '[did] not mean not eating peas off the knife but a responsibility towards one's fellows that indicate[d] the grains of leadership'.[85]

This reference to not eating peas off your knife was a cultural reference to the working class whose behaviour was associated 'with cheap restaurants that had dirty tablecloths, uncouth waiters, and chipped dishes'. In Philadelphia in the 1880s a restaurant owner even went so far to eject anyone who ate food off their knife to attract a higher class of patron.[86] Laughton Mathews' reference to this indicates the stereotypes of class present at the time, whereas well-bred ladies would never have dared eat off their knife; it was seen as more common for the working class. In making this comment, she demonstrates that she was not interested in facile indicators of someone's character, rather their actual capability.

In June 1942, waiting lists of women wishing to join were so long that applicants were restricted to specific qualifications and criteria, as previously discussed.[87] Sheila Rodman applied to join the WRNS in 1943 when she was 17. She recalls that when she turned 17½ (in mid 1943) the WRNS closed applications for new recruits for six months.[88] Voluntary recruiting was re-opened for women under the age of 19 on 3 January 1944.[89] Sheila eventually joined the service on 31 May 1944 and attended her initial training at Balloch Castle, Loch Lomond, Scotland, having travelled up from her home town of Sheffield, where she had been working as a laboratory assistant and typist for James Neelam and Co. Steelworks. Her initial training was similar to those women sent to other centres. She remembers scrubbing many stairs from six o'clock in the morning. 'They deliberately gave us these jobs to test our mettle, I think'.[90] After her training Sheila was selected to train as a Wren Ordinance (armourer) and was sent to HMS *Fledgling* for a six-month course in how to maintain the guns on Fleet Air Arm planes.

Alongside this 'official' side of the service that aimed at the same time to discourage unsuitable recruits and bond new Wrens, thereby building a sense of common identity, there were also stories of women trying to level out their differing backgrounds. It was an attempt to build alliances and friendships or to scare off those who did not conform. Rites of passage formed a common way of doing this. In most cases these were performed through pleasant social gatherings, which included going to the first dance or down the pub with new Wren colleagues.

There were also more direct and harsh ways of forming a common identity. Issues of living with a diverse range of people meant those with body odour or who did not look after their appearance were soon noticed. Christian Lamb, in her book *I Only Joined for the Hat*, which provides a personal account of being a Wren, remembers: 'some [girls] were wedded to their vests which they had been wearing all day, keeping them on even under pyjamas ... Putting your bra on outside your vest then of course comes naturally.'[91] Christian is unclear why these women did this, but she talks of sharing rooms with women from diverse backgrounds. Wearing a vest would have helped some women, who may never have undressed in front of others, as would have been common from those of boarding school backgrounds, to maintain their modesty. It may have also provided a shield from the ridicule some women felt they might receive if they revealed their bodies.

Differences in how women from various backgrounds viewed their own bodies were noticeable. Summerfield notes that many of the women she interviewed emphasised their bodies and appearance being brought into line.[92] Processes to do this were often demeaning and cruel for women bearing the brunt. Betty Calderara recalled: 'we did have one or two 'off' ones, but it didn't last long. One or two people we threw in the bath because they were so grubby. You know it's like boarding school. You have to live with it'.[93]

Summerfield discusses the instances of women being thrown in the bath as a process that:

> Focused on bringing deviant members of their groups up to standards of behaviour, which they felt they themselves embodied. These stories described stemming a tide of pollution, literally with soap and scrubbing brushes, in acts which were also ritualised and symbolic. [...] They focused on symbolically and materially on bodily hygiene and manners, matters of immediate and daily concern to women living together in close proximity in the forces.[94]

Bringing women up to standards of cleanliness favoured by the majority matched the femininity of the WRNS as expressed through its uniform and rules about personal presentation, for example, hair not being allowed to touch the collar. Priscilla Inverarity writes of her experience of initial training, where 'every morning we had "Muster", in other words we had to parade in a courtyard and be inspected by a group of rather terrifying Wren officers, who ticked us off it they thought our hair was too long or our shoes were not sparkling with polish'.[95]

The sense that one 'had to live with it', as Betty put these types of events, reflected practices in other institutions at the time, such as boarding schools, where rites of passage were important to form bonds of reliance. Such bullying was often short-lived when conformity was achieved. They also reflect the way in which the service 'levelled up', drawing women from a variety of backgrounds to a similar standard of behaviour.

Presentation was very important for many of its members. Coming up to these standards provided women with a sense of pride and belonging whilst also promoting a distinct expectation of behaviour. Once barriers of appearance and body odour were overcome, relationships were formed based on strong bonds of loyalty and affection.[96] Christian Lamb felt her horizons had been broadened as it was the first time she 'mixed on completely equal terms with girls of all classes'.[97] Christian was from an upper-middle-class family, who had just passed her exam to enter Oxford just as the war began. She reflects that the women she came to live with all settled down quite harmoniously despite their differences.

The ethos of the service encouraged cooperation and teamwork. Jeanette Wakeford believed the service helped bring people together, especially in the first two weeks of hardship and cleaning. This made them more tolerant of differences as 'you all had to knuckle under and you know, room inspections and things like that. You had to pull together to make it good.'[98]

Claire James also made a similar comment in her interview, believing the service helped to broaden her outlook by giving her the opportunity to mix with all sorts of people. She believed women got into the service because of their education, which led to a real mix of individuals from all sorts of backgrounds. Claire did not believe there were any social barriers that divided people.[99]

As can be seen, especially in the early stages of a Wren's career much was being done to shape the new recruits into the image of the service. The two weeks' probationary period was suitably tough to put off those women who would not conform to the ethos of the service. Attrition rates for women leaving the WRNS after the probationary period have not been found; however, accounts by servicewomen and officers do not indicate that many people left or were asked to leave after being appointed as Wrens after the first two weeks.

Officers' Training

WRNS officers, following the few initial direct entrants in 1939, as previously discussed, were always selected from the lower deck. Unlike the other women's services, Wrens could not apply for a commission themselves. They had to be nominated for the officer's training course, in some cases having discussed this with the ranking officer where they were stationed. In the early years of the war, when the service was small enough, each potential officer would have to go through a selection board, headed by the Director, her Deputy, Angela Goodenough, and Staff Officer, Lady Cholmondeley. Technical qualifications, Laughton Mathews argues, were never enough to automatically guarantee a Wren a commission. The board was looking for OLQ (officer-like qualities), which included the ability to take responsibility for women below them in rank and a sense of leadership. Laughton Mathews notes, 'sometimes the holders of very high intellectual qualities went on the rocks as officers because they lacked ordinary common sense and the ability to hitch their knowledge and their dreams to reality'.[100] The occasional women who were appointed because of technical qualifications were never more than Third Officers. The Director stated she was not happy with this situation, as she wanted good leaders over and above technically competent women, but the massive expansion required of the service necessitated the situation.

At the end of 1940 there were 561 officers, compared to 8,587 in 1945. The Director noticed that differences between the officer recruits of 1917 and 1939 varied more significantly between the older women than the younger. The women in their late forties were very different to those in the first war. Many of them had business and professional experience, with many officers having held important positions in civilian life and were used to responsibility.[101] This reflects a change that had occurred in the interwar period with more older married women entering and staying in the workforce than they had in 1914.

Many of the original officers were the daughters or wives of naval officers. In the first year of the service 48 per cent of new officers were from this background.[102] Laughton Mathews faced problems with 'Third-Officer Mrs Captain' with the early Cypher officers.[103] During the war this disparity diluted significantly as recruiting from the ranks soon solved this problem when all officers had to be promoted from the lower deck. The length someone would remain as a rating before promotion varied, for example, 'the daughter of a Peer might stay longer in the ranks than a more gifted "self-made" messmate'.[104] The important factor was whether an individual was suitable to lead a group of women, not who she knew or how many qualifications she had achieved.

Peggy Scott discusses how the relationship between officers and ratings in World War II was different from the first. She includes the observation of Superintendent Joan Carpenter who was a Wren in World War I, who stated, 'the attitude of the Wrens today in approaching an officer is quite different from ours in 1918. It is much more democratic; there is more feeling of equality'.[105]

This sense of equality, which came through many times in the interviews and was supported by memoirs in archives, helped foster good relations between officers and ratings, leading to strong working relationships. For officers, it was important to be inclusive and this was emphasised within the training and was reflected in their selection. Kathy Baker reveals the service was not exclusive, despite its reputation as the 'superior service'. It comprised a range of women from many backgrounds, including 'totally uneducated fishermen's daughter[s] from Grimsby', who were 'lovely'.[106]

When serving as Third Officer, Officer in Charge, in a small Wireless Telegraph station in HMS *Proserpine*, Wick, Scotland, she had to look after 25 to 30 Wrens and recalls everyone 'mucking in'. She would drive to Wick or Thursow to buy provisions for the cook, for example. Officers were not there to be high and mighty, but rather to lead and encourage the women under them. It was also not always easy for them. Kathy recalled her time in Scotland as the loneliest period of her life as she was the only officer and was told to have a distanced relationship with her ratings. She also spent many days alone, driving the van round the countryside to try and get enough food as only a very limited amount of naval supplies reached them. WRNS officers, therefore, had to have a certain amount of resourcefulness and courage to undertake their duties.

The Director played a pivotal role in shaping how the service would later grow based upon her initial involvement in selecting officers determined the WRNS culture as numbers grew. Christian Lamb, who had direct contact with Laughton Mathews in the first year of the war, having worked in WRNS HQ from 1939, recalls how officers were selected for the service and the importance of the Director's vision in recruiting particular types of women:

> Vera Laughton Mathews was a remarkable woman [...] she knew exactly what sort of WRNS she wanted from the start, and fought all the regiments of bureaucrats and civil servants singlehandedly to get it right. A dedicated, hands-on person, she did everything herself, interviewing and choosing her closest staff officers [...] These colleagues all became great friends and stuck with her through thick and thin.[107]

The first Officers Training Course began on 30 October 1939 at Greenwich, by agreement with the Admiral President of the Royal Naval College, Sir Charles Kennedy-Purvis. With the service having only begun recruiting a month before, this demonstrates the foresight Laughton Mathews had when setting up the service before war broke out.

Laughton Mathews and Goodenough had expected opposition to Wrens being allowed to billet within the Naval College, but 'there was no opposition at all'. In early 1940 she thanked Kennedy-Purvis, stating:

> How thankful we are that at that decisive moment, there was a broadminded man in that high position, someone who could welcome women into such a sanctuary of naval officers without thinking the world was going to end.[108]

His answer, Laughton Mathews recalls, with a 'twinkle in his eye' was 'I've always been a bit of a bolshie'. High-ranking officers such as Kennedy-Purvis, open to the WRNS and what it could do for the navy and war effort, provided the service with the legitimacy and support that helped it prosper. Allowing WRNS officers to train at Greenwich provided them with a strong relationship with the navy. Christian Lamb recalls her training in which

> [O]ne was to learn not only how to become an Officer but hopefully a 'lady' too. There were other things you apparently needed to know, besides not to eat peas off one's knife. The lectures we listened to varied from the utterly boring to brilliant, with one on Navigation and Admiralty Procedure in the latter category. Admiral Sir William Goodenough did not so much seem to lecture as simply tell us things we might find useful in the Navy, the Proper Navy of course.[109]

The close ties forged between the RN instructors and WRNS officers throughout the training programme at Greenwich, and later Framewood Manor, bonded the two services, with a strong emphasis on instructing new officers further in the traditions and procedures within the RN. Between 1940 and 1945 Superintendent Elsie French oversaw the course. French would prepare reports for each candidate at the end of the two-week course in preparation for the selection board meeting, carefully commenting on the merits of each individual.[110]

The training was put on a revolving system, with a pass out ceremony each week, ensuring a certain number of officers were ready to meet the demands of the navy. In the early days of the Officers Training Course Laughton Mathews recalls having been able to remember the names of all new officers, as she, along with Goodenough and Lady Cholmondely had interviewed them all.[111] Later in the war, this would cease as the service grew.

WRNS officers were encouraged to think of their promotion not as a reward for good service but a 'grave responsibility' to care for the ratings in the service and encourage a high standard of values.[112] This attitude reflects the 'exclusive' perception of the WRNS, with its high standards and sense of moral duty. During a House of Commons debate on 7 March 1944, unquestionably late into the war, Samuel Viant, MP for Willesden West, questioned this perception. He stated that he had received reports that the selection board for officers was putting these questions to candidates: '"What is your father? Who are your bankers? What was your school?" and, finally, "Who recommended you?"'[113] He goes on to claim to have been inundated with letters that indicate the main qualifications for a commission were 'a good social standing in private life, a private income, a higher school education, influential relatives or friends'. Albert Alexander, First Lord of the Admiralty, responded:

> I really must interrupt my hon. Friend. I was commissioned from the ranks in 1916 or 1917. I was not asked what my bank balance was, but I was asked exactly what we ask the WRNS today—who are your bankers, and do you wish your money, when you get your commission, to be paid through a bank or paid direct?[114]

Questions that might have been interpreted as promoting social exclusivity were being used to find out practical information about the backgrounds of applicants such as this. This criticism was investigated by Alexander and the backgrounds of successful applicants were found to be very wide-ranging and mixed in terms of social class, demonstrating yet again how, even for officers, class was not a defining feature of selection. It was essential that roles were filled by capable women. Officers were needed for a range of work, two-thirds directly replaced male officers and a third worked in WRNS administration and welfare roles.[115]

Sybil Riley joined the WRNS in early 1941 as a pay ledger writer. After six months, the Paymaster Captain and Wren Officer in Charge of the Sparrow's Nest, Lowestoft, recommended her for a commission. At the end of her two-week Officer Training Course she was interviewed by the Director. Sybil recalls:

> The interview was most unpleasant. It seemed that nothing I said was right and finished by her saying that she was very doubtful of my ability to be an officer. At twenty-eight years of age, a mother and wife of an Army Chaplain I had mixed with many people and had lived in Shanghai for three years, which no one else had done.[116]

She took a very dim view of the Director, whom Sybil believed was critical of her because she was Church of England, whereas Laughton Mathews was Roman Catholic. There is no corroborating evidence that the Director allowed her religious background to influence her selection of officers. However, a friend of Sybil's claimed Laughton Mathews 'was a bigoted RC' and that she 'knew of only one such [Church of England officer] that had been commissioned'.[117] Whether this was in any way true is doubtful as Sybil was then interviewed by Lady Chomondley (Laughton Mathews' right hand on the officers' selection board, who was originally Lady Rocksavage – the person who had supposedly come up with the idea for the World War I WRNS) and was appointed as an officer. Perhaps a clash of personalities between the two women was more likely, as in her memoirs Sybil Riley demonstrates herself to be as obstinate as the Director.

For much of the war, individuals working and being trained at Greenwich were not allowed to sleep above ground. Instead, they slept in the catacombs below the building. In the autumn of 1940 when bombing was particularly bad the cadets and staff both slept and worked in the vaults.[118] Elizabeth Dunkley was sent to Greenwich for OTC in January 1941. She remembers they 'lived in Spartan conditions with snow on the ground and slept in a cellar where there was a hole blown at one end in a previous air raid'.[119]

Greenwich was the location of Officers Training Course until April 1944 when bombing forced the service to move into new premises at

Framewood Manor, Stoke Pogues. In December, it returned to London to New College, Hampstead and in June 1945 was restored back to Greenwich.[120] From the beginning of the war until the end, 8,587 WRNS officers and cadet Wrens passed through the Royal Naval College.[121] The course allowed new officers to learn 'the tone of command and physical presentation of self which constituted the performance required of them'.[122] New WRNS officers had been shaped in the likeness formed by Laughton Mathews and her Superintendents and Chief Officers. This likeness referred to a sense of integrity and ability to lead others, which was not a product of the background of the individuals selected.

Reasons for Joining the Service

All of the women interviewed were under the age of 24 when they joined the WRNS and all but one signed up after 1941. The justification for joining the service had a lot of similarities within this age group and would probably have been very different for women joining in their middle years. Most gave a reason for why they joined the service but others just saw it as a natural choice. Within the archive sources and memoirs a few women had also set out their reasons for selecting the WRNS.

For some of the interviewees, including Betty Calderara, Jean Atkins, Nancy Jennings and Mabel Langdon, it was the influence of their parents and naval connections that prompted them to apply to join the service. As the last child in a large family, Betty hoped that by joining the WRNS she would be stationed somewhere close to home in Lewes. She also liked the look of the sailors whom she would watch march by when she was in Brighton as the officers training centre was at HMS *King Alfred* in Hove.[123] Jean had no real opinion of the service before applying but her father had always been interested in 'naval things' and the 'naval connection' of the WRNS appealed more than any of the other women's services.[124] One Wren who had an actual naval connection was Nancy Jennings, which, given the unfounded belief that this was important, as discussed earlier, actually made her unusual among the interviewees. She wanted to join the service because her father was a RN Officer, who was recalled in World War II. She saw joining the WRNS as 'natural' and applied in 1939 for any job that was open.[125] Mabel Langdon also had a naval background, as her mum had been one of the first Wrens in World War I; for her, the navy 'always came first', which she links to her mother's role in the first war.[126]

Image and reputation were also important reasons that swayed some people's decision to join the WRNS. The perception of the WRNS being the 'best service' was the main reason Nina Adams and Norma Deering signed up to be Wrens. Nina perceived the WRNS to be the 'senior service'. She gave up her job as a secretary because she hoped the WRNS would enable her to travel. Indeed, she ended up being posted to Egypt and Palestine.[127] Helen's mother thought the WRNS was the best service with a nicer type of girl. And Sarah Abbott was initially going to join the WAAF but the girls in the queue at the recruitment office put her off, as she decided 'she didn't like the look' of them.[128]

Other reasons related to the visual appeal of the WRNS uniform or having seen a friend or sister as a Wren. Jeanette Wakeford knew she would have to join up eventually and chose the WRNS over the other services because of the uniform. She regards her decision as 'quite a shot in the dark!' but on the whole had 'a good time'.[129] The chance to have a good time was one of the reasons Amanda Davies applied, seeing the potential for meeting lots of men. The uniform also helped sway her decision because unlike the other women's services you could wear silk stockings. In addition, Amanda perceived the service to be the hardest to get into because it was voluntary and very popular. This appealed to her.[130]

Uniform was a key motivator for many women, with its obviously feminine appeal. However, others liked the idea of being able to wear bell-bottoms in more manual jobs, drawing in women who were not necessarily taken by the glamour of the skirt and jacket. Christian Lamb tells of how the Director employed a 'top designer to create a uniform, based on that of the WRNS in World War I ... and which included the splendid tricorne hat [worn by officers]'. She states in her tongue in cheek manner that she had 'always been extremely hat-minded' and this became her main reason for applying to join the service.[131] When working in WRNS HQ, sorting through applications, she notes:

> The enormous waiting list of applicants wishing to join the WRNS was, in fact, very much dependent on the uniform- smart, dark, navy blue, plain jacket and skirt, whose straight line concealed deficiencies in one's figure, and topped with either the sailor hat or the distinctive tricorne hat − the effect was a winner. The ATS and WAAF were unlucky in that their less attractive khaki and air force blue had wide waistbands, which tended to exaggerate their hips.[132]

The use of uniform to lure in prospective applicants was, on the face of it, quite frivolous but worked as an effective tool to attract a 'type' of woman. The uniforms of the WRNS and WAAF, which were regarded as more flattering, promoted an image of elegance not present in the khaki of the ATS. In the early years of the war its uniform only came in three sizes, small, medium and large, which meant some new recruits described their uniform as 'stupid and inelegant' or 'awful'.[133] The 'glamour' presented by older women in flattering WRNS uniform offered some younger women a glimpse into a world of adulthood that corresponded with their concepts of feminine identity.[134]

The military uniform of the three women's auxiliaries, and in particular that of the WRNS, is quite contradictory. On the one hand, it conjures up a military status at odds with femininity: 'the wartime emblems of citizenship, which restrained the visible signs of feminine difference'.[135] As the war progressed it did this even further with Wrens in mechanical and outdoor roles increasingly having to wear boiler suits and bell-bottomed trousers with shirts. Yet contradicting this, the uniform conformed to the expectations of femininity of the time, with the glamorous image of the WRNS uniform that Christian Lamb highlights. This public persona helped to construct a narrative about the nature of the WRNS that maintained a feminine façade, even when the jobs of Wrens moved beyond this. Bell-bottoms were an interesting addition in 1941, because on the one hand they were essential for the job women had to do − you could not work upside down in an aircraft in a skirt — and yet they challenged social norms — it was still very uncommon for women to wear trousers socially. Jean Matthews found her bell-bottoms really comfortable and easy to put on if you wanted to quickly pop out to get something. However, when she came home on leave, her father demanded she take hers off, saying 'don't ever let me see you in those things again'. He regarded them as a bit risqué and not befitting his daughter.[136] This aspect of the uniform only really fitted the image of the WRNS when put in the context of women 'doing their duty'; they were not for public display in a general setting. The WRNS uniform, therefore, straddled the careful boundaries of cultural acceptability. In making its 'official' uniform particularly feminine leaders normalised it within a military setting. This allowed them to present an aura of respectability in their public image whilst also enabling them to undertake the military duties they increasingly came to carry out.

As some oral testimonies and Christian Lamb's memoirs reflect, the WRNS uniforms highlighted the way this clothing has come to symbolise the service and become a form of memorial, indeed a metonym for 'Wren-ness'. The uniform signifies what the service stood for in its members' eyes, asserting a glamorous image that has been maintained and reflected in the oral testimony, but also the sense of having been part of something greater than themselves. In 2005, the first official memorial, The Monument to the Women of World War II (sculpted by John W. Mills) was unveiled in London's Whitehall. Peniston-Bird argues that this memorial has not been without controversy, depicting, as it does, an abstract interpretation of the contribution of women to the war. The bronze comprises 17 representations of women's wartime lives, including the great coats of the women's auxiliaries and the hats, coats, handbags and of women's attire at the time.[137]

The chosen design has created heated debate due to the diverse range of roles in the war, which have been placed alongside each other, exposing differences in experience and perceived status. Debate has also arisen because people and groups have 'personal investment in these symbols', which may not be represented in new images such as this.[138] A former Wren, for example, complained that the representation of the WRNS as a great coat hanging on a hook was an 'affront' as they always wore their uniforms with 'great pride and treated them with care', hanging them up on a coat hanger with the buttons done up. Another woman criticised the imagery of the auxiliary uniforms for the lack of femininity, arguing 'when we volunteered and willingly gave our service, we were nubile; and dare I say, beautiful young women. We did wear trousers on night duty, but at other times we were smart and glamorous in our neat uniforms.'[139] This commentary serves to confirm the argument that the WRNS has come to be memorialised in this way. Its uniform and crest, which replicates that of the RN (an anchor with a crown around the middle with the addition of a wren bird at the top) have come to signify all the WRNS saw itself as and has been maintained in the imagery and commemoration of the service. The Association of Wrens, for example, still uses the crest as its logo. Contradictory images of this, as some have found on the 2005 memorial, have countered the dominant narrative of what the WRNS has come to stand for: glamour, togetherness and service.

The importance of uniform and appearance for some of the women is not surprising given the age of most when they signed up. Many had been relatively sheltered in their home and school lives, and joining the WRNS was seen as a chance to have fun and gain freedom. Several of the interviewees, including Pam Marsden, had seen their friends having a great time in the service.[140] Pamela Bates wanted the chance to leave home and meet some men.[141] If we compare the experience to today, joining the WRNS at 19 was the equivalent of going to university, a chance to get away from home and the restrictions of parents. A sense that work would have to be done, and that it was ultimately important, was there, but given the relative youth of most of the interviewees the focus was much more on having a 'marvellous time', as Martha Rose put it.[142] In the 1930s it was very unlikely that a young single woman would have lived alone or with friends rather than family, so joining the services represented a massive shift in lifestyle.[143] Despite the presence of the war, many respondents stated in their interviews that they felt a degree of separation from what was occurring in the news about the conflict, and their own role in the service.

For others, the reasons for joining were less flippant than uniforms and meeting men. Claire James thought she would be able to get a better job within the WRNS than the other women's auxiliaries because it was voluntary and allowed her to have a say in her choice of category. She did not wish to end up in a domestic or physical job, which was more likely in the ATS and a given in the land army.[144] Josephine Rayne also favoured the uniform but wished to get away from home, having lived with her grandmother since she was 15 months old. The service was her chance to gain freedom and try something new.[145] It was also a way to avoid or hold off social convention. Joyce Tapp in her memoirs talks of how:

> For many girls war service was their first experience of life away from home ... until the outbreak of war life for girls was narrow. They were expected to remain at home until marriage, go out to work if necessary.[146]

Service life allowed many women to branch out on their own and develop their own identity and sense of self, away from their parents and friends at home.

The effect of parents on the choices made could also be very profound. Based on her interests, Beatrice Parsons felt the WRNS was the right service for her. At the time, the only categories that were open were cook and radar mechanic. The latter required her to have higher maths, which she trained herself for, taking the exam before she was called up to the WRNS a year after applying. Her father, with whom she lived following her parents' divorce, 'was very annoyed' when she got her calling up papers at the age of 21. His objection led both of them being called before a tribunal that dealt with cases of people who would not or could not participate in war service. The argument he made for Beatrice not being able to be called up was that he needed her to look after him. Once the tribunal board found out how old he was, and that he was capable of looking after himself, they decided against his claim and Beatrice was allowed to join the WRNS.[147]

It seems that Beatrice's father was not against her joining *per se*, as he was ex-Army; the problem was in leaving him alone as he had got used to having his daughter at home. His attitude reflected the pre-war norm of unmarried women being expected to look after parents requiring care. Her story touches on how this norm had been adjusted. The employment exchanges came to treat young women who did not have children under 14 years of age as 'free agents', Summerfield argues, 'contradicting older understandings of a young woman's embedded place within her family'.[148]

Summerfield goes on to explain in *Reconstructing Women's Wartime Lives* that some individuals advising the government on the recruitment of women had doubts about Labour Exchanges behaving in this way. Discussion centred upon young women holding a different position in their families than young men. Mary Sutherland, Chief Women's Officer for the Labour Party, argued that these gender differences linked 'young women – and their parents', indicating that parents were more willing to surrender their sons than their daughters for war work.[149] This pre-war narrative was overturned and parents were expected make sacrifices in their war effort that included allowing their daughters to be conscripted. Images of the ATS portrayed in posters used the caption 'they can't get on without us', moving the rhetoric away from young women being at home with their parents toward being completely invaluable to the war effort.[150] The WRNS used a slogan with a similar emphasis on the crucial need for women to support the war: 'Join the WRNS and free a man for the fleet'. Summerfield highlights the importance of the media in portraying this sentiment. 'The message was simple. The patriotic parent would let a daughter go wherever the state required.'[151]

Parental influence in the case of the interviewees tended to be positive and the women, on the whole, were supported in their decision to join the service. In the case of Pam Marsden, her father was against her joining the WRNS owing to 'some of the things he thought went on'. Pam did not elaborate on this, but it obviously did not influence her decision.[152] Summerfield discusses the rise of the 'free agent' in the late 1930s: young women who had detached themselves from the expectations of their parents. One of her interviewees, Ann Tomlinson, who joined the WRNS in 1942, left school with the qualifications for university entry. With the prospect of the international situation declining she chose to go into work as a secretary. Describing herself as a young woman she said, 'I wanted to . . . do my own thing.'[153] The impact of education and an increased expectation that young women would work after leaving school was a greater sense of independence for some women. Having their own money and prospects provided some women more choice about their futures.

The requirement to do some form of war work when the National Service Act was introduced in 1941 provided many young women with the ability to 'do their own thing' and a choice in the type of work that suited them.[154] Many WRNS applicants imagined they would join one of the women's auxiliaries, choosing between the three. Only a few considered nursing or manual labour in farming or factory work. The voluntary and selective nature of the WRNS was a big draw for some, over the other two auxiliaries, because as Joyce Wheatley puts it when discussing her own reasons for joining, '[the WRNS] had a reputation of being more difficult to get into, a more desirable service to be in and less "rough" than the ATS at that time!'[155] This view, alongside favouring the uniform, became significant justification for signing up to be a 'Wren' for young women aged between 17½ and 21.

There were some women who felt they had been born to have a life serving the Royal Navy. M. Pratt could not wait to join the WRNS, her 'favourite service', at 17½. In the six months between leaving school and being able to join up, she attended a training course in communications at Chiswick College to provide herself with more skills for her chosen category. She learnt how to communicate with merchant and naval shipping using coded signals in morse, flags and broadcasting, in addition to learning how to maintain the machines used on board ship. When she was eventually called up she was assigned to be a signals Wren.[156] As it would for any job, determination shown through gaining more training before being called up stood women in good stead when joining the WRNS as it demonstrated the type of commitment required for the service.

Another Wren, Rozelle Raynes, equally convinced she was born to a life working at sea, states from the age of three that she had decided she wanted to work on a boat in a busy port. Throughout her childhood she spent a great deal of time rowing a sliding seat skiff on the Serpentine in Hyde Park. Because of her age, 17½, Rozelle was able to wait until a job opened up in the category of boat's crew and in September 1943 she was made a stoker.[157] Rozelle recognised she had an idealised view of the Royal Navy, which she was unable to be swayed from. Her older and more experienced friends in the boats crew shielded her 'from the tougher aspects of service life'.[158] Her job was always more important than her social class and she found her life in Southampton suited her more than the parties at home.[159]

The lack of importance of class background meant the WRNS allowed some women to flee a life of poverty and restriction. Phyllis Damonte wrote in her memoirs that the WRNS became her way of fleeing a husband whom she did not love and an impoverished background. She had married her husband to give herself more opportunities, having been a sweat shop worker in London prior to the war, working from 8 a.m. to 6 p.m. making dresses for 1/6 pence. She states, 'I grabbed at his proposal like it was a life line and indeed it was . . . I didn't love him and with hindsight I know he didn't love me.'

She saw little of her husband once he was sent abroad with the Royal Navy. Eventually, she went to live in Newbury after being bombed out of London and sought work. Phyllis ended up as a temporary Grade 3 civil servant clerk in the Victualling department at the Admiralty. When the WRNS put round a call for women to apply to go to Ceylon (Sri Lanka) she applied and was accepted, 'I was running away from the man I didn't love and didn't intend on ever being his wife again. So, I was going to hide in the uniform of a Wren, until I could sort myself out.'[160]

The motives for women joining the WRNS are many and varied and probably only a few views are represented here. Several factors have arisen throughout the course of this discussion, however. These include the image the service presented, both in terms of uniform but also in terms of the type of women who were selected to join. The selective nature of the service made it a popular option, playing into the perception of it as the 'superior' women's auxiliary service. Connected to this was the ability of applicants to have some say in what category they were assigned to, although this did not always work out. A sense that the service was also a 'leveller' was important because the focus on skills and experience meant working-class women who had been employed prior to being called up were not barred from becoming Wrens. This was important as it meant that women like Phyllis Damonte were able to leave restrictive lives, providing them with opportunities they would never have had.

CHAPTER 6

Disrupting the Combat Taboo

The WRNS saw numbers double from 1941 to 1942 and ultimately increased from around 10,000 in 1941 to over 66,000 in 1944.[1] 1941 was a turning point in pushing 'the acceptable limits of women's work outward, to the frontiers of active combat'.[2] It also saw Wrens being deployed across the globe as part of the Royal Navy's operational duties. The female combat taboo, that had excluded women from the potential to kill in war, was carefully maintained during World War II. 'It was not considered appropriate [...] for women to have combatant roles.'[3] Enloe has argued that the biggest problem with the concept of the combat taboo is the lack of a clear definition of what is meant by combat.[4] DeGroot builds on this, indicating that it allowed military officials to 'exclude women from combat status even though they might be, to all intents and purposes, participating actively in the killing process'.[5] The taboo came to be seen as being linked to women firing or releasing weapons, rather than the technical and mechanical functions they performed that actually allowed killing to occur. He explores the example of the mixed-sex anti-aircraft (AA) batteries that came operational in August 1941. Female members of the ATS

> participated actively in combat, came under fire and suffered wounds and fatalities as a result of enemy action. But, because this service threatened the combat taboo a clever distinction was made so

that women could remain, at least in theory, non-combatants. They
were prevented from loading or firing weapons (they merely aimed
them) in order to maintain the illusion that they were not actually
firing.[6]

Careful political calculations were made to avoid the possibility of
women being seen to be taking on combative roles. In the case of the
AA, debates on including women in mixed batteries and the
possibility of them using weapons took until 1941 to conclude.
Summerfield and Peniston-Bird argued that World War II 'was one
of the most contradictory periods in British history for the
boundary of male and female roles'. At the same time that women
were allowed to work in anti-aircraft units they were also arming
bomber plans and maintaining and repairing military equipment.[7]
The Home Guard, they argue, embodied this contradiction as the
presence of women in the organisation were resisted from
the government and military hierarchy, despite it being part of
the Army. The main objection was the necessity of Home Guard
members to bear arms, from which women were excluded.[8]

   Yet, by 1941 a greater number of women were taking on quasi-
combatant roles, such as Wrens performing highly technical,
mechanical roles. Subversion of the combat taboo was done secretly.
The most famous example is the case of female SOE (Special
Operations Executive) agents who infiltrated occupied France.
Pattinson indicates these women were parachuted into France to
take up saboteur roles within a resistance group, adopting the role
of local women. They risked being arrested, tortured and executed
behind enemy lines. By being trained, as they were, in silent killing
techniques, their roles fundamentally crossed the combat taboo.
Thirteen female SOE agents were killed during the course of their
duties, further undermining the idea that women were non-
combatants. The role of these women in the war, Pattinson argues,
has attracted a lot of interest in popular culture and film.[9]

   Less well known is the case of the Operation Outward Wrens who
were used despite the combat taboo, although not to the degree of
the SOE agents. These Wrens both actively constructed and released
weapons, in the form of 10–12 foot wide balloons with trailing

incendiaries across the Channel. They were also 'taught to handle and fire Lewis guns and rifles in defence of the site' (a golf course in Felixstowe).[10] Interestingly, the women who worked in this 'dangerous work' did not really see it as divergent from the acceptable roles of women.

Technical and Operational Duties

1941 and beyond saw the start of the remit of the WRNS widen further into technical and mechanical roles, involving the service far more in operational duties. Stanley Holmes MP for Harwich, summed up the responsibility the service had assumed by March 1943 in a House of Commons debate:

> They are now employed in more than 60 categories, and have taken over much technical and operational work and many posts of considerable responsibility. Practically all the new categories allotted to the WRNS during the past year have been of a technical nature. The Wrens have responded enthusiastically to these new calls and have taken intensive courses of training.[11]

1941 was the year the decision was made by the Admiralty to replace all appropriate RN naval base men with Wrens.[12] Numbers of women in the service also doubled between 1941 and 1942 (10,653, to 22,898).[13] As discussed in Chapter 4, a large number of new categories were created at this time. Many of these were associated with the defensive and strategic responsibility of the Royal Navy. They were not the ancillary roles typically open to Wrens at the beginning of the war, such as office workers or domestic staff, although these still accounted for the largest numbers of Wrens, with 30 per cent in domestic roles.[14] These new categories were not 'duties conventionally applicable to women', stated the Commander-in-Chief, the Nore, and were taken on, Laughton Mathews believes, because of the efficiency of the WRNS to replace men in shore-based duties.[15] New technologies, such as radar and meteorology, had a part to play in this expansion because they required increased labour that was not front line.

The war in the Atlantic and the widening of the conflict into the Mediterranean also increased the need for servicemen overseas and Wrens to provide the support infrastructure in these new bases.

Mechanical categories

Maintenance and mechanical roles became more commonplace by 1942. Wrens were becoming qualified in newly created categories and in some cases were fully replacing men in pre-existing mechanical and maintenance duties. In the case of qualified ordnance, Wrens were training RN ratings and officers and maintaining equipment needed for the RN and Fleet Air Arms campaigns. Challenges did exist for some women. It was not the case that they were always welcomed into these new roles by their own officers and other male personnel. Being able to take on a masculine category was challenging for a few.

Summerfield discusses the experience of Ann Tomlinson, who had been working as a secretary at the BBC before volunteering to join the WRNS as a mechanic in 1941. She was initially selected to become a writer, as a senior WRNS officer warned her against deserting a gender-conformist role. The main aspect of this warning, Ann remembered, was the officer saying how awful the weather was in the job. It made her more determined to become a mechanic, and she later reflected that the training 'was a gruelling course but very interesting'. She felt the role put her 'in almost what I would consider a fighting capacity, or at least enabling the fighting to go on.'[16] This view was shared with others who felt that, by taking on a mechanical role, they were more directly linked to the war. Women varied in their attitude. There were those who were not afraid to challenge gender roles in the aim of giving service to their country, whereas others, such as the officer in the case of Ann's experience, were happier maintaining a gender-acceptable role during their war service. The WRNS provided scope for both.

Sheila Rodman joined the WRNS in 1944 after working as a secretary in the James Neill Steelworks in Sheffield, having left school at 15. She asked to join the Fleet Air Arm and was trained in ordnance. It was 'The best of both worlds' in her mind as she had been in the Junior Air Corps before joining up, but preferred the

WRNS uniform.[17] Her role was to maintain the weapons on Fleet Air Arm planes when they returned from combat operations. The training course for this job was six months at HMS *Fledgling* in Mill Meece, North Staffordshire. This was the first purely WRNS technical training establishment for air mechanics, commissioned in April 1943 during the 8th Army's new offensive in Tunisia.[18] Its initial role was to train Wren Air Mechanics who eventually provided the navy a saving of 25 to 30 per cent in labour. In all, 3,000 Wrens were trained at *Fledgling*.[19]

There were four different types of Air Mechanics: airframe (A), engine (E), electrician (L) and ordnance/armaments (O).[20] '(L) tested electrical fittings, did minor repairs, overhauls and signed airworthy certificates; the (A) and (E) did the same service for airframes and engines'.[21] Peak numbers reached 1,581 in 1944. Sheila said only 'the brainiest' were selected to be electricians. They needed to have a higher-level school certificate in maths or physics. However, all women applying to be air mechanics had to have the equivalent of GCSEs. Unsurprisingly, very few had relevant work experience before joining and were trained on the job. They were expected to learn a complex new skill in six months, demonstrating the need for Wrens who were intelligent and able to take in a lot of information in a short period of time.

Sheila recalls her training as an ordnance mechanic, where she learnt about guns 'of all descriptions'. 'From rifles, right through to the Hispano cannons in the wings' (which were installed on Spitfires). 'We had to know how to take these guns apart, clean them, put them back together and so on.' She goes on to talk about how dangerous the Hispano cannons were because of the large steel spring inside which they had to press into the gun. If these flew out 'it would cut you straight through the body'. Subsequently, these were replaced with the Browning 303 machine guns. Later training included how to load a torpedo and put detonators on bombs. The final part of the course was about rockets. The maintenance of such weapons put Sheila within the realms of the combatant. She was loading and repairing weapons that would ultimately be used to kill, much as her male equivalent on a ship would have done. The difference was that he would have been regarded as a combatant, she was not.

After her training she was posted to HMS *Jackdaw*, just south of St Andrews, Scotland, where she was only one of two Wren air mechanics. They mainly worked on Barracudas, the 'flying bedsteads' as she called them 'because they were really battered old things', and the occasional Swordfish plane.

> Very often I would be in a huge aircraft hangar. The aircraft would be waiting, in line there, and so I would have to clamber up into the cockpit, sort out the jettison buttons, which were what they jettisoned the bomb with ... but mainly I would clean the guns in the wings and at that time [...] I would [...] get the guns out and strip them down and we had long cleaning, metal rods.[22]

She goes on to talk about how important it was to make sure the gun barrels were all spotlessly clean to avoid damage or blowback.

Sheila was transferred to the category of writer in early 1946 when the base was mothballed. The air mechanic category had been shut in July 1945 and would become redundant in the next six months. Many of the maintenance and defensive roles were also discontinued at the same time, including, boats crews, gunnery control, maintenance, net defence, qualified ordnance, ship mechanic and torpedo Wrens.[23] With women still having time to serve they were reassigned to more traditional roles like writers or stewards as the service contracted, indicating a return to the pre-war realms of acceptable roles for women.

Claire James, Pam Marsden and Beatrice Parsons were all radio mechanics. Pam and Beatrice were both trained to fit radar systems. The training condensed a three-year course into six months at either Battersea or Chelsea polytechnic. Pam attended the former. Owing to the need for radar mechanics at the time, Pam did not have to do the two-week probationary training and was made a Leading Wren straight away, indicating the importance of radar to the RN and Fleet Air Arm.[24] Radio mechanics were then sent to HMS *Ariel* for three months' 'hands-on' training.[25]

Beatrice had joined the WRNS in August 1943 aged 21. Her job was similar to Pam's early work, in that she initially maintained radar systems on Swordfish and Barracuda aircrafts on the Fleet Air

Arm Base HMS *Ariel*. She was later transferred to the Royal Navy and stationed in Portsmouth, initially to install radar technology aboard ships.

Her job at Portsmouth involved testing 'air search' radar equipment, installing it on vessels, carrying out emergency repairs and occasionally testing the sets within a three-mile radius of the base. She mainly worked on corvettes and frigates. There were very few Wren radar fitters in the dockyard as women were prohibited from working there, Beatrice claims, until 1944. The reason was that there were no facilities for women in some parts of the docks and a fear that there were no female doctors should they be injured. This anecdote reflects wider concerns about women's employment that required changes in the infrastructure of employment opportunities for women, no different to factories needing to provide facilities for women, yet much harder to achieve in a dockyard.

Beatrice's job was hazardous; firstly, the machinery would need to be installed in an electrified small wire mesh room on the ship where formerly the obsolete system was housed. She would replace this with the radar system that included a magnetron that produced the pulses to detect objects. This had to be linked to an antenna, which meant Beatrice had to climb the mast to reach the crow's nest to connect and tune the transmitter to the frequency of the system below. She would also have to oil a sump that was connected to the system. She remembers being on a Canadian ship and nearly getting blown off: 'we were making a noise and all this smoke going over [. . .] and there were all the ratings down there, killing themselves laughing and these Wrens on the top'.[26]

It was a very technical job that required a good knowledge of electronics. For example, Beatrice had to know how much piping she would require to carry the data collected from the aerial down to the receiving room, whilst also maintaining the frequency along it.

Claire James had a different experience to the other radio mechanics; although she started in this role she found the nine-month course very difficult. She recalls 'just about scraping through the last few exams', 'and on the last one I did really badly and I thought, well this is it, I'm not going on with this'. Claire was transferred in 1944 to be a plotter in Dover. Both of these roles required higher level maths but the less physical nature of the plotter role suited Claire better as her asthma had got very bad near the end of her exams. It affected her ability to do the job well as so much of it was outside.[27]

D-Day and the fall of Germany

Claire's role as a plotter at Dover reflected the huge role the service played in operational duties. The involvement of the WRNS in the build-up to D-Day, in particular, and following the invasion of France, demonstrates how roles created between 1939 and 1943 converged with the largest mobilisation of men in the war.

Daphne Coyne was working as a plotting officer at this time. She was stationed in Fort Southwick, which had become the combined HQ for the invasion of Europe. She found the expansion of the operation fascinating and was on duty the night the invasion started. As a plotter, each ship and vessel had a model on a large map of the English Channel. 'It was a breathtaking sight even in model form, and in the knowledge of what was happening out at sea hard to credit.'[28] She said it was very hard to plot once traffic started flowing to and from France.

Jean Atkins had been posted to HMS *Lynx*, Dover, in June 1943 as a meteorological Wren, having joined the service a year earlier. This category had been formed in 1942. Eventually, WRNS personnel were at most of the Fleet Air Arm stations at home and three officers and eight ratings served in South Africa.[29] She would serve there until gaining a commission in August 1944. When interviewed, Jean talked of how her role included plotting weather charts from information that came in on a teleprinter. The plots would have to be drawn by hand every three hours. This would allow the forecasting officers (which Jean later became) to join up the lines of equal pressure to get a picture of the weather. The charts were drawn for the whole of the country and relevant information sent to various naval and fleet air arm stations across the UK.

In the build-up to D-Day she carried out her work in the casements in Dover. There was a small Met office there and she remembers it being different from having worked in similar stations.

This was because, with the preparations for D-Day developing, the navy wanted to build up a picture of the weather in the Channel, rather than across the country. This meant recording the sea and fog levels and creating swell forecasts. There was only Jean and her friend Millie working for one Met Officer who also doubled up as the Flag Lieutenant for the Admiral. She recalls the lead up to D-Day being very busy:

> and of course very restricted movement, you weren't allowed to go on leave for quite a bit, or travel around much, and one day I went into work, and because you got to know the sentries, and the sentry was chatting and he said 'have a look at those barges in the harbour', so I had a good look at them and I suddenly realised that their sides were flapping. They were mock barges to make the Germans think that was an invasion fleet building up in Dover harbour when of course they never went from Dover.[30]

The whole of the south coast was closed at the end of May for security reasons. Wrens were not allowed to leave the closed area to go home for any reason. Post did not carry any return address. Jean recalled that she never really felt scared, all through this time. 'We had tremendous confidence in the British forces.' Some women, Mason notes, were very fearful, as they knew boyfriends, husbands and brothers were in the invasion force.[31]

Other women were directly involved in the preparation of soldiers and sailors for the operation and with the traffic to and from France afterwards. Judy Botting had been serving in HMS *Tormentor*, Southampton, as a qualified maintenance Wren. She was responsible for making sure the landing craft for Operation Overlord were in good repair. Judy worked in the engineering stores and in the Linatex shop (a type of rubber). Her recollection was of the build-up to D-Day where the huge number of landing craft lined up along the coast:

> They said you could have got on a landing craft at Southampton and you wouldn't even have to get on the floor 'til you got as far as Portsmouth there was so many there and they was all filling them up and getting them all ready, all day long and that is something.[32]

Maintenance became a very important role in the WRNS, which helped support the RN in a variety of ways. Olive Newman was at Portsmouth at D-Day, 'from then on for several weeks it was all feverish activity, the huge landing ships coming in empty and going out again laden with tanks, lorries, guns and troops. Hundreds of soldiers cheered and waved to the Wrens, probably the last females they saw for some time.'[33]

The WRNS was given a lot of responsibility at this time. First Officer Margaret Drummond had received 20 copies of the Naval Plan for D-Day two months before. She was the head of section in the office of the Commander-in-Chief for Plymouth and was responsible with her staff for issuing charts, typing and issuing sailing orders and allocating berths to ships. 'They knew all that was going on.'[34]

Laughton Mathews discussed the work of the WRNS officer who held the most responsible operational post during this time. Chief Officer Parker was appointed to the staff of the Commander-in-Chief, Portsmouth, as the Assistant Staff Officer Operations in April 1944. From D-Day plus one onwards, Park was taking turns in keeping continuous watch on the balcony overlooking the plot of all the British and half the American Task Forces and subsequent convoys across the Channel. Her responsibility included keeping all shipping protected and maintaining all anti U- and E-boat patrols in the Channel and assault areas. The job became increasingly more complex when the Atlantic troop convoys started to use the Channel ports and had to be met and escorted.[35]

For some Wrens, it was the most involved they felt during the whole war. For many, like Jean Atkins, there was not a sense of fear. The seduction of war, as described by Elshtain, allowed people to locate themselves 'inside' its 'prototypical emblems and identities'.[36] This allowed women to assume the roles of both pacifist and militant, helping men to overcome a great evil. 'And the WRNS at home no longer envied the WRNS who had gone overseas' claimed Mason.[37]

International Service

The expansion of the service overseas was very significant in bringing women closer to the conflict and in requiring them to take on quasi-combatant roles, often out of necessity rather than having been planned beforehand. Having begun to replace male service personnel in all shore establishments in the UK in 1941, the WRNS began to send women to locations internationally where they could help with the administration of naval and joint operations bases. The biggest roles were for writers, wireless telegraphists, domestic branch and stores workers.

Overseas service became a popular option for many Wrens who favoured the prospect of travel and being able to carry out their work in the wider arena of war. In 1942 the expansion of Wrens in international locations began. The first of many drafts was sent to Alexandria, Egypt. The WRNS then expanded out to naval establishments in Port Said, Cairo and Suez. The first unit of 30 WRNS ratings in Singapore, which had been evacuated to Colombo, Ceylon, on 3 February 1942, had to be evacuated again following an attack on the city on Easter Sunday by Japanese forces. They went on to Kilindini, Kenya, which became the HQ for South East Asia Command (SEAC) for a time.

The second draft of Wrens was destined for Alexandria. Laughton Mathews states when they got as far as South Africa:

> they were stopped by orders of the Commanders-in-Chief, Mediterranean (Admiral Sir Andrew Cunningham). Half went on to Singapore to join the first party and the others returned home. Five years later I heard Lord Cunningham refer to this incident in public and say . . . 'I was wrong'. He had thought women could not stand up to the rigours of a war zone. 'But', he said, 'they could and did.'[38]

Opposition to women serving in the Mediterranean was soon quashed. Later in 1942, a small group went to Basra and the first draft for South Africa left in the summer. The close of 1942 saw 211 officers and 741 ratings serving in 11 locations, the largest group being those serving at HMS *Nile* in the Mediterranean and HMS *Assegai* in Durban.[39] When the Suez Canal opened again in 1943 many more women were sent abroad to start replacing men in preparation for the second front.[40] The end of the war saw 6,000

Wrens[41] serving in 37 overseas shore establishments.[42] This did not include the various mobile naval parties in France and Germany following D-Day or Wrens sent to locations in the United States in 1941 and Australia in October 1944. In Germany, post-VE Day, Wrens served in Minden, Hamburg, Wilhelmshaven, Cuxhaven, Bremen, Hanover, Kiel and Berlin.[43] Compared to the other women's auxiliaries, the WRNS had a much larger proportion of servicewomen in foreign locations.[44]

As with the selection of officers, Wrens were carefully chosen to go overseas. Jean Matthews, when interviewed, remembered going to a selection board where she was questioned for her suitability. She said 'they were very careful [about] who they sent abroad'. The Chief Officer also asked her what her parents thought about it: 'and I said, well my father's not that happy but my mother said "I'm not going to tell you to go because then if something happens to you I'll blame myself". She said that "if I was your age I would want to go"'.[45] This extract clearly shows, again, how the views of parents toward their daughters, in this case Jean's father, were being challenged by the service. Although interested in the view of Jean's parents, the Chief Officer would not have been deterred from posting her abroad. Intriguingly, Jean's mum did not go against her decision, which may show that many women, even those in their middle years, had begun to shift their views of what it was acceptable for young women to do. Nina Adams's mother was also supportive of her being drafted overseas and 'encouraged me to do that sort of thing. She loved travelling.'[46] There were instances when women would choose not to be drafted overseas, such as Josephine Rayne, who would have wanted to except that she had promised her grandmother that she would not.[47] The drafts of Wrens were always volunteers. No serving members were forced to go overseas.

Uniform was different for Wrens overseas. The women were issued with three white dresses, in addition to skirts and shirts. They also had a white cover on their hat.[48] Joan Dinwoodie who sailed in early 1942 received 'awful uniforms made from heavy white drill, white cotton stockings, white canvas shoes'. Priscilla Inverarity's kit contained 'two pairs of white woollen knickers!

And a regulation white skull-cup to put over our navy "pudding basin" hat once we reached the tropics.' Uniform, by 1944, had improved with the introduction of white dresses and ankle-socks.[49]

International service brought some women far closer to the war than they had experienced on the home front. The ratings sent in the first draft to Singapore had complained when selected that they would miss the excitement of the conflict in Europe because they were going so far away (at this point Japan had not entered the war). This all changed when they were later evacuated from the occupied island. They ended up being some of the last to leave because of their role in maintaining wireless communication with the outside world.[50]

In late June and July 1942, the Middle East service was evacuated from Alexandria when the German advance threatened Egypt. Beryl Lacey, who would eventually become a Superintendent was a Third Officer Quarters Assistant, wrote a full account of the hectic withdrawal:

> The atmosphere became pretty tense on Sunday. The telephone buzzed a good deal but there was no real question of leaving [...] We arrived in the docks and found everyone boarding in an enormous long train of iron cattle trucks; a few officers in each, and ratings, with mounds of luggage. There were a lot of civilians [...] We finally left at 5.25pm. The heat was frightful.[51]

After a night in Ismailia, the Wrens sailed for Suez, reaching it at eleven in the morning.[52] The main group were accommodated on a ship in the harbour at Suez, while small numbers were sent to work in the naval offices set up in Port Said, Ismailia and Cairo.[53] Following the evacuation, the Admiralty put in place a policy that stated women should not be sent to locations where there was the possibility of them falling into enemy hands. However, in the event of things going wrong, Wrens would be required to remain at their posts, just as the men were expected to.[54] This policy further indicates the duality of Wrens being both non-combatants and simultaneously also members of a uniformed military corps with responsibility to their role.

Lengthy travel was a characteristic of international service with long journeys even before work began. Sheila Hamnett's journey from Liverpool to HMS *Tana* (Kilindini, Kenya) took four weeks and she recalled problems with getting water to wash.[55] Kay Tomlin remembers Elsans (chemical toilets) being set up in 'the minutest cabinets erected in one of the gun rooms'. She found the sanitary arrangements a source of amusement, such as having to hold down a chain in the showers made for someone six feet tall.[56] Kay was only five foot two inches tall, according to her certificate of service.

Cramped conditions and a lack of basic services were a common experience for Wrens en route to their eventual bases. M. Pratt wrote in her memoirs of her experience of travelling on the liner 'Orduna' from Liverpool to HMS *Klindini*:

> Excitement quickly died down as we stepped aboard and inspected our allocated quarters – twenty-one of us were to be crammed into a four berth cabin on a lower deck opposite the bakery![57]

When the ship pulled away from the dock many of the Wrens aboard wondered why they had volunteered in the first place. The six-week journey had further trials. Her convoy was the first to enter the Mediterranean since the occupation of Northern Africa and France by Italy and Germany:

> The next few days were to prove very tense – noise on board had to be kept to a minimum and we were ordered to remain in our scratchy bell-bottoms day and night, ready for any emergency.[58]

After making it to the Suez Canal the atmosphere on ship was more relaxed. However, after exiting the canal they were met by another convoy and at that point the heat became 'intolerable' because of the overcrowding on board. Many people were taken ill and two seamen died and were buried at sea.[59]

Overseas service was both challenging and hazardous for many of the servicewomen. Challenges included the heat and tropical diseases in places like Colombo. In her memoirs, Sheila Carman

worked for the early part of the war in Special Duties X for
Bletchley Park and towards the end of the war in Europe she
responded to requests made for Wrens to go overseas. She was
posted to Colombo. At the time it took six weeks aboard ship to
travel from the UK. When there she completed the same work she
had been doing at home, attempting to break Japanese codes, rather
than German ones, using Holerith machines instead of the bombes.
Sheila recalls a number of trials Wrens had to face when in
Colombo. For one:

> Our reception in Ceylon was not always welcomed. As we went from
> our Wrennery to the WT [wireless telegraph] station, the bus was
> occasionally stoned, particularly when it was dark. I can remember
> an incident when a Wren, riding her bicycle down a quiet road in
> the daytime, was pushed off her bike by a young Singhalese man.[60]

Jean Matthews, when stationed in Ceylon, also recalled not being able
to go out after six in the evening unescorted for their own protection.
Before she arrived, her group was given a talk about how to behave if
they found themselves in a Ceylonese home because the women did
not have the freedom women had in Britain at the time.[61] This may
explain the attitudes experienced by Sheila Carman.

Sheila Hamnett had a different experience when stationed in
Durban. She found the beginnings of apartheid very worrying
and talked of an instance when an Indian woman was thrown out
of a queue at the post office.[62] For many Wrens international
service brought them far closer to internal political troubles
and the wider conflict in ways they had not expected when they
signed up.

This was not always a common experience. The first draft sent to
Malta in January 1944 were greeted by 'everyone they met' when
they went out in the town. This included servicemen wanting news
of home and Maltese welcoming them as liberators because the siege
had just been lifted:

> Some of us worked at St Angelo. Our first morning on duty was
> bright and cold, with a bitter wind, but there were queues of sailors

standing outside the clothing store as word had got round that we
had brought fresh supplies.

Many of these men had no shoes or underclothes, just a boiler suit
with a blanket round their shoulders. They were survivors.[63]

The role of some servicewomen in the latter stages of the war was
to help with the withdrawal of service personnel in post-conflict
areas and with the reconstruction of countries ravaged by war. The
Wrens sent to Malta shared this role, as did those sent to France and
Germany.

Further challenges of overseas service included bugs in tropical
countries, which were a major problem. Sheila Carman recalls:

> I remember having a drink with friends in a large hotel and on lifting
> my arms from the chair, they were covered in bites. This happened in
> the cinema too which made for an uncomfortable film![64]

Kay Kerrvish described her time in Ceylon as 'pretty grim':

> For the first time I realised that mosquito nets also helped to protect
> us from the rats that ran all over our rooms at night, knocking down
> the photos of our friends and family and eating anything from soap
> upwards and downwards. The toilets were great pits dug down
> through the hills ... The stench was incredible.[65]

Illness from tropical diseases was also a further trial with many
service personnel falling ill from dengue fever or blisters made from
the bites of a small spider.[66] Sheila Hamnett contracted malaria
when in Mombasa (her posting after Durban).[67] Kay Kerrvish noted
'most of my friends finished up in hospital [...] I soldiered on apart
from a short bout of dysentery.'[68]

Following the fall of Singapore the SEAC was transferred from
HMS *Kilindini* after three months to Ceylon. M. Pratt was amongst
the Signal Wrens transferred to the new location. Despite Wrens
regularly travelling in HM troopships in convoys, they would
occasionally be transported in destroyers. Her group were sent on
HMS *Chitral*. Unusually, the orders were given that all Wrens were

to be treated as matelots 'swabbing the decks, cleaning quarters and latrines and sleeping in hammocks'. She recalls their presence aboard causing widespread dissent. Two days out from Mombasa, a German U-boat was sighted in the distance. Normally, a fast destroyer would give chase but because there were females on board they had to return to harbour to await safe passage. 'Our names were mud, though most of us would have relished a good scrap at sea!'[69] This attitude indicated how the role of women varied with circumstances. Although still protected from the front line, the fact that the Wrens were treated as matelots rather than passengers indicates the way in which the navy could sometimes alter ideas about the role of women in the service. However, it strictly maintained its rules about the exclusion of women from sea service.

This was not the same experience aboard all craft. Kay Tomlin travelled back to the UK in August 1946 from HMS *Lanka*, Ceylon, on an aircraft carrier. There were only 20 women (WRNS and VADs) on board with nearly 3,000 men. She said they were treated 'more or less like lepers, only being allowed aft on the flight deck on a roped off portion slightly bigger than a tennis court, [and] not allowed to mix with the men at all'. She recalls being surprised by this complete segregation but there was a 'dark secret' for their seclusion. Kay was told that news of a WRNS officer who had been 'attacked by a monster' from the lower deck on another ship, had got into the newspapers back home. As such, the captain decided not to take any chances and therefore put in place rigid rules for the women aboard.[70] Such a story, and the possibility of it occurring, was another reason Wrens were excluded from serving on board Royal Navy ships for so many years. There was either the potential of impropriety from men who would take advantage of women on ship, or in the case of M. Pratt's experience, women would be viewed as inadvertent potential troublemakers whose presence would disrupt the normal running of the ship's business.

Propriety was of great importance to the navy and WRNS. Sheila Hamnett recalls having been sent to London on 6 April 1943 to wait a week for the next convoy. She had lectures during this time: 'we had [a] [. . .] talk by a shrunken female who urged us to drink our lime juice, whilst abroad, to control our sexual urges.

This was alright but I didn't know what she meant by "sexual urges"'.[71]

Patricia Pern was also told 'the hotter the climate, the hotter a man's passion. Beware!'[72] Obvious steps were being taken to protect the virtue of British women abroad, which reflected the desire by the service to protect the reputation of its servicewomen whilst also maintaining its image. However, as Sheila recalls, there was a great deal of naivety within the groups of younger Wrens.

Overseas service was not always challenging. Many Wrens had a very good social life in their various locations. M. Pratt remembers not having to do any work for the first three weeks when her convoy arrived at Mombassa. Those weeks involved 'fantastic beach parties, picnics, dances and just one whale of a time'.[73] Wrens who served in the Far East also gained a few perks that women at home would not have had. Pratt was able to buy many clothes, shoes and the ingredients for her wedding cake in the Indian bazaars because of a lack of rationing, having been re-stationed after Ceylon to HMS *Garuda* in Coimbatore, Southern India.[74] In Ceylon, Jean Matthews stated she had 'a very good time'. She was able to go to the Toc H Club several times a week and was regularly invited to dinner dances at local hotels.[75]

Near its conclusion, the war was brought home to many when serving overseas. When Jean Matthews was in Colombo the real tragedy of war hit her. When not on duty, she was helping the Red Cross with the prisoners of war returning from Japanese camps. Men would come ashore where they were entertained by Wrens and given food and clothing. Nancy's role was to sort through the thousands of letters and telegrams for those on board. She would take the mail out to the ships and would be surrounded by the men not well enough to go ashore:

> You can imagine their delight, I mean they were so pleased to see us and they huddled around wanting to know what things were like back home and had such and such a place been bombed and had they been getting enough to eat. But there were those who lay in rows on the deck just too ill to care, all life gone from their eyes, which was a terrible sight.[76]

The role of the WRNS continued to be important even at the end of the war. Helen Clarke and Sophie Richardson had both been Special Duties Linguists, translating German communications in Y stations in various locations around the UK. They later became translators for the Nuremberg war crime trials in 1945/46. Helen was interviewed and had also provided a copy of her eight-page memoir about her service up until the Nuremberg trials in *They Listened in Secret*.[77] Sophie's husband gave details of her war service, believing, quite rightly, that her and Helen's unique experience at the end of the war was a significant story that needed to be shared.

Helen and Sophie were in the first contingent of WRNS sent to Normandy after D-Day. They lived in a rather basic old farmhouse in Courseulles and worked in a dug out constructed by the Germans. It had various alcoves 'in each of which someone was busy doing something'. Helen recalls the group being a 'motley crew', made up of various services all working together. Work was limited as the Western Front became more distant. Wrens were not allowed to follow the advancing Western front in groups of less than 50, and there were only four in Helen and Sophie's group of SD linguistic Wrens.

After some months, up-to-date German papers were found and the entire German naval archives were sent to the basement of the Admiralty stationed in the German naval HQ in Rouen. Helen and Sophie's team went to work evaluating the content of each file. Helen was working on documents concerned with war crimes. Among the 50,000 files found were some containing the evidence required to try 22 men at the Nuremberg trials. In these files she found evidence for the collusion between Quisling and the Germans before the invasion of Norway and the identity of the U-boat that sunk the *Athenia* on the first day of the war.[78]

When the Americans found out that the Admiralty had all the archives and that the Special Duties Linguist Wrens had found relevant evidence, a 'very personable Commander who was particularly interested in our little group, knowing how short of translators they were in Nuremburg in advance of the trials, asked if we would like to go and work at the trials and we said yes'. Helen talks of how he had to use a lot of charm to get Laughton Mathews to accept. When the group went to the trials they were in uniform but were part of the American

Delegation and as such had a strange dual role where they looked like Wrens but were not sanctioned by the service. This provided them with a lot of perks, including being able to stay in the Grand Hotel (which was for officers; they were only petty officers), eating five-course meals and receiving a 200 cigarette ration a week.

Sophie and Helen worked in the office of Airey Neave who served on the tribunal. He later wrote a letter of reference for Sophie in December 1950 when she was applying for civil service posts. The letter, kept by her husband, gives a very good indication of her role in the trials. This is a previously unseen document, which has been transcribed in full below (it includes her maiden name):

> To whom it may concern,
>
> Miss Sophie Glazier worked for several months under my direction during the trial of the major German war criminals at Nuremberg in 1946. I was particularly concerned at that time with the assembly of the evidence for the defence of the SS and other so called criminal organisations. Miss Glazier's work entailed the summarizing of statements [...] for the assistance of the judges. She acted as interpreter of the views of the tribunal on many complicated points to the German defence counsel few of whom understood English.
>
> In general, I found Miss Glazier to be a hard worker with plenty of natural intelligence. She showed tact and did not lose her head. She is in addition to being a German speaker, a very competent office worker. In my opinion she is a suitable candidate for a branch of the civil service. *Airey Neave*[79]

Sophie and Helen played a significant role in the prosecution of the German war criminals. They had to collate the relevant evidence, transcribe it and provide continuous transcription for the judges and court. The work was almost constant with translations being made throughout the trial and in the evenings in preparation for the next day. The work was also harrowing. Helen recalled in her interview:

> We were sort of the first people who saw the pictures [of the concentration camps], and they were horrific. Though in fact I think when we were working out there [...] everything in court had to be

in four languages. So whatever language it started in, it had to be translated into three others and most of it was German because they had never thrown anything away, so they'd more or less produced the evidence against themselves! [...] And if the officials wanted it next day, you'd stay up all night and translate it until it was done! And then you were allowed to go into the court to see what happened. Which was very interesting, but after, I mean it was extremely boring being in court otherwise! That's because, the poor old German lawyers, they hadn't got a leg to stand on, but they made the most of what they had. They nit-picked like mad.[80]

Helen also reflected that it was important that everything said at the trials was recorded so that there was a true record of what had occurred. The involvement of these four SD linguist Wrens in the trials demonstrated the role servicewomen had come to have over the course of the war. Although always restricted from the front line, they were not prevented from service in a significant and harrowing, concluding episode of the war that brought about the prosecution of a key number of German war criminals.

After eight months working at the trials, Helen was demobbed in June 1946. Sophie stayed in Germany and went on to work for the Control Commission from 1946 to 1950, helping with the reconstruction of the country. Sophie's continued service corresponded with the maintenance of the WRNS which, following the end of the war, was not disbanded like its predecessor in World War I but changed status from auxiliary to permanent service.

The overseas service of the WRNS subverted the non-combatant role of women in the military as it placed them within the realm of conflict. It did every time women travelled on ships to a new base through occupied seas, in the role they would take on aboard ship (in some cases) and by coming face-to-face with the consequences of war: prisoners of war and war crimes.

Wrens as Combatants?

The obvious involvement of the WRNS in the many and wide-ranging roles that involved them far more greatly in combat operations as the war progressed serves to demonstrate the way in which the WRNS came to take on roles that can be viewed as quasi-combatant (as did its counterparts). There were also roles that were more clearly combatant. This history of the service has been more hidden from general knowledge than, say, their participation in the build-up to D-Day or their international service, which has come to form part of popular memory.

Wrens at sea

As previously discussed, Wrens would travel in various ships to their overseas deployments and most of the time they were carefully looked after or restricted from interacting with the ship's crew. However, cypher officers were often sent to work on troopships crossing the Atlantic so that they could translate the cyphered messages into plain language. Nancy Jennings did this once in June 1943. She said that this was a 'perk' for those officers who had done really well; except she did not really think it was a bonus as 'it was very dangerous'.[81]

Elizabeth Dunkley, a cypher officer, was posted to the USA in May 1941 where she worked in the British Embassy in New York, dealing with a backlog of secret messages about British naval ships being refitted in US ports, supplies to the UK and intelligence about U-boats likely to attack convoys. Later she attended a communications staff conference in August 1943 where she encrypted and deciphered top-secret communications between the Allied Chiefs of Staff, Churchill and Roosevelt. Returning aboard the battleship HMS *Renown* to the UK in August 1943, she sent signals on behalf of Churchill who was on board with his wife and youngest daughter.

In December 1943, she was selected to attend the Chiefs of Staff Conference in Cairo as part of the communications team for several high level meetings. She seems to have been travelling with, or at least was moved to assist, Churchill following the Tehran meeting. After this summit, Churchill developed pneumonia and was taken to Marrakesh to recuperate. 'As an emergency measure, I and five other Wrens officers were embarked on HMS *Penelope*, a light cruiser at short notice and started a wild dash from Alexandria round the

Mediterranean, intended to deceive the enemy as to the whereabouts of the Prime Minister. Meanwhile we maintained radio communications for Churchill.'[82]

A woman working aboard a RN ship was very uncommon and in the case of Elizabeth was due to her particular role as one of Churchill's cypherers. However, the inclusion of a cypher officer was more common on troopships. In early 1943, the War Cabinet approved the deployment of WRNS Cypher Officers and Coders aboard the 'Monster' troopships[83] such as the *Queen Mary* and *Queen Elizabeth*. Teams were made up of two to four officers and six coders. Some women did short trips, like Joyce Openshaw, whereas other Wrens would serve at sea for up to seven months. Laughton Mathews notes this was a 'most sought-after line of work, and a rota was established' to allow all qualified women to get a chance to serve at sea.[84] This was a small but significant departure from the 'Never at Sea' motto of World War I WRNS. It was not something expected in the early years of the service and underscored the contradictions in status of the service throughout the war.

Under the Geneva Convention, Cypher Officers would have been regarded as combatants as they were undertaking activities directly involved in combat operations and were wearing uniforms that distinguished them from the civilian population. Where the Royal Navy made the distinction was that the ships the Wrens served aboard were not involved in front line operations, as they were troopships. However, these women were clearly involved in military action. The Director felt in later years, 'not even in my most optimistic moments could [I] have visualised' Wrens both serving on troopships and crewing 'His Majesty's Warships when returning from service overseas'.[85]

Soon after the Cypher Officers were approved to work aboard the monster troop ships, writers were approved.[86] Stanley Holmes, MP for Harwich, made a request for women to serve at sea in the House of Commons on 10 March 1943. He started by discussing how much the remit of the service had widened since 1939 and went on to argue:

> I have said that the original appointment [of the WRNS] referred to establishments ashore. The first point I want to put to the Civil Lord

is whether that can now be modified and whether the WRNS can go afloat. I can quite believe that in the Spring of 1939, when the Service was instituted, the Admiralty felt it was unnecessary for women to go afloat. I think all of us would have said so, too, at that time; but during the past few months we have heard from the Secretary of State for War and the Minister of Labour how great is the shortage of labour and how necessary it is for us to release every young man who can be spared for the purpose of combatant service in one of the three services. Moreover, we have seen in industry accomplishments by women that have surprised all of us. In all trades women are today doing jobs, which, before the war, it was thought that only men could do, and they are doing them thoroughly well. Surely, the Admiralty, in its turn, must consider whether there are not afloat jobs such as communications, supply and clerical work which could be done by women, so releasing young men for harder service.[87]

His suggestion was that women serve aboard the larger ships because they would be easier to adapt. He goes on to talk about how proud members of the WRNS have been able to 'work and fight' side-by-side with the men in the Royal Navy. This notion of equivalence between the WRNS and the much larger RN was clearly in the minds of some Members of Parliament.

The Civil Lord of the Admiralty Sir Richard Pilkington responded to the request for women to serve aboard ships:

'Can the WRNS go afloat?' he asked. The answer is that the principle of Wrens serving afloat is not objected to by the Admiralty. I have no doubt that if you gave the WRNS half a chance, they would be perfectly prepared to sail a battleship. In fact, when the Wrens go overseas now they do take part in service on the ship and help the men in a good many ways day by day. But the real difficulty about this proposal is accommodation on board. In all designing today the utmost and absolute economy of space has to be effected, and quite obviously if women and men are serving alongside you cannot have the same economy of space as if there are men only. That is the real objection to my Hon. Friend's suggestion, but at the same time I can assure him that if, when and where it is found practicable to employ Wrens afloat that will certainly be done.[88]

There is no question in this discussion of the exclusion of women based upon physical grounds. Christopher Dandeker explains, 'of the many reasons the military developed as a male preserve, the first was human sexual dimorphism and the greater upper-body strength required to wield clubs and swords, and bear the weight of body armour'.[89] The ability Wrens had shown to 'help the men in a good many ways' had managed to quash this traditional argument. The main explanation used for the exclusion of women on ships was the practical issue of a lack of separate facilities. This would come to be part of the same argument used until 1990 when Sir Archie Hamilton, Minster for the Armed Forces at the time, announced the decision to allow women to serve at sea.

There is also the question of why new ships were not constructed to provide space for both genders. This would relate more significantly to the issue of the involvement of women in the military after the war. Segal argues that 'when there are shortages of qualified men, especially during times of national emergency, most nations have increased (and will increase) women's military roles'.[90] The reduction in the need of postwar personnel resulted in the exclusion of women from sea service. That the potential for women serving at sea was raised in the House of Commons in 1943 shows how serious the labour situation was at that point in the war. Laughton Mathews recorded that the Admiralty rejected requests for Wrens to go to sea beyond those roles approved on troopships. However, there were some instances, where other authorities, such as Commanders-in-Chief, would not ask permission and would send Wrens on day exercises on ships and in submarines.[91] The *Never at Sea* moto of World War I WRNS had become somewhat of a misnomer by the end of World War II. However, this ad-hoc, limited and pragmatic bending of the taboo was soon ended and maintaining the service placed back within the realms of the non-combatant.

Operation Outward

The movement of Wrens into a clearly combatant role came in 1942 under the cover of the category boom defence (which was another category in and of itself). This role was a cover for an operation called 'Outward'. After piecing together evidence about what was once a secret category, it has become apparent in this research that this was one role where Wrens held combatant roles, not in terms of front line action, but through the distinctly military nature of their work.

Sheila Bywater was given the choice of station X or confidential operational duties when interviewed to be a Wren. She opted for the latter and was sent to Felixstowe to work in a station linked to HMS *Beehive* on the doom defence project. Outward was a purely offensive operation. Sheila explains how the Wrens set about releasing eight-foot wide balloons filled with hydrogen. These had one of three trailing attachments including, trailing wire, incendiaries and phosphorous bottles, which would slowly drop once they had reached height. The intention was to cause damage to crops, electric power cables and cause fires across Germany. This was different to the barrage balloons the WAAF operated, which involved attaching large blimps to long cables to ensnare low flying aircraft.[92] The Outward balloons had a massive potential for destruction; in the final analysis of the operation it is written, 'quite apart from countless incidents, a power station (about the size of Battersea Power Station) was destroyed and assessed as being equal to the loss of a big ship'.[93]

Records indicate six naval and marine officers, seven WRNS officers, 80 Royal Marines and 140 WRNS ratings were employed in the operation.[94] The construction of these very dangerous, huge and highly flammable balloons was done entirely by the Wrens. The Marines cleared fishing vessels in the 'sink at sight' zones around Felixstowe and helped to release the balloons, as they were hard to handle when the attachments were added. They operated in all weathers as long as the wind was blowing the right way.[95] A. Porter recalls that the balloons 'frequently caught fire landing us in hospital covered in gentian violet, or acriflavine, with no eyebrows and front hair – but nothing too serious', with some Wrens ending up in hospital with burns.[96] During the war 99,142 balloons were launched, 45,559 trailing wires and 53,543 carrying incendiary bombs.[97]

Operation Outward highlights the thin line between the role of combatant and non-combatant that some Wrens held during the course of the war. Although not a front line role, this operation was obviously offensive in nature as it involved the destruction not only of land and buildings, but also potentially of life. Women were directly involved in using weapons, rather than just making or maintaining them, which could be regarded as no different from the release of a torpedo if the report of a power station, equivalent in importance to a battleship being destroyed, is taken into account. The secrecy of the job and perhaps also the distance of the women from the consequences of their role is what allowed this category to continue, much as the SOE agents challenged the combat taboo. These were 'temporary transgressions, less disruptive, however, in their understatement'.[98]

In addition, Sheila says that Wrens defended the station, operating two Lewis machine guns.[99] This means that the Wrens would have had training in the use of rifles and machine guns when they were recruited to the base. Laughton Mathews claimed that this was a unique situation. It was the only station to be defended solely by Wrens throughout the whole of the war. Laughton Mathews argues it would have meant employing men just for the purpose of defending the base, which seemed like a waste of resources. She goes on to say that 'this was approved and in being before the employment of servicewomen on lethal weapons was discussed interdepartmentally and prohibited'.[100] The navy and the WRNS had taken advantage of a situation that arose, that commonly would not have been allowed, both in the defence of the station and the nature of the work itself. The secrecy of the category is what would have allowed this to happen, unlike the women in the ATS who were banned from handling weapons on anti-aircraft sites.[101] Notions about the acceptable role of women in war meant that the actual contribution of some servicewomen was marginalised and not recognised.[102] In the case of Operation Outward it stayed secret for decades to come.

The secret nature of Operation Outward would explain why Wrens defending the base never became a controversy in the media, unlike the ATS in the very visible anti-aircraft batteries, as no one, except those with security clearance, would have known. It also highlights how high-ranking officers in the Admiralty and WRNS were more closely linked in making decisions about widening the remit of the service than at the beginning of the war. A high level of trust was afforded the WRNS to carry out such an operation. There is little question that these women would have been regarded as 'delicate'. In fact Laughton Mathews, when she visited the Operation Outward Wrens, said they looked like 'Amazons', 'lined up in the field in bell-bottoms and navy blue jerseys'.[103] Such images also help to subvert the combat taboo – rather than being regarded as delicate women, they were seen as super-human. This addresses the somewhat abnormal image often linked to women who take on roles that challenge dominant gender narratives.

A particular type of woman had to be selected for this job, owing to its potentially violent consequences. Few of the accounts about Operation Outward actually reflect upon women's potential to kill. Instead, tales were filled with humour, with stories of Wrens who got told off for writing rude comments like 'take this you bastards' and 'death to all Germans' on the balloons.[104]

Braybon and Summerfield discuss how in a variety of roles during the war 'some women were worried by the thought that their work would contribute to killing people'. Mary Maberley, who made shell cases at an ICI factory in Sutton, remembers: 'You didn't let it get to you that it was going to kill women and children. You would go berserk if you did. You felt that it would fall over a military target.'[105] Some women found it important to distance themselves from the result of their work. Women also had other reasons for helping to manufacture weapons. Summerfield details the reasons Moira Underwood chose to work in an ordnance factory. She recalled seeing crippled ex-service men after World War I:

> And they used to look at you and say 'I fought for you [. . .] I nearly gave my life for you' and I used to feel so awful [. . .] I thought if ever we have another war, I'm not going to have anybody telling me that. I'm going to say 'yes I did my bit too'.[106]

The desire to be close to a combat role provided some women with a direct sense of both having 'done their bit' and of identifying with male relations who were serving in the military or who had been killed during the conflict.

It is worth noting the contradiction between women being directly involved in the killing process of war and the portrayal of women as 'beautiful souls', as described by Jean Elshtain.[107] It could be argued this image was being socially reconstructed so that although women were not combatants they were still being directly involved in the war machine. In the case of the maintenance Wrens, they were constructing and maintaining weapons and tools needed to search for other vessels and planes. In the case of Operation Outward, Wrens were deploying the tools to cause mass destruction of property and life.

Yet, as Elshtain describes, the reconstruction of this social identity after the war allowed what women really did in a time of war to remain hidden. The normative identity of 'beautiful souls' 'function[ed] to re-create and secure women's location as non-combatants'[108] thus placing their involvement in activities such as armourers and boom defence as just deviations from the 'normal' pattern of female behaviour, necessary in a situation of total war. Owing to the secrecy of this operation, the public never had to reconcile the work of the Outward Wrens with the glamour and femininity presented by the wider WRNS. However, images of women who went against the pre-war norms of femininity were widely presented to the public and were able to be reconciled because of the important war work women were doing. The iconic photos of Wrens working in bell-bottoms, jumping from boats, and undertaking manual work, in Lee Miller's work is proof to this.[109]

Any woman with a manual job who spent most of her day in bell-bottoms challenged any sort of belief that Wrens were concerned with appearance over substance. Femininity was increasingly being put aside when on duty in favour of an operational role that was more directly involved in the mechanism of war. A range of manual jobs emerged during 1941 and 1942 that played around the edges of the combat taboo, including the category of qualified ordnance in September 1941. These Wrens were instructed to maintain guns at training locations. J. E. Pritchard was in this category:

> There were only 200 of us in the service and we did all our training
> at the Royal Naval Gunnery School on Whale Island. As far as I
> remember the course was about six weeks, during which we learned
> about all the guns, from pistol to pom-pom; how to strip them
> down, clean, oil and ensure they fired.[110]

In not firing the arms in combat, these Wrens' managers ensured
that the women sidestepped the combat taboo as their role was
ancillary, rather than combative. Wrens were also employed on
gunnery sites as analysers, range finders and range takers at anti-
aircraft targets. Two WRNS were trained at the Gunnery School in
1943 to strip and reassemble rifles and familiarise themselves with
firing procedures. They became Inspecting Officers on Defensively
Equipped Merchant Ships (DEMS).[111] Boats Crew Wrens had to
know how to use the Lewis guns fitted to the larger boats in areas
vulnerable to air attack.[112] There are no reports of Wrens ever firing
them and women were only ever placed in locations where direct
conflict was unlikely. In the case of the Inspecting Officers, their
role as Inspectors on merchant ships made their role no different to
that of air mechanics who checked and repaired weapons for Fleet
Air Arm aircraft. Such inconsistencies demonstrate what Peniston-
Bird regards as the 'fuzzy' boundary between the sexes in the realm
of the combatant in World War II.[113]

1942 was a key year in the changing nature of the WRNS,
making it a far more technical service with a direct role in the
support of operational duties. It moved far beyond the civilian
status it held at the beginning of the war and as this chapter has
indicated, moved into quasi-combatant roles and in some very
small instances were given combatant duties. These were hidden
from public view to avoid challenging the combat taboo of roles
acceptable for women to take on in conflict.

CHAPTER 7

Social Perceptions and Relationships in the Service

World War I had left men's masculinities in doubt. They had been traumatised by conflict and, as Summerfield argues, sought to reassert their dominance 'in view of the apparent increase in women's power during and after the war'.[1] This led, in part, to the firm reestablishment of pre-war norms of gendered identity, placing women back within the domestic sphere. The crossing of gender boundaries in World War II represented a change in these interwar values, opening up greater freedoms for women. However, in some respects attitudes toward gender identity were carefully maintained, such as the secrecy surrounding Wrens in semi-combatant roles or their marginalisation from the actual contribution they made to the war.[2] Strict conventions about gender were still adhered to. '[W]ithin the women's auxiliaries, where rampant promiscuity was allegedly the norm, there was in fact no great loosening of morals . . . romance blossomed more than passion exploded'; 'purity remained important and marriage sacred'.[3] Summerfield asserts that the preservation of military masculinity and non-combatant femininity helped to maintain social order.[4] Nonetheless, serving in the auxiliaries allowed women to express their patriotism, something they had not been able to do before. DeGroot argues that women had not been regarded as true citizens before this point and the war allowed them to express their national identity.[5] Their greater involvement in society became entrenched from this point.

None of the women interviewed for this book saw their involvement as a feminist attempt at empowerment. The relative youth of most of the women interviewed meant their participation in the war as Wrens was much more linked to: 'doing their bit'; pride at being able to contribute;[6] growing confidence;[7] or being able to have more freedom.[8] The war provided many Wrens with a sense of autonomy, yet the clear bounds of the service provided restrictions of behaviour that protected women. Some had never travelled independently nor been able to go out with friends in the evening. Making the steps into adulthood was the initial challenge for some, as the service provided them with freedom from their parents and it offered them new life experiences. Those in mechanical roles had to contend with working with men who were not fit for or were too old for combat duties.[9] They teased and bullied the Wrens. However, the women often showed themselves to be much more hardworking and skilled, brushing off the misogyny they experienced with humour.

The war also opened up the adult world in other ways. It was the first time many had really thought about relationships with members of the opposite gender, knowing little about sex. Other adult matters, such as marriage, would come along during the course of the war for some. Facing the behaviour of 'lusty young men', who on the whole were honourable, would figure in the experience of others.[10] For a few they would hear stories of pregnancy and homosexuality. The war provided the opportunity to learn a great deal more about the world than many of the women had experienced before.

The Social Life of a Wren

The social life was a very big part of service life for Wrens. Going out with friends and boyfriends was seen as part and parcel of service life. Jean Atkins remembered her timidity at going out each evening without needing her parents' permission, such as to the cinema. Her 'fairly strict nonconformist' family would have been critical of her behaviour. Yet, as she said in interview, 'I soon got over my qualms.'[11] Becoming an individual with the ability to make decisions about how social time was used became an important developmental experience for some women.

Sheila Hamnett was stationed in Dundee and found the Wrennery very sociable and a bit like boarding school. There was always an activity on a Saturday night:

> We had lots of 'boyfriends' whilst in Dundee. I remember we once totted up the number of men called 'John' with whom we'd been going out and it came to twenty-six. It was all very innocent though, just ships that pass in the night.[12]

Going out with boyfriends for many Wrens was about having someone to dance with or buy you drinks, rather than finding a husband, although this was important for some women. Time had a lot to do with whether relationships developed between couples. Betty Calderara stated in her interview:

> There was always a man somewhere to take you out. You didn't last long between boyfriends, you had one that went on draft and within fourteen hours somebody said, 'what are you doing tonight?' So it was a pretty gay life.[13]

E. Sealey said she got engaged three times during the course of the war, explaining it was 'not unusual [...] for young people in those days'.[14] This reflected DeGroot's assessment that the war, rather than promoting promiscuity, allowed romance to blossom.[15] For most, the goal was having a good time, although military life did represent a sexual awakening for many.

Dances were a common way for male and female service personnel to meet. Jean Matthews went to a lot of American socials when stationed at Gayhurst Manor, as part of her Station X work for Bletchley Park. There was also a dance at Gayhurst every month and regular shows. She felt she had a very good social life.[16] This was a common theme of the interviewees. Even if they did not like dances, the women would engage in other activities, such as watching a film at the cinema, going to the theatre, visiting the local town for a cup of tea, or just walking and cycling around the area where they were stationed. Leisure time made it possible to get away from work or do something in between watches.

In some cases, the presence of Wrens caused a stir at dances when the number of women was small in comparison to the men on base. When M Pratt was stationed in Ceylon:

> A 'ship's' dance was held once a week, to which local girls from the village and half-castes would be invited – but white girls were more of a novelty, and our appearance at dances caused endless trouble and fighting until, after two such occasions, we were banned from attending these hops. The chaps in the W/T office, however, respected our presence and we very gradually became used to being so outnumbered.[17]

Wrens were often important for helping to maintain morale just by being present, especially overseas, as in the case of Pratt being allowed to attend the dances after being initially banned. Women who served internationally provided a sense of normality and a connection with home for men who had been at sea for months. Pratt talks about the banter that went on with men on the base she worked on in Ceylon: 'to get to the W/T office we had to walk right through the camp, which attracted wolf whistles, much chatting up, and singing of appropriate songs as our names became known'.[18]

When it might be assumed that having a small number of Wrens in overseas bases could have led to difficulties between the women and men, Laughton Mathews believed that the women provided a 'definite incentive to better conduct among the men'.[19] Lieutenant Commander Jack Neale of the RNVR felt that the Wrens provided a form of safety valve after being on ship. The servicewomen, who were all in their late teens or early twenties, 'acted as kind nursemaids to us all, cheerful, conscientious and very skilled'.[20] The morale Wrens overseas provided is also indicated in Laughton Mathews's conversation with a naval officer from Gibraltar who, when she asked if the Wrens stationed there were being 'spoilt' (as in indulged) said, 'Oh no! But if one wants to make a date one had to book three months ahead.'[21]

A good reputation was very important for many women and was reinforced by the service and Royal Navy. Patricia Manley-Cooper in her *People's War* account said she and her friends tried going to Saturday dances a few times 'but the sailors instinctively knew we were "nice" girls and weren't up for what they wanted and never asked us to dance, so we gave up on that'.[22] Maintaining a respectable reputation meant that going out in the evening with a man was 'very innocent' for most. Joyce Tapp highlighted this issue in her memoirs:

> As I have seen it expressed elsewhere of girls in wartime – 'there were those who did, and those who didn't'. This should not be forgotten went for the men as well. I think most of them were in the second category with some hopeful not to continue in it. Most of the girls I knew were in the second category.[23]

She went on to discuss 'a tendency to close ranks against the others, when identified', highlighting how peers used social control to challenge the behaviour of women 'who did'.

This is not to say all Wrens acted with propriety or were glamorous. In a letter dated 19 September 1941, a Wren discussed the 'boys', aged 16 to 20, training on the base to become warrant officers who 'have learnt plenty of techniques from the local tarts who hang around the poor lads ten-a-penny'. The Wren did not think that the men liked the tarts very much, but was critical of how these non-servicewomen's behaviour affected 'their boys'. It is not made clear who these women were, but they were from the local area. To express their femininity and challenge the 'tarts' she states, 'we are all going to wash our most glamorous undies tomorrow early and hang them out in the laundry to dry and show the boys what pretty little things we wear'.[24] This blatant display to the men was set as a challenge to let them know who was more sophisticated. However, the hanging of one's knickers in public cannot be seen as much different from the advances of the 'tarts'. What this does show is that no matter how much the service prided itself on strict behaviour, it was still made up of a whole mix of women and, as Joyce Tapp said, there were some that did and some that did not. The overriding image in the memorialisation of the service, characterised in many of the interviewees and archive sources, was that Wrens were sophisticated and deserving of chivalrous attention. The other fact that is reflected is that a great many were relatively young, and like Patricia Manley-Cooper, were 'nice girls', with the emphasis being that they were only 'girls' in their own eyes, not women of the world.

Older Wrens and officers would have been more exposed to the wider potentials of adult behaviour. Prostitution was scorned but also pitied by some of the WRNS officers. J. Hodges, a First Officer, was 'disgusted' by the 'endless tarts' in Liverpool who would constantly hit on black American troops. She said the girls had lived very restricted and deprived lives, so it was not unsurprising that they took advantage where they could to gain silk stockings and cigarettes. Her view of sexual matters was more liberal than many of her contemporaries. She claimed that all the American women's services were issued with contraceptives, 'why the hell weren't ours?' And she saw many Wrens get involved with married men during the course of the war. However, she still had very high standards for the women serving under her. When she was sent by Laughton Mathews to find WRNS quarters in Germany at the end of the war she told her Wrens in no uncertain terms that 'any infringement of discipline would lead them to being put on the first plane back to Britain'. Reputation was absolutely essential.[25]

Sexual Relationships and Pregnancy

Whilst sexual relationships were obviously going on, as this was just a fact of human life, there were a great many Wrens who were very innocent about such matters. Gwendoline Page knew little of sex before she joined the service. She was very surprised when the WRNS doctor gave an illustrated lecture.[26] Sheila Rodman discussed her own innocence at the time, having joined the service at the age of 20: 'our parents didn't tell us anything. I mean, how on earth some of us survived I'll never know. We've had many a laugh of it since.'

She did not know of anyone personally who had 'got [themselves] into trouble' as she called it. That contemporary euphemism was code for becoming pregnant out of wedlock. Sheila assumed that if a Wren did get pregnant 'they were whisked away very quietly, and we never knew'.[27] This suggests that the service tried to maintain the innocence of younger Wrens, some of whom were only 17 ½ when they joined.

Daphne Coyne, in her memoirs, talks about her first posting to HMS *Skirmisher* as a messenger. She worked with a male counterpart called Alfie who was a similar age to her. As she put it: 'Alfie was as ignorant and unsophisticated as I was and we spent our time swapping harmless jokes, doing card tricks and writing letters.'[28]

This extract serves to highlight how stereotypes of servicewomen and men, as found in the Mass Observation surveys,[29] were ineffective for explaining the behaviour of most male and female service personnel when they were together. In the case of Daphne and Alfie, their innocence was shared and reflected a social norm for many young people at the time, who were not exposed to the same information about the adult world as young people are today. It also echoes the formation of 'relations of women and men on a healthy and normal basis', discussed by Laughton Mathews.[30] There is always a tendency when talking about the relations of women and men in wartime to talk of the extremes, 'sexed up American GIs' or prostitutes profiteering from a prevalence of randy soldiers on leave.

This is not to say that Wrens did not come across men who wanted more than a night out dancing. Pamela Bates remembered some of the sailors, when they came back at the end of the war, 'were rather short on sex' and had expected to be able to easily get a girl 'because they'd all read that the Americans laid every single girl in Britain'.[31] She had to inform them that this was not the case. On a number of occasions she and her friends had their arm grabbed by a sailor who would say 'back of the ambulance' indicating that was a location for quick sex. Feeling very embarrassed, they reported this to their Chief Officer.

Rare accounts of rape reflected attitudes in wider society about the responsibility of women and men in sexual relationships, not reflected in the regulations of the WRNS. E. Sealey recalled in her memoirs the sad occasion of:

> a nice, unsophisticated Wren, who went to a 'hop' down at HMS *Grasshopper* [Weymouth]. A sailor with whom she had been dancing, asked to take her home. On the way, she permitted him to kiss her. He then raped her. She reported it the following morning and he was charged, but acquitted, the judge ruling that, because she'd permitted the kissing, she'd encouraged the consequences [. . .] I felt so sorry for her, her reputation in ruins through being a little too naïve in a male chauvinist world.[32]

WRNS officers could not always protect their Wrens from the threats of the world and if taken out of their area of responsibility were not always able to protect the reputation of the women serving under them.

For most, their relationships with members of the opposite sex were far from those above. Sheila Hamnett remembered there always being activity outside the Wrennery on a Saturday night, including the police arresting prostitutes, when she went on to say, 'it didn't bother us much – we didn't know what prostitutes were!'[33] The innocence of Hamnett and her friends speaks much of the limited knowledge most Wrens had about the less virtuous aspects of life.

The WRNS took great pains to protect its members and maintain the high standards it expected. Sheila Rodman, for example, stated, 'we never had our virtue attacked! Because we were well defended!' She was speaking here about VE night when the matelots were issued with rum and 'we knew what might happen later on that night'. Indeed, later 'we were brought in by the Petty Officers and locked into our cabins for safety!' The Nissen hut she was in had windows that opened outward all along one side:

> And one of the funniest sights I've ever seen was one of my mates, on the top bunk diagonally opposite me who was by a window. Every time a head appeared through the window, with the effort to try and climb in, a navy head, she would bonk it with a slipper![34]

Although Sheila saw it as ironic that they were locked in for safety, it does indicate the fear that her Petty Officer had for the young women she was responsible for. It may have been an overreaction of her PO, but reflects the importance placed on the protection of younger Wrens.

Betty Calderara spoke in her interview of regularly going to a dance hall in Brighton. She describes how 'much more healthy' relationships with men were then compared to now. Dances would be attended by groups of Wrens who would travel to and from their Wrennery together. For Betty there was an expectation that the men would behave in a gentlemanly manner. Pamela Bates told of how the sailors 'were all lusty young men', who would try and peek in their windows when they were getting changed, 'but they were honourable. But nowadays, sadly, people are not quite so honourable.'[35]

Of course, there were instances of pre-marital sex, pregnancy, sexually transmitted (venereal) diseases and extra-marital relationships. However, these were not widespread within the WRNS. Few of the interviewees could recall women they knew who were in any of these categories. When women did discuss this behaviour it was often someone they had heard about from others. This was still a time when sexual morality was very important to many people, male and female, who did not agree with pre-marital sex and placed more importance on courting. Contraception was also limited and ineffective. Pamela Bates recalls the biggest fear was falling pregnant:

> of course we were all terrified, because [...] if you found yourself pregnant, oi, yoi, yoi! With the Wrens, I only ever knew one got pregnant. And she was sort of removed quietly.[36]

Even those who would have wanted to have a physical relationship with boyfriends were very fearful of the consequences. As such, pregnancy was not a common occurrence in the service. Kathy Baker, as an officer, stated 'very very few Wrens were pregnant', though she did have to sit in on at least one interview with a First Officer, when stationed in Chatham, for a steward who was clearly pregnant.

Wrens who became pregnant were discharged on compassionate grounds and were helped by a welfare officer. Officers could go on leave or apply for a discharge at their own request. A letter was sent to the Ministry of Labour to say they could not be put in full-time work anywhere else.[37] They were not disciplined. Pamela Bates stated, 'you see [. . .] the good reason for going in the WRNS was that you do not have to face court martial or anything like that' because of the voluntary nature of the service and because it was not subject to the Naval Discipline Act.[38]

Pregnant women would be given extra ration books and their remaining pay. The discharge did not mean that the women could not return. It was very important not to put SNLR (services no longer required) on the service record because this effectively ended their service career. Hodges made this mistake and got told off.[39] However, if women hid their pregnancy their record would be made SNLR and they received no benefits. Muriel James knew of a Leading Wren this happened to who was five months pregnant when the Second Officer escorted her to the hospital. She also talks of a Wren telephonist who was able to work up until six months when she was pregnant because she had been honest about it and was sent to a mother and baby unit for unmarried mothers to have the baby.[40]

Laughton Mathews was of the opinion that the man and woman should both be held responsible for pregnancy:

> The Wrens were urgently needed for essential national work. That was their purpose and the fact that had to be recognised. They were not placed there merely as a temptation to weak husbands, as some unhappy wives seemed to imagine. We expected Wrens to behave properly, but that did not mean we put all the blame on the girl if things went wrong.[41]

The regulations regarding pregnancy were drawn up early in the re-formation of the service. Laughton Mathews notes that unmarried members were discharged but were deemed 'suitable for re-entry' in appropriate cases where there were no other disciplinary offences. If officers were accepted back they had to start again in the ranks.[42]

This policy and the extract above indicate a fairly liberal view for the time, based on an understanding that people could make mistakes and women and men were equally responsible in matters of sex. The main aim of the WRNS leadership was to 'try and equip' Wrens against enticement, 'so that in a time of temptation they can protect themselves'.[43] Although not in favour of contraception, the views of the WRNS leadership foreshadowed future beliefs about sexual matters and pregnancy. For its time, it was ahead of wider social values. Allowing unmarried Wrens to return after the birth of a child, who was possibly adopted or looked after by a family member, may also demonstrate the expediency of the war. Women were 'urgently needed'. Therefore, even the most sacred realm of motherhood was being militarily, as opposed to socially, adjusted to fit the requirements of the war.

The rating Kathy was helping to interview was asked if she knew who the father was: "Oh well ma'am you see it might have been a soldier or a sailor but he had his hat off so I don't know!"[44] This funny anecdote notwithstanding, not knowing who the father of a child was could make things very difficult for unmarried mothers financially and socially. According to Braybon and Summerfield, although there was still 'plenty of disapproval [...] the "sinful" were still expected to be penitent'. Yet there were a range of welfare organisations and arrangements for unmarried women who would be able to get a second ration book, find a nursery place and have lunch in a 'British Restaurant' for 1/6d.[45]

In 1945, the numbers of illegitimate children had more than doubled from 4.4 per cent in 1939 to 9.9 per cent. Braybon and Summerfield indicate this increase was not due to 'the loosening of moral standards', but instead the difficulty of making the birth of the first child legitimate through marriage. This was owing to the way in which couples were thrown together because of the war but also separated abruptly. Another change related to the war was the number of illegitimate children born to married women, 'half of them servicemen's wives', who had to wait for the husband to decide whether the child would be taken on as their own in 'his' home or adopted.[46]

Sybil Riley worked on HMS *Chrysanthemum*, initially as assistant paymaster, but later as the drafting officer for the gunners who were placed on merchant ships. She found the job very harrowing as many men she came to know never returned. Sybil also came across several instances of unfaithful relationships that had resulted in illegitimate children:

> Some young men who had entered into a hasty marriage when called up returned to find an unfaithful wife. Sometimes an illegitimate baby would be there; sometimes these were looked after by relatives until the man returned for duty [. . .] I did my best to console and to consider all aspects with the unhappy man. Most men were against bringing up someone else's child until I pointed out the innocence of the child in such cases and what sort of mother would his wife be if she cast her child off? Would he have married such a woman? The result was many baby photographs and many slice of christening cake after subsequent leaves. In defence of the young errant wife one has to consider that letters were difficult and her man may not even be alive.[47]

Sybil's commentary is interesting because she considers all sides of the story, from the innocence of a child who needs its mother, to an unhappy husband who felt betrayed by his wife, to the wife herself who should be forgiven, as her actions were the results of the challenges of war. She indicates a great deal of understanding, which reflects a view that it was the war that had caused the situation, through the strain it had put on people's relationships, many of whom had married hastily in the first place.

Cases of illegitimate children were not the only occasions in which Sybil became involved in the relationships of married people. She had one instance when a woman had travelled down from Leeds looking for her husband. He had been unable to send the money for their council premises, which was a common problem when men were at sea. This had led to three weeks being unpaid. The contents had all been taken and the woman evicted. The Captain wrote a letter to the housing association for the local council and the firm, which sold the furniture on a mortgage scheme (known as the Never-Never) and her house was restored to her.[48] Not only were women waiting to hear from their husband, boyfriend, brother or father they also had to deal with financial issues they had no control over. Waiting for news of a husband or fiancé in the military provided Wrens with additional stress throughout their war service.

Husbands

Only a few of the interviewees had a long-term boyfriend or fiancé when they were in the WRNS. Betty Calderara was married in 1943 at the age of 21. She met her husband in 1941. He was a torpedo officer and they met during a drama production when she was stationed as a writer at HMS *Vernon*, Roedean School. He was sent overseas to the Far East in November 1944. She described the 'little traumas' she faced each time he was relocated. She was distraught when he was sent to the Far East because she was relocated at the same time to HMS *Collingwood*, with no friends or family nearby. When he returned nine months later: 'that was another trauma, incredible. I hadn't seen him for nine months, because before when he came into port I saw him over the years, although we were separated for three years.'

She was staying with his parents and she planned to go and meet him at the train station. His father said, 'Oh I'll come with you.' 'As I walked home with him, it was quite a long walk from the station to the house, just holding his hand I couldn't say a word because father in law kept talking all the time. Never quite forgave him for that.'[49]

Separation was very hard for Wrens whose loved ones were parted from them. Joyce Openshaw was never able to forgive her Chief Officer when posted to Greenock. She had refused Joyce leave to attend her brother's belated 21st birthday party. He was killed a few weeks later.[50] This experience is contrasted with her wedding to her long-term fiancé who had left the UK in 1940 for the Middle East and was later posted to Ceylon. They eventually married on 24 February 1945. This was the happiest part of the war for Joyce. These contrasts were typical of how wartime was portrayed in the media, great loss mixed with romantic love. Rosamunde Pilcher's novel, *Coming Home* demonstrates this dualism in the character of Judith Dunbar who became a Wren. She lost her first love after he committed suicide following his experience in the Battle of Britain but later fell in love with her future husband who was in the navy through chance meetings when they were on leave.[51]

Jeanette Wakeford had known her husband her whole life and during the war had to contend with him being a prisoner of war for three years. She would occasionally get letters from him, which offered her some solace. Jeanette found that time very hard, not knowing what was going to happen. When the POWs were eventually released they married in December 1945.[52]

Being in the service was a good way to meet your future husband. Josephine Rayne met hers when she was still in the WRNS at a New Year's Eve party when her mess was invited to join his mess. He was an officer in the army who had fought in Italy and got very bad dysentery and was sent home. They married in February 1946.[53]

When Pam Marsden decided to be transferred back to secretarial work after being a radar air mechanic she ended up working in London where she met her spouse-to-be. She had been working in the Ministry of Aircraft Production and her future husband was an air engineer officer. They met in 1945 but were separated for a time because she had to go home to look after her mother. When she returned she found herself in the office next to him. They got engaged on 7 January 1946 and were married on 11 May the same year.

There was a misconception that Wrens who got married had to leave the service.[54] This was not the case as it would have led to problems in maintaining consistent personnel numbers. Not all women agreed with this policy. In the case of an officer who requested to work at HMS *Owl* in Fearn, where her officer husband (who was a lower rank) was stationed, the refusal by the WRNS leadership meant she walked out. Challenges to regulations were swiftly punished to avoid precedence. The Superintendent asked Captain De Courey to ban her from the base but he allowed her to access the mess. The service got its own back by refusing to civilianise her. She got no ration book or clothing coupons, an 'altogether embarrassing affair, but only a minor blot in the general picture'.[55]

At the end of the war, marriage could be used as a reason to leave, but not before. Married women were readily accepted to join the service. Laughton Mathews stated that the issue of whether to enrol them never arose. Even women with young children were not barred from volunteering. The Director thought it would have been hypocritical of her to impose this rule when she herself had young children.[56] There were some objections to this decision and it was a problem that recurred through the years but the labour situation allowed it to be discarded as a concern.

Boundaries

Clear boundaries of behaviour were established for servicewomen. These indicate the desire of the WRNS leadership to allay the fears of parents whose daughters had volunteered for service life. This was certainly a problem in the ATS. Noakes refers to regular references made in Leslie Whateley's memoirs, through her time as Deputy and then later Director of the ATS, of the problem of overcoming parental resistance to their daughters joining the service. She believed this was due to a 'whispering campaign' that attempted to publicise examples of inefficiencies in the corps related to middle-class girls being exposed to working-class women who were viewed as immoral. Wellbeing also seemed to be a major issue. This was addressed using a variety of propaganda tools produced by the Ministry of Information. Noakes includes a copy of an advertisement in *The Evening Standard*, in 1941 that states:

> You, her mother and father, need have no fear for her whilst she is away from you. Careful measures have been taken to ensure her health, happiness and wellbeing ... And as a high standard of conduct is required by the ATS, your daughter will be in good company and make good friends.[57]

The protection of the moral and social wellbeing of ATS recruits is clearly highlighted here. It also returns to the discussion in

Chapter 5, about the resistance some parents held to their daughters joining the women's auxiliaries.[58] This focus on wellbeing and care aimed to smooth the contradiction between the traditional social narratives about the role of young women in society, who, on the one hand, were in need of protection within the home of their father or husband, and, on the other, were necessary tools of the state to wage war. There is a definite sense this article, and others like it, was being aimed at middle-class girls. Some parents feared the ATS in particular would bring their daughters into contact with unsuitable working-class girls. The protection to which the article alludes aimed to show the service would do all it could to prevent potential immoral influences that young middle-class women could be exposed to.

The ATS was always quite wrongly dogged by an image of immoral behaviour. In fact, DeGroot states it was much harder for ATS women to be promiscuous than for factory workers because of the highly controlled environment.[59] It was found in the Markham Committee report, published in 1942, that many of the claims about the ATS stemmed from public perceptions about the social class of the women in the service. Crang shows the report recognised 'standards of sexual behaviour' had changed massively in the previous generation and it was inevitable that 'some recruits would bring into the military fold "loose habits" acquired in civilian life', but that this was confined to a very small proportion of the whole.[60]

Unlike the WRNS, as argued previously, the ATS reflected the 'army's class structured division of labour' that meant those from lower-class backgrounds ended up in domestic roles.[61] The view of women from lower social class backgrounds, therefore, had a large role to play in the way in which the ATS had to repeatedly challenge claims of depraved behaviour. Noakes claims these views could be very extreme. In the Mass Observation survey on the women's services, the view of the ATS varied from 'rather rough' (a common view of the interviewees) or, in one case, 'a load of whores'.[62] The Markham report did much to challenge these views. The claim that servicewomen were promiscuous was unfounded as they had far smaller rates of illegitimate pregnancy compared to the civilian population, 0.6 per cent as opposed to 2.1 per cent.[63]

The WRNS never had to contend with such vehement criticism. On one hand, not relying on mass conscription like the ATS, this may have been due simply to being a smaller, voluntary and more selective service. On the other, however, the way in which the service was established in the first place by the Admiralty and Civil Establishment (CE) certainly built boundaries of behaviour within the WRNS that helped to preserve the femininity of its recruits and maintain its reputation as a service with a moral compass. Laughton Mathews welcomed the Markham report where 'the slanders on the Women's Services were entirely refuted'. She went on to state:

> Obviously with a body of women already nearing the 100,000 mark [across the three services], it was impossible not to have some loose behaviour. The point stressed by the [Markham] Committee, and in which I fully concur, is that this is a human factor and not a service one, and that the discipline, work and good comradeship of service life tend to put the relations of women and men on a healthy and normal basis.[64]

The Director was not naïve about the nature of male/female relationships, favouring instead an environment where there were clear boundaries, healthy working relationships and education. The leadership of the WRNS was not going to allow it to gain the reputation the WAAC held in World War I, whether this was based on reality or not. The concern about ATS had shown that public perception was an important dimension in the formation of reputation, or the damage of it.

One view of sexual matters that the Director held very strongly was that providing 'prophylactic packets' to servicemen led to temptation and undermined the 'self-control of young inexperienced boys'. She thought that 'the best way to get a high standard of conduct was to expect it'. The Director challenged various RN officers (and her own, such as Hodges) who suggested Wrens be offered contraceptive measures, arguing 'we expected a very high standard of conduct and the Wrens knew it, and in overwhelming numbers and often in very difficult conditions, they lived up to the high name and reputation which they themselves built for the service'.[65] Despite having quite a liberal view for the time, Laughton Mathews was still bound by the morals of her tenents of faith as a Roman Catholic.

The Royal Navy also took the responsibility of Wrens working on their bases very seriously and, in most cases, reinforced the attitude of the WRNS. Naval Petty Officer W. Churchouse, an instructor at the first WRNS air mechanics training station, HMS *Fledgling*, recalled strict rules about the 'handling of Wrens'. Relationships were forbidden on the base. He remembered one occasion when a male colleague was seen holding hands with a Wren on one of the grassed areas of the station. A few days later he was drafted to sea.[66] Whether this was a true story does not really matter. That it became part of the folklore of HMS *Fledgling* serves to indicate that careful measures were taken to avoid women and men going beyond a working relationship.

Boundaries did not just apply with respect to sexual relationships. The lives of Wrens were carefully controlled to reinforce the 'very high standard of conduct'. Wrens had to be back on base by a certain time if they went off base in the evening. Josephine Rayne found the social life 'terrific' but having to be in by ten o'clock was strange for her at the age of 24.[67] Joyce Tapp's testimony indicates the restriction the service placed on Wrens:

> Discipline was far tighter than most modern girls would accept. Twenty-one was then the age of majority and the officers of the armed services are traditionally regarded as being in *loco parentis* in respect to members who are minors. This discipline was applied to all other ranks in the WRNS, without regard to age or marital status. We were locked up in our quarters by ten every evening. Two late passes a week until eleven o'clock were allowed. These had to be pre-arranged. [...] We had to report to the regulating office on going out and coming in. Cheating, though not unknown, was not generally practised. Blackout arrangements added to the hazard of climbing through windows![68]

The behaviour of Wrens was an important factor for the service's officers who placed restrictions on behaviour as both a form of protection of young women but also a way of avoiding temptation. If Wrens were late back they were 'put on charge'. When Beatrice Parsons did this once she was made to clean all of the windows on the outside of the Wrennery wearing a gas mask. Her friend was made to clean all of the cutlery in the house. They were also deducted pay and lost leave privileges.[69] Gwendoline Page had to stand on parade as a defaulter and was lectured by the First Officer for coming back five minutes late. She saw this as an 'unfair indignity for the sake of a few minutes'.[70] Such punishments were common and were used to reinforce the behaviour the WRNS officers expected from their ratings.

However, Wrens who exhibited good behaviour were rewarded. World War II saw the introduction of good conduct stripes for the first time. Just like the men, a chevron was given to women for the completion of good service and another for good behaviour. Until 1946, Wrens gained one chevron for the completion of three years' service, a second after eight, and a third after 13 years. For Wrens these were blue, rather than gold.

Lesbianism

Boundaries also existed in relation to acceptable relationships between women in the service. During the interviews, the subject of lesbianism arose out of discussions about reasons why women would be transferred or in connection to discussions of naivety. In both cases there was a sense of innocence that aimed to contextualise what has become commonplace today within the experience of their twenty-year-old selves. Reflections, based upon the homophobia of the time, were not in evidence. Instead, the recollections were used as a way of showing how different their experience of being young people was to now.

Beatrice Parsons remembered sleeping in a bunk with her friend Nan because she was always so cold. They would both be wearing balaclavas and gloves; 'that's how romantic we were, we were so cold there'. One day somebody else told her that 'you better not let anyone see you, getting in that bed'. She had no idea what lesbianism was at the time and could not understand why she was being made to feel that she was doing something wrong.[71] DeGroot argues that many working-class women had never had a bed to themselves and the terrible cold of some barracks meant the occasional sharing of a bed seemed a natural solution.[72] For Margaret Boothroyd, sleeping on the top bunk with her friend Laura Mountney was a necessity because of all the mice running around on the bedroom floor.[73]

Summerfield found similar testaments from an ATS interviewee who also recalled creeping into someone else's bed because she was so cold. The statement 'we weren't doing anything wrong [. . .] I don't know about anyone else', Summerfield notes, indicates this woman did not think it was appropriate to enquire about what anyone else was doing in bed. She suggests women sharing beds were practices that ATS Privates collectively concealed from their officers, just as they did about eating sausage sandwiches in bed.[74] The feeling that Beatrice had not done anything wrong by warming up in bed with a friend reflected the sense by women that their actions were innocent and based on friendship rather than sex. Beatrice did not have any idea what the connotation of her behaviour was. It was others who were making it out to be something bad.

Sheila Hamnett was equally nonplussed when stationed at HMS *Cressy*. She recalls there being a real mix of Wrens, 'married, sophisticated, thick, naive'. 'We had two girls who stuck very close to each other, went to the bathroom together and never left each other's side. There was a lot of whispering about them but I knew nothing about lesbians until much later.'[75]

The confusion for many of these Wrens lay in the problem that they did not realise what the issue was. For Beatrice, sleeping in another girl's bed was a solution to a cold winter. Sheila never found out at the time why two girls spending so much time together was taboo.

Norma Deering, in her interview, discussed how the service viewed lesbianism: 'There was this case of two lesbians, two girls were found in one bunk together, they were separated of course, one was sent somewhere else, that was terrible in those days.'[76]

Instances were obviously dealt with swiftly by WRNS officers, resulting in the separation of women suspected of homosexual acts.

Whether or not this was an official policy has not been unearthed. It is unlikely, owing to the disrepute it could have caused the service. However, this course of action fits within wider societal views of the time about the immorality of homosexual behaviour. Women were always excluded from the legislation that made illegal any sexual act between males from 1885. Relocating servicewomen would have been a simple solution that would not necessarily have required explanation or official disciplinary action. It served to balance societal prejudice whilst maintaining an image of propriety.

Relations with Male Personnel on Duty

In addition to forming relationships with men in social situations, many Wrens worked with males on an everyday basis. Attitudes of male service personnel towards Wrens varied. Some were openly hostile at the beginning of the war to women replacing men in shore duties. Others welcomed women and set about placing them into more and more roles. Those who originally did not like the idea of women doing 'men's work' very often later changed their minds. Sybil Riley met a man after the war, whilst on holiday in Wales, who had been the Commodore-in-Charge at Lowestoft when she first joined the service. He told her how Laughton Mathews had visited him to talk about having Wrens on his staff: 'he was extremely angry at the idea that women should be considered fit and able enough for a naval establishment. He refused to consider anything so preposterous.'[77]

Such negativity was not uncommon and reflected a normative discourse within wider society about the role of women in society. One view was that women should not participate in military matters, especially those that were secret. Jean Matthews talked about a senior officer who saw Wrens recruited to Station X as a substandard alternative to male personnel. She said some of the older men had fears about whether the 'girls' could do the job and whether they could be trusted.[78]

There was also a view that the WRNS was interfering in the historically male domain of the Royal Navy. At Newport, a Commander-in-Chief had told Laughton Mathews he would 'fight against having Wrens to the last ditch'.[79] Rear Admiral Sir Wellwood Maxwell held a similar view at the beginning of the war. She had written offering the help of Wrens, but received only the brief reply 'that when he wanted Wrens he would ask for them'. At the time he would rather 'be put in a ditch by a man driver than have a Wren'.[80] In this case, a matter of principle was more important than the recognition that a woman could do a job just as well as a man.

Some stations were also very female dominated, with few male personnel. The wireless telegraph station in Bower, Caithness, that Kathy Baker was in charge of as a Third Officer, only had two males and 30 females.[81] She recalled having to report to a Captain in Lyness (HMS *Proserpine*). This is an account of one of their meetings:

KB: There was the captain sitting at his desk, without looking up;
Captain: 'Good morning Third Officer'
KB: 'Good morning, sir'
Captain: 'Any pregnancies?'
KB: 'No sir', *silence* 'Thank you, sir,' and I turned and left. Well, I thought – very odd. Well, the next Friday exactly the same thing took place, so when I came out I said to the PO outside; 'I say PO [why] do you think the Captain asked me, were there any pregnancies?'
Petty Officer: 'Oh' he said 'you don't want to take no notice of him, he's had no experience of Wrens, you know he's frightened of you and your girls.'
KB: So the next Friday the same [occurs], so I advanced two paces nearer to his desk and said loudly, assuming him to be deaf, 'I understand sir, it takes two sir, and I have thirty Wrens and only two Chief Petty Officer mechanics both much married.' He was so astonished he looked up and saw this rather pathetic little thing, really, my hat and top and so on. I just stood there and he suddenly, he probably had children of his own, and he said 'come and sit here.' And he was lovely, from then on. You see, sometimes people respond if you stand up to them.[82]

Some Wrens had similar experiences facing, initially, some animosity towards their presence or at least, in the case of this captain, a general lack of understanding as to the purpose of the WRNS. That an older officer could make such an assumption, although not commonplace, speaks of some expectations people held about the behaviour of servicewomen.

These views were very often overturned as the war progressed or at least pushed to one side for the needs of the conflict. Sybil goes on to say how the Commodore she talked to later regretted his attitude: 'When the Wrens arrived, without his approval, he found they did twice as much work as the men in any given time, made far less fuss and were more reliable.'[83]

In 1946, Admiral Burnett wrote to Laughton Mathews saying that 'the WRNS continuing as a peacetime service was one of the best things' and 'what a long way it seems since our first assembly of ladies of all ages and sizes at Chatham and what a branch of the service you have built up'.[84] In this letter the Admiral indicates that the service had grown to be seen as a branch of the wider navy rather than an appendage that placed members into stations whether the Commanding Officer agreed or not.

Hard work was one way the Wrens overcame the views of certain RN officers and ratings. When stationed in HMS *Kilindini*, Ceylon, M. Pratt worked in the Wireless Telegraph station. The male Petty Officer in charge remarked 'Wrens [were] no substitute for my lads'. His attitude 'brought them up sharp', and they became determined 'to make him eat his words!' She added, 'we were soon on very good terms' with him.[85] At HMS *Fledgling*, where Sheila Rodman was stationed for air mechanics training, some male instructors who had previously trained hundreds of men had admitted 'they were not looking forward to training girls'. Despite their misgivings, the instructors were all reported to be enthusiastic about the results they were getting and the attitude of the Wrens to their work.[86]

Proving you could do the job was a significant way for Wrens to overcome negative attitudes or to enable them to dismiss the negativity of the men they were working with. In all of the literature and primary sources the majority were determined to show they could carry out their role just as well as the men. Knowing this would be the case, especially in categories where women were carrying out

traditionally male jobs, women were given the impetus to perform
their duty as they had been trained to. There is an overwhelming
sense that the women wanted to prove themselves and to do a good
job. Some were taken advantage of because they were more
conscientious. Summerfield provides the account of Felicity Snow
who said that a job would sometimes come up and the men would
just walk away and call out for the women to do it. Women then did
it because they were keen to 'keep [their] image up'. Such accounts of
lazy, resentful and inadequate men allowed the women to reconstruct
their wartime experience as 'proud and patriotic workers, more than
capable of doing a man's job'.[87]

The other way to challenge these types of men was by standing
up to them. This was what Kathy Baker had to do to the Captain
who repeatedly asked her if any of her Wrens were pregnant.[88] She
also discussed another similar occasion, recalling the story of Mary
Pelow who was commissioned as a Special Duties Linguist in a
listening station on Rum in the Inner Hebrides:

> And on one occasion one of her girls kept saying 'I can hear that
> there is E-boat so and so' [...] they got the next station to try, so
> they got a fix on it, so she rang the duty officer at the Admiralty who
> said 'oh it can't be we've had no information' [...] Well she said 'I'm
> prepared to absolutely swear something is there, we can hear it.'

The duty officer did nothing about it but the Wrens in the listening
station could still hear the E-boat going up and down:

> So she rang the duty officer again and said, 'I'm sorry sir but there
> really is activity there, we can still hear it all.' So finally he said,
> 'well, all I can say Third Officer is that if I arrange for a corvette or
> something to go out from Hull or Grimsby [...] to get a fix on it
> and there's nothing there you may well be court martialled.'

In fact, there was an E-boat. Mary was prepared to stand by what she
believed they were hearing and a fast motor torpedo boat was sent to
disperse it. Despite his initial threat, the officer who had been on
duty recommended Mary for an MBE, because, as he said, 'it takes

moral courage for a young women officer to stand up to a tough senior officer'.[89] Whilst it took time, the WRNS eventually proved itself in situations like this, challenging the view of some that women were emotional and incapable.

On the whole, most of the interviewees did not recall any problems with male officers. Claire James did not work with many as a plotter but those she came across were 'great'; 'they cooperated with us really well'.[90] Nancy Jennings felt women were treated well but she thinks the RN officers 'thought we were a load of rubbish really!'[91] This belief may have been due to Nancy joining the WRNS when it was first reopened at the beginning of the war. As the service developed so too did attitudes, because later she talked of how respected the service was by the RN.

Some Wrens were put in charge of male ratings. Pam Marsden, as a radio mechanic, ended up in charge of around nine men when stationed in Rothshire as a Petty Officer. To begin with, the men hated the idea that a woman was in charge of them and had shown them up by fixing the air-to-surface vessel radar equipment on four or five grounded planes. Later in her interview she talked of how they got used to her being in charge. Most of the time they had very little to do with each other as each person had their own job. Relations became more normalised as they got to know each other and 'one little chap got a crush on me. It was after I'd got the aeroplanes going. I had the best clean bike on the station. So that was all right. Didn't encourage it any further than a crush.'[92]

Pam's experience typified most of the interactions the Wrens had when working with men. However, teasing was very common. Martha Rose, when in the boats crew, used to get picked on a great deal. She took it in her stride, having three brothers. This sort of interaction between Wrens and RN ratings happened most in categories where they worked closely together. Sheila Rodman had a lot of fun with the men she was stationed with as an air mechanic. She thought herself lucky, as some women posted on their own with lots of men were not treated very well. Sheila was a constant focus of pranks and amusement for the men. When she would clean down the guns she would have to take them to a big hut with vices attached to benches all round the room, which were quite high up:

> Now, working, we wore overalls [...] bell-bottoms, like the men [...] And these overalls were men's. So when we climbed into them there was loads of what the navy called 'redundant stuff' [spare fabric] [...] The back, there was an awful lot of spare, dangling off our bottoms. So one of their favourite torments, when we weren't busy, was to grab the spare, the 'gash', at the back, put it in the vice on the bench, turn it up and leave you dangling![93]

To her this was all in good humour and indicated the inclusive approach many stations had to Wrens working alongside the men. Summerfield discusses the way in which such memories may indicate a 'wrestling' between the memories of being tested versus the positive experience they had of working in a category of their choice.[94] For Sheila, however, teasing was part of service life and proved that Wrens were part of the crew. They were 'one of the boys', so to speak, and some saw it as a good way, or indeed the only possible way, of cementing an effective working relationship.

Sheila also talked about being trained by men when stationed at HMS *Fledgling*. She felt even when it seemed like they were bullying the Wrens by giving them nicknames, often this was used as a way of pushing them to do better and forming them into a working unit. Her Chief, Chiefy Bones, as they called him, used to call one girl in their training group, Mabel, the 'Bloody Dumb Blonde!' Sheila said Mabel was 'lovely'; in fact, 'all the girls were lovely'. [95] They took the teasing and name-calling in their stride. It was an expected part of service life, especially when they joined a mechanical category.

Perceptions of women being a nuisance both emotionally and in their inability to do 'men's work' soon gave way to an acceptance that most Wrens were more than capable of doing their job to a high standard without getting pregnant in the meantime. Pamela Burningham worked under a tough old Chief Petty Officer who, to their faces, would say: "Girls in the navy – whatever next? Flighty young things, can't expect them to do a man's job properly." 'But one day we overheard him and another Chief talking in the boson's stores and were surprised to hear him say: "Don't you criticise them girls. Better than your lads in many ways. Do their jobs well, they do." So we knew he was an old softie really.'[96] Negativity soon gave way to necessity, if not acceptance, by all Royal Navy officers. It also drove the women to prove doubters wrong. Pamela Wootton and four other Wren airframe riggers built a Swordfish frame from scratch when her very negative lieutenant in charge set to test the mettle of the women under him. It took them months but they did it, although Pamela did end up in sickbay for a fortnight.[97]

Despite the banter, RN personnel would also stand up for the Wrens. Betty Calderara kept navy lists at HMS *Vernon* for men arriving for training and being relocated after. Every afternoon she would put up a large board in the corridor that gave the men their duties. This would often result in 'awful language'. One RN officer, walking past, heard this and tapped Betty on the shoulder, saying 'do you stand for this?' He shouted at the sailors 'keep your mouths shut in front of the women!' The presence of Wrens often provided RN officers with a way of making their ratings behave better. This was not to say this RN officer did not also engage in 'teasing' women. Betty went on to talk about a time a Wren officer was drilling them. He said to her 'for heaven's sake woman you turn round like a fat cabbage in a high wind!' Betty thought he was naughty for talking to her in front of them like that, but it offered a bit of light relief.[98]

Not all of the men were pleasant. E. Ridley worked as a cook at HMS *Kestrel*, Worthy Down, after joining the service at the end of the war in 1945. In her memoirs she notes, 'most of the lads in the servery had been through the war and were just filling in jobs while awaiting demob'. She only came across one person who resented being in the Navy, 'he was a real troublemaker':

> The first time I was sent to work in the PO's galley I was on duty with the Leading Wren. We had just 'scrubbed out' after the dinner hour and I had gone into the rest room with the Leading hand from the servery to discuss a forthcoming function. I had stayed in the galley and sat on the side waiting for the floor to dry. The door

opened and a crowd of lads came in on 'jankers' [men who had privileges restricted as a punishment for behaviour] and we had to find them jobs to do. They seemed a friendly bunch and they came across all talking at once. I asked them to stand still or they'd have the deck to scrub again. As soon as I'd said this I felt a terrible blow on my mouth. It jerked my head back and for a moment I couldn't move. Everyone had stopped talking and one of the other lads helped me to stand up. I went to the WRNS room on very wobbly legs. One look at me, and the Leading hand went to see what had happened and the President of the Mess sent for. The other lads told him what had happened and they all said I hadn't done or said anything to warrant him hitting me. But it seems he was a person always lashing out with his fists and now he was on another charge.[99]

Such experiences were not common, and in the case of Ridley this violence did not seem to be caused by what she said or did. Very few incidents like this were found in the interviews or archives. Relationships between women and men were carefully controlled, as discussed earlier in the chapter, and were based upon certain expectations of behaviour.

This control of male/female relations was reinforced in a number of ways. Some of the interviewees had little or no interaction with male personnel on duty even when they worked in proximity to each other. Helen Clarke and her fellow WRNS in one Station Y location were not allowed to even speak to the sailors. They worked in another house and they had to swap over at break time: 'they walked through the garden to our house, and we walked through the garden to theirs. We had to go the other side of the rose bushes. I've no idea why ... There must have been some antediluvian people there!'[100]

Her reference to out-of-date views may indicate the presence of WRNS officers who were more traditional in their perspective. They may have thought that not allowing the two genders to meet would have removed any form of temptation. It is not clear whether something had happened on the station before to warrant this rule. Helen did not know of any reason why it was in place. She just thought it was funny. Later postings for her were much more free.

The men were not immune from name-calling or being picked on by their colleagues, particularly when men ended up in jobs Wrens had taken over. This extract indicates that teasing was common in the service when men ended up doing jobs that came to be feminised, such as the boats crew. Pamela Burningham had a male coxswain on the first boat she served on as boats crew. This 'very nice leading hand' called Nobby Clarke, had been assigned shore duties as 'he had been through some bad times, surviving being torpedoed on a Russian convoy'. His mates would call him Wren Clarke and teased him about being with the girls. This soon stopped, but Pamela thought he enjoyed it in the end.[101]

Sometimes women would surprise the men. Pamela recalled collecting an officer off a ship in the Solent. The weather was very bad with strong winds and rain blowing in sideways. The female crew were all wrapped up in oilskins. The officer was 'removing his wet raincoat when he suddenly saw [our dog Susan] at his feet. Turning around he next saw that the deckhand was a girl and finally – to his horror, judging by his expression that the helmsman was a helmswoman.' He had been out East since the beginning of the war and had never heard of Wren boats crews.[102]

The number of Wrens working in Royal Navy roles and in a range of traditionally male categories by the end of the war provided a challenge for men who had been in the Far East either on ships or as prisoners of war for much of the conflict. They had to readjust their pre-war conceptions of the role of women in a military context. Around VE day, Daphne Coyne met some newly released POWs who had come for training in the tactical unit. She explains how different they were from other male officers. For one, they had pre-war accents, 'even their jargon and expressions were five or six years out of date and delivered in extreme public school accents'. She went on to say 'I think the casual attitude between women and men in our Mess slightly shocked them.' She believed the men were disappointed at the things that had changed.[103]

During the six years of the war, and beyond, preconceptions of many naval men and particularly officers had broken down. These POWs had pre-war attitudes towards women. That they were shocked indicates how much male and female relationships had changed during the war and in service life. It may partially explain the continuance of the WRNS postwar. Those six years had served to reduce the gendered oppositional relations between women and men in a military context in a way the WRNS in World War I had not been able to do.

Relationships with Female Officers

Working with men was part of some women's service life. Most typically, however, women would work with other Wrens, who would be the people with whom they socialised and lived. Wrens also had to contend with their officers. Just as with any institution, relationships with superiors varied. Some had a good relationship with their officers, some were openly cheeky towards them, and there were those who recall some of their officers with open hostility. There were also the women who were officers themselves who offer us a different view of Wrens with 'stripes' as snobs and bullies.

Wrens recalled having to salute officers. Wendy Ferguson remembered walking with a bundle of parcels and a Wren officer accused her of not saluting. 'So she dropped the parcels and saluted.' 'That's one of the sort of things that annoyed me', she said. 'Some women made marvellous officers, but others thought they were the Queen!'[104] There were definitely a number of officers in the WRNS who took discipline very seriously, even in situations, like Wendy recalled, when there was little need. Waller and Vaughan-Rees noted it was more likely for Wrens to be 'put on charge' when they were in larger stations.[105] It tended to be more relaxed in smaller locations, much as it had been for Kathy Baker when she was in charge of 25 to 30 Wrens at the Wireless Telegraph station in Caithness, although for her, contempt worked in the opposite direction. She did not discuss pulling any of her 'girls' up on charge, but she did talk about a Leading Wren cook who she said 'had a very obvious contempt for officers in general'. Kathy did not find this surprising as she was only in her early twenties, whereas the cook was in her late forties. A lack of life experience on Kathy's part played into the view of this Leading Wren. She also discussed the challenge of being in charge of women of a similar age and educational experience to her own. The need to maintain proper discipline without alienating herself and appearing stuck-up put a big strain on her.[106] Here was a woman who treated her contemporaries with respect within their officer and rating relationship.

Betty Calderara, when asked about her officers, said it depended a lot on the individual. She had a very nice Wren Officer when she was at HMS *Vernon* in Portsmouth. She used to run a dance group and regularly organised entertainments for the troops. In contrast to this, Betty also remembered 'one awful woman' who was 'frightfully stiff and starchy' and never said hello. Betty had tried to petition her to allow her to stay at HMS *Vernon* but the officer drafted Betty to Collingwood. This was the weekend her husband was sent to the Far East.[107] These sorts of decisions could taint memories of officers, just like the Chief Officer whom Joyce Openshaw would never be able to forgive because she did not allow her to go to her brother's birthday shortly before he died.

Some Wrens were constantly getting into small amounts of trouble. Claire Lowry found herself getting called to the local WRNS office to face the officer in charge for various indiscretions noted by the Petty Officer Wren. These transgressions included her wayward hair not being far enough above her uniform collar, wearing pink nail polish, while occasionally she would feel 'like making [. . .] up with brilliant lipstick' (making the situation worse for herself). Each time, she would be 'thoroughly told off' and perhaps lost a few privileges.[108] Exemplary punishments and discipline, especially on large bases, were used as a means of controlling behaviour. They also provided distance between the officers and ratings and an aura of authority.

Pamela Bates said she and her friends 'were always rather patronising to our officers'. The reason was that whilst she was working at Station X, Bletchley Park, very few of her officers actually knew what she was doing. This allowed her to get round various rules and regulations through, as she put it, 'pontificating' to them. She had been on leave the day the war in the Far East ended. The expectation would have been for her to return to base. However, she and her friend decided to have 24 hours' extra leave. They returned back to Bletchley and were told to go to the Regulating Office where they were told off for being late back. Pamela managed to avoid punishment by presenting a telegram to the Chief Officer that she had been given in May when the war was won in Europe. She argued that as the war was now over this telegraph to have 24 hours' leave still stood. The officers did not really have anything to say to this. As Pamela put it, 'I had them, so we were home and dry, no problem.'[109]

Patricia Manley-Cooper recalled not taking life at all seriously when in the service. She states, 'we were treated as children, having to be in quarters by 10 p.m., and so we behaved like children'.[110] Wrens and their officers could mirror the boarding school dynamic, with Wrens challenging their 'prefects' and 'mistresses' by being cheeky.

For others, the relationship with their officers was a positive one. Jean Atkins talked about how at Christmas time when she was stationed in Donibristle the officers, as in all the forces, would serve up Christmas dinner to the ratings also arranged shifts to help everyone get some time off during Christmas Day. She remembered it being a very 'jolly' and 'enjoyable time'.[111]

Challenges could also come when Wrens were promoted. Daphne Coyne discussed the trials of being a young officer when she was sent to Newcastle after attending the officers training. She was only one of 20 and all the officers were much older than her. She recalls, 'here was a hot bed of bitchiness, jealousy and knitting patterns'.[112] She was only there for around six months before being relocated to Fort Southwick.

Officers, despite having more power and responsibility, could still behave in a similar manner to some of their ratings. Again, it depended a lot on the individuals themselves. Daphne appears to have been quite surprised by the behaviour of the women she worked with in Newcastle. Age may have influenced some of this. She was trained and came up through the ranks of the WRNS. In many respects, having been trained by Chief Officer Bell in her late teens, she exemplified the behaviour the WRNS leadership expected from its membership. Laughton Mathews notes how women who had joined the service as pre-war local entry officers or probationary direct entries 'were a very mixed bag' and some 'distinctly difficult'.[113] Although it is not clear whether the officers Daphne was discussing had come from this group, there is a sense that some of the older officers could be a bit 'difficult', as Laughton Mathews put it, because they had not received the training of later officers. It was also more challenging to select entirely suitable women at the beginning of the war because of the immediate need. Just as in any institution, the characters within varied. Daphne's experience seems to have been unusual, and for her war career it certainly was.

The WRNS did much to protect the reputation of the service and of the women serving in it. The auxiliary was, on the whole, a nurturing environment for young women, many of whom were given greater freedoms than they had at home. It maintained high standards of behaviour in all areas of their working and social lives. This considered, pastoral and highly regulated approach meant the service did not have the same reputation the ATS was dogged by. Wrens also felt they had a good experience in their service careers. This was a common reflection that may have been linked to their role, location, relationships, social life or more. Their presence, which was characterised by hard work and dedication, helped to break down the negativity of some naval men. Other challenges came in the form of an awakening of sexual knowledge and experience. This was, on the whole, quite innocent. However, for the Wrens who did encounter sex-related problems, the service did much to try and support them, even letting unmarried women who became pregnant return to service if they wished. The service was not unaware of the nature of human relationships, yet it did much to try and prepare and support the women in its care in a manner that was progressive for the time.

The Service Postwar and the Impact on the Wrens

The national security situation in both wars was essential for the genesis of the WRNS, as it was for the other women's services. This was the overriding reason why centuries of naval tradition were overturned in favour of allowing women to serve as a part of the RN. Although women were still barred from sea service during the two world wars (other than a few exceptions), the WRNS pushed the boundaries of what women could do in naval services. This participation of women in the armed forces forever left the door open, leading to the maintenance of the women's auxiliaries after World War II.

It was announced that the WRNS would be maintained in a government White Paper on the future of the services as a whole on 30 May 1946.[1] This continuation of the services was the consequence of a different set of circumstances. Fletcher believed this occurred because the WRNS had taken over the majority of the shore support functions from the Royal Navy and as such had become an integral part of the navy.[2] This view reflects what may have been the assumption of its World War Two members idea that it was a reward and a recognition.

Kathleen Sherit paints a different picture, stating, 'the Admiralty argued that every woman would mean one less man available for ships in an emergency. At most, it might want a small permanently employed nucleus of women to organise and train a larger [female] reserve.'[3] This position reflects Admiralty reluctance to take on the expense of retraining anyone who could not be readily switched to a combat-ready ship. This was part of the views collected from the three armed forces in the report by Ralph Assheton, the Financial Secretary to the Treasury, on the future of the women's auxiliaries in 1943.[4] The report concluded that a smaller body of women in each of the services would need to be retained postwar to help with its immediate aftermath.

At the end of the war the Admiralty was unwilling to maintain the WRNS, which was similar to the initial view of the RAF. However, whilst the air force argued that the reason for ending the WAAF was due to the higher costs of employing women because their turnover was higher, Sherit argues 'the Admiralty's assessment of Wrens was expressed in damning terms as being up to 25% less effective than men in most trades and never more than 10% superior where they were deemed to perform better'.[5] This view was voiced in evidence given to the Royal Commission on Equal Pay, stating the issue was Wrens related to their:

> lack of physical strength and inability to stand up to prolonged strain, inferior mechanical aptitude, lower capacity for the application of knowledge, inclination to get flustered in emergency and more easily discouraged when up against difficulties; lack of capacity for improvisation; unwillingness to accept responsibility and inability to exercise authority'.[6]

This view is particularly derogatory when the evidence collected for this book indicates the achievements of the WRNS and the positively expressed opinions by members of the Royal Navy about the women who worked as Wrens. Such a discrepancy suggests either one person's misogyny or a hypocritical collective reneging on the navy's usual approving stance, in the face of increased pay. When questions of cost became the point of focus for the armed forces rather than the national security situation it was easy to dismiss the work of women as something that had been tolerated, rather than as something that was celebrated.

The initial plan to demobilise the WRNS in March 1947, owing to the Admiralty Board's calculation that the budget available would be too limited to maintain the service and because of the assessment of the capability of women, was challenged in March 1946 by the personnel department's view that women could be useful to release men for higher value work.[7] The opinion of the Admiralty Board was in opposition to the Army and later the RAF who had come to the conclusion that they wanted to maintain a war footing as they did not think they would get a year's grace, as they had in 1939, to rebuild the numbers of personnel.[8] The Admiralty Board's attitude, on the other hand, reflected the pre-war principles that female participation in supporting the navy was only for the duration, particularly as women were barred from sea service. This echoes Segal et al.'s assessment that women only come to be seen as useful for the military if their use outweighs their cost.[9] With questions of equal pay being raised at this point, retaining women would have been seen by some members of the board as antithetical for an armed force focused predominately on sending men to sea.

Accommodation and employment costs came to be the biggest reasons to end the WRNS with First Lord of the Admiralty, Albert Alexander, the chief proponent of this view, believing the Admiralty 'should not be too ready to follow the other Services in this matter'.[10] Although reluctant, the Admiralty came to agree with the RAF and Army that the women's services would be retained. However, there is a sense that they were pushed to take this stance as they would have been the only armed service not to.[11] The making permanent of the WRNS, therefore, was due more to the wider circumstances of postwar planning on the part of the RAF and Army rather than being driven by the Admiralty itself.

Employment in the armed services fell from half a million at the height of the war to 60,000 in 1947.[12] June 1946 saw the WRNS numbers reduced to 15,000. Reducing it to just a fifth was consistent with the contraction of the military more widely, which concurs with Segal's assessment that changes to the purpose and function of the armed forces led to modifications to the involvement of women.[13] The 129 WRNS categories in the war were cut back to 55 post-1945, with the most iconic role of boats crew disbanded along with most of the technical jobs. The service would not see women being able to apply for the range of work they had access to in World War II until 1990 when they began to achieve complete equality to the RN as part of a necessary shift in its demographic patterns.

The postwar maintaining of the women's auxiliaries was unprecedented. Perhaps smaller in scale than some hoped, their continued presence represented a historical shift in the role of women. Yes, still in a supportive capacity without parity with men, particularly in terms of pay and responsibility, but still there, which was more than could be said for the end of World War I when women were unceremoniously excluded from the military.

Women's military roles became embedded postwar. Carreiras argues that 'the growing number and diversification of women's military roles' has come to be 'both a symptom of and one of the most visible consequences of change in the armed forces'.[14] Increased parity with the Royal Navy came in the 1970s. 1970, the same year as the Equal Pay Act, saw Wrens allowed all-night-leave, the same as men. However, the most significant event in this decade was the WRNS own regulations being superseded by naval regulations from on 8 April 1976.[15] This reflected the increased responsibility the service was taking on within the RN and reflected changes in equality legislation in wider society with the need to create equal systems for recruitment and treatment across the male and female services with the WRNS ceasing to be civilian.[16] Equality between women and men in the armed forces grew as changes in gender equality shifted in wider society, as Carreiras highlights.[17]

The changing purpose of the military is integrally linked to widening access policies within a society. The national security situation is also highly significant in determining the nature of the armed forces, whether essential – as was the case in the world wars in Britain – to a structure that is far more occupational (with entering the military viewed as a career rather than the result of conscription). Changes in women's roles in society cannot come overnight because of the many facets that are present within society: family, education, employment, demographics, and the economic and national security situation that all have to be taken into account.

Together with being physically maintained postwar, the WRNS –
alongside the other women's auxiliaries – also continued to uphold
its distinctive identity, despite being a much smaller organisation
than it was in World War II. This conflict had seen it develop a sense
of proud purposiveness instilled by its female leadership, pushing the
bounds of the roles women could assume. The WRNS had challenged
the combat taboo by taking on increasingly militaristic and
combative, if not front line, roles throughout World War II because
of the way the Admiralty afforded the WRNS' leadership latitude in
a time of extreme need for personnel. The WRNS leadership
developed a service with a distinctly hardworking identity that
pushed its remit beyond the feminine function envisaged by its Civil
Establishment managers at the beginning of the war. Unlike the
WAAF, which was embedded in the organisation and administration
of the RAF, the WRNS developed a meritocratic culture led by
women who had formed and shaped the service.

Whilst it was true that the service included a greater number of
middle-class women, they did not obtain their position because of who
they knew. Social status was not important to becoming a Wren, or
indeed an officer. Instead, the education and character of the women
was far more significant. The dominance of middle-class women was
due to the ability of these women to stay in school longer or gain
relevant training. Yet this did not prevent a woman with suitable
experience or skills being accepted by the service. The WRNS
provided many women with social mobility, promoting those with
'officer-like-qualities', who had served on the 'lower deck' as ratings.

The image of the WRNS has been iconised through its uniform.
However, the uniform also demonstrates a duality of male and female
wartime roles; the role of the combatant and non-combatant. WAAF
members wore the same uniform as their male counterparts, the
difference being skirts not trousers, proclaiming an alleged equality of
status.[18] The WRNS uniform, on the other hand, was glamorous and
feminine, emphasising that these service personnel were first and
foremost women. Yet it also asserted the WRNS's military role. Wrens
had equivalent ranks to the RN by 1941, although without matching
titles, which were visible on their naval uniform. In technical and
mechanical roles, they would wear the same bell-bottoms as the male

workers. Whilst femininity was being maintained, women's bodies were also being utilised as part of the machine of war. This demonstrates the complexities in trying to classify the difference in social position of women and men in the war. It is too crude to just see women as subordinate and non-combatant.

What was less known is the way in which the WRNS moved beyond the typically glamorous persona, they were put into increasingly dangerous and combative roles as World War II progressed. In doing so, they forever left the door open to the future involvement of women in the armed forces postwar in a way that was unprecedented. Many of the most dangerous jobs assigned to Wrens in the war did not get official sanction from the Admiralty first. Rather, such pioneers were put in place by naval officers as experiments sanctioned by the Director, some kept secret from wider knowledge for years to come. In making such pragmatic moves, some of the naval officers were complicit in the expanding roles of Wrens that were neither dismissive of the potential of women workers nor domineering, allowing WRNS officers to train men and expect the correct response to their rank.

The WRNS leadership knew this could only be for the duration. Society would not tolerate the continuation of women in militarised roles postwar when it was likely that more questions would be asked about what they were doing. Contraction of the three armed forces would have also made the widespread inclusion of women in all aspects of the military untenable, if not for cultural factors, then definitely for financial ones. Whilst it took time to fully develop its identity in World War II, the WRNS maintained a fierce independence throughout, something that would continue in the postwar period.

The Legacy of the Service

The impact of the WRNS stretched far beyond the sustained inclusion of women in the military post World War II, despite the service having a predominately administrative function. Being a Wren had a personal legacy for many of the women who served in the Women's Royal Naval Service. For some this was in minor ways; for others, it helped to change fundamental aspects of their lives. Martha Rose sums up the juxtaposition of these experiences. She did not think being in the WRNS had much impact on her later life although it has left her with lasting friendships with other Wrens. Yet there was also a sense of pride that she could share this experience of having been 'the Wrens' with other women. She also regarded her time in the service as a 'tremendous experience'.[19] Her discussion serves to highlight that whilst the impact of being a Wren may not have always been palpable or articulable, it was something significant.

The debate about whether the wars, in particular World War II, acted as a 'watershed' in the position of women in society has become unresolvable. This is in the main due to the way in which current cultural narratives about gender are applied to historical events.[20] Marwick is critical of the 'revisionists', including feminists and socialists, in their fervent opposition to the idea that World War II did not have any 'identifiable consequences'.[21]

Marwick sees this as an issue relating to their ideological views that saw only total transformation, such as the abolition of gender inequality, as the truest form of impact.[22] Taking such a strong position, he believes, means that these historians miss out on the smaller changes that have affected the lives of those involved. The evidence collected for this history confirms this argument, showing social change as a result of war does not necessarily need to be all-encompassing or revolutionary. It can be incremental and diverse, rather than universal. The evidence also counters Harold Smith's argument that 'the war's most important legacy was a strengthening of traditional sex roles rather than the emergence of new roles'.[23] Whilst it cannot be disputed that traditional gender roles were reasserted at the end of the war, when looking at women who were Wrens, small changes should be taken into account, as Marwick advocates. The impact of the war on some women's lives was profound and allowed them to move beyond what they and their family members would have expected for them prior to being in the WRNS. Of greatest significance was the possibility of choice that the war opened up.

The interviewees all tended to highlight the personal significance of having been a Wren. It took Beatrice Parsons away from a 'dull life'.[24] For Josephine Rayne, the service removed her from her 'rather sheltered background.'[25] Nina Adams similarly thought her life would have been narrower, with the expectation that she would have just married a local chap rather than choosing to travel. Helen Clarke noted more generally that joining the services allowed women to broaden their horizons beyond their local community, seeing it as a tremendous opportunity.[26] Jean Matthews felt privileged to have been in the WRNS, seeing it as 'quite an experience' that gave her much greater freedom and boosted her confidence having been 'very shy'.[27] Similarly, Norma Deering felt being a Wren allowed her to gain a lot of confidence due to living away from home.[28] And Jeanette Wakeford believed the Wrens had influenced her life choices in the future as it made her 'stand on her own feet and make decisions'.[29]

Kathy Baker identified service life as having an impact on women's postwar lives. She stated, 'it enabled a lot of people to acquire self-confidence and belief in their capacity that possibly they might not have had at school'. Following World War I, Kathy argued that there was a greater presence of women in employment but they had to choose whether to work or have a family. Following World War II, she thought this distinction began to be eroded. Society no longer found it odd if a woman wanted to combine a career with a family. Kathy joined the careers service after the WRNS and met a great number of women who were looking for a career. This might have been in jobs still regarded as feminine, such as teaching, yet there was a far greater desire by women to combine a family and career.[30]

Jean Atkins reflected this feeling; she was able to get an ex-service grant to go to university and was able to train to be a dietician. Many women benefited from these grants. Jean would not have had the opportunity to go to university without it. Having worked full-time before getting married, she only took four years out of employment to have her children. After this, she always worked part-time before retiring. She was encouraged back into work by the doctor who had run her dietetics course, believing 'being at home looking after kids was just sitting on your backside doing nothing!'[31]

Some women found it hard to settle at home following the war, having had greater freedom in the WRNS. Claire James felt like she had lost touch with people when she came home mainly because 'they didn't know what my life had been. I'd led a totally different life to anybody at home. I'd gone through things people at home hadn't.

I found it very difficult, settling back.'[32] Sheila Rodman similarly took a year to get used to civilian life as she missed 'being by the sea and all the fun'. She ended up working as an Education Officer from November 1949 to April 1956, having done an Educational Vocational Training course before leaving the WRNS. She found the work very interesting and enjoyed earning her own income. Sheila left the job on health grounds, rather than due to having a family.[33]

Marriage would often put paid to women's employment, either through the choice of the couple, or in the case of Nancy Jennings by her husband not wanting her to get a job.[34] For Sophie Richardson the marriage bar in the civil service in the 1960s meant she had to give up her career when she married Matthew.[35] A mood had changed, however. Amanda Davies thought women realised they were worth more than they had been before the war. They 'wanted to earn some money, have a job'. She always worked part-time as a music teacher, which allowed her to balance family life with a job.[36] These women are now reflecting with the benefit of hindsight. However, this was their life and reveals the changes that were happening in women's lives at the time.

The impact of the independence service life provided might have also had an impact on their parenting. This could be a very important reason for the rise of the teenager in the 1950s and the 'free love' generation of the 1960s. Betty Calderara believed women joining up enabled women to have an individual identity, separate to men, rather than being 'just the little lady at home'. This was something that stayed with them, leading to the greater independence of women. She considers this was half of the problem with latch key children, the use of contraception and what she saw as the 'deterioration of family values'. Betty felt the war made some parents, including herself, more immature because they were more individualistic than their parents, or particularly their mothers, but they had also missed out on the formative years when they would have learnt cooking and so on from their mothers.[37]

The service did try and help the great many women who had married young during the war and had no training in running a home. Kathy Baker remembered that the education branch of the WRNS at the end of the war would take a mobile cookery van and teach Wrens basic pastry making and baking. This idea of individualism for women was not a concept that figured in the mentality of pre-war women, particularly those who were married with children. In terms of a change in the nature of femininity, this represented a distinct shift that would not be altered.

The memory of individuals who were Wrens have come to be reshaped by their later lived experiences. Yet public memory of the service is, on the whole, very positive. This, it can be argued, is the result of the strong ethos the service built and the iconic image it formed. Whilst the impact of being in the service might be seen as minimal by some women, there is a sense in the personal testimonies that they felt part of something very positive. Being a Wren allowed women to express their patriotism, to 'do their bit', widen their horizons and learn skills they may not have done in their civilian lives.

The significance of particular individuals in the creation of the WRNS has also been very important in forming an understanding of the nature of the organisation. This book has had to rely very heavily on the public testimony of Katharine Furse and Vera Laughton Mathews for the very reason that there are not many sources that deal directly with the administration of the WRNS. Whilst their memoirs will inevitably reflect their own personal perspectives, they are still invaluable sources because of the women's vantage point as wartime Directors from which they could observe the whole organisation. These two women were crucial to determining the nature of the service. The WRNS developed a very distinctive identity that helped it to assume a sense of being the 'superior' women's service alongside its sibling the Royal Navy.

The WRNS has never been in the limelight within the histories of the women's auxiliaries in World War I and World War II, being the smallest. Nevertheless, as has been demonstrated, it has a fascinating history that does not necessarily match up to later versions of how it has been remembered. Far from being socially selective, the WRNS allowed women to develop and grow. It had a strong ethos and maintained a high reputation throughout both wars. The WRNS, along with the other women's auxiliaries, helped push the bounds of what women could do within conflict.

NOTES

Introduction

1. Notable works include: Lucy Noakes, *Women in the British Army: War and the Gentle Sex, 1907–1948*, new edn (Oxon: Routledge, 2006); Tessa Stone, 'Creating a (gendered?) Military Identity: The Women's Auxiliary Air Force in Great Britain in the Second World War', *Women's History Review*, 8/4 (1 December 1999): 605–24.

2. Including: Ursula Stuart Mason, *The Wrens 1917–77: A History of the Women's Royal Naval Service* (Reading: Educational Explorers, 1977); Chris Howard Bailey and Lesley Thomas, *The WRNS in Camera: The Work of the Women's Royal Naval Service in the Second World War* (Stroud: Sutton Publishing Ltd, 2000); Marjorie. H. Fletcher, *WRNS: A History of the Women's Royal Naval Service* (London: Batsford Ltd, 1989); John Drummond, *Blue for a Girl: The Story of the WRNS* (London: Cox and Wyman, 1960); Graham Bebbington, *The Fledglings* (Leek: Churnet Valley Books, 2003); Katharine Furse, *Hearts and Pomegranates – the Story of Forty Five Years 1875–1920* (London: Peter Davies, 1940); Vera Laughton Mathews, *Blue Tapestry* (London: Hollis and Carter, 1949).

3. Suzanne Stark, *Female Tars: Women Aboard Ship in the Age of Sail* (London: Constable and Company Ltd, 1996), p. 1.

4. Ibid., p. 2.

5. Jo Stanley, *Cabin 'Boys' to Captains: 250 Years of Women at Sea* (Stroud: The History Press, 2016).

6. N. Rodger, *The Wooden World: Anatomy of the Georgian Navy* (London: Fontana Press, 1988), p. 76.

7. Ibid., p. 77.

8. Stark, *Female Tars*, p. 3.

9. Stanley, *Cabin 'Boys' to Captains*, p. 25.

10. Stark, *Female Tars*, p. 51.

11. Dudley Pope, *Life in Nelson's Navy*, (London: Chatham Publishing, 1997), p. 171.

12. Stark, *Female Tars*, p. 51.

13. Jedidiah Stephens Tucker (ed.), *Memoirs of Admiral the Right Honorable, the Earl of St. Vincent* (London: Richard Bentley, first published 1942), p.120.

14. Stanley, *Cabin 'Boys' to Captains*.

15. Noakes, *Women in the British Army*.

16. Jean Elshtain, *Women and War* (Chicago, IL: University of Chicago, 1995), p. 183.

17. Gerard DeGroot, 'Arms and the Woman', in Gerard DeGroot and C. Peniston-Bird (eds), *A Soldier and a Woman: Women in the Military*, 1st edn (London: Routledge, 2000), pp. 3−18, p. 7.

18. Ibid., p. 8.

19. Barton Hacker, 'Women and Military Institutions in Early Modern Europe', *Signs*, 6/4 (1981): 643−71, p. 666.

20. Eva Isaksson (ed.), *Women in the Military System* (Worcester: Billing and Sons, 1988), p. 1.

21. Stanley, *Cabin 'Boys' to Captains*, p. 34. This status would continue as the WRNS in World War II would remain a civilian organisation as it did not come under the Naval Discipline Act in 1941.

22. Bailey and Thomas, *The WRNS in Camera*, p. 97.

23. Ibid., p. 3, p. 103.

24. Mason, *The Wrens*, p. 107−8.

25. This section has been influenced by research for the author's Master's dissertation: Roberts, 'Why was the decision made to implement female sea service in the Royal Navy?', Kings College London, 2008.

26. Ibid. In 2007 for her Master's dissertation, the author obtained the following documents via a Freedom of Information Request: 'Employment of WRNS Personnel in the RN' (Memorandum by the Second Sea Lord, January 1990); 'Employment of Women's Royal Naval Service (WRNS) Personnel in the Royal Navy', Executive Summary (Annex A of 1990 Memorandum by the Second Sea Lord, March 1989).

27. Such as: Stanley, *Cabin 'Boys' to Captains;* Arthur Marwick, *Women at War, 1914−18* (Glasgow: Fontana, 1977); Gerard DeGroot and C. Peniston-Bird, (eds) *A Soldier and a Woman: Women in the Military*, 1st edn (London: Routledge, 2000); Janet S. K. Watson, *Fighting Different Wars: Experience, Memory, and the First World War in Britain* (Cambridge: Cambridge University Press, 2004).

28. The WRNS as part of broader historical comparisons can be found in the following: Penny Summerfield, *Reconstructing Women's Wartime Lives: Discourse and Subjectivity in Oral Histories of the Second World War* (Manchester: Manchester University Press, 1998); Gail Braybon and Penny Summerfield, *Out of the Cage*, 1st edn (London: Pandora, 1987); Noakes, *Women in the British Army*; Stone, 'Creating a (Gendered?) Military'; Jeremy A. Crang, 'The Revival of the British Women's Auxiliary Services in the Late

Nineteen-Thirties', *Historical Research*, 83/220 (1 May 2010): 343–57; Jeremy A. Crang, '"Come into the Army, Maud": Women, Military Conscription, and the Markham Inquiry', *Defence Studies*, 8/3 (1 September 2008): 381–95. The WRNS as part of popular fiction can be found in examples such as Rosamunde Pilcher, *Coming Home* (London: Hodder & Stoughton, 2005).

29. Such as the film itself: *The Imitation Game*, Nigel Farndale, 'The Imitation Game: Who Were the Real Bletchley Park Codebreakers?', *Telegraph*, 31 July 2016, available at: http://www.telegraph.co.uk/films/2016/07/31/the-imitation-game-who-were-the-real-bletchley-park-codebreakers/ (accessed 6 June 2017).

30. Including Gwendoline Page, *They Listened in Secret* (Wynmondham: George R Reeve Ltd, 2003); Michael Smith, *The Debs of Bletchley Park* (Aurum Press Ltd, Aurum Press, 2015).

31. Smith, *The Debs of Bletchley Park*, p. 3; Sinclair McKay, *The Secret Life of Bletchley Park: The History of the Wartime Codebreaking Centre by the Men and Women Who Were There* (London: Aurum Press Ltd, 2011), p. 49.

32. BBC *People's War, Fact File: Royal Navy*, available at: http://www.bbc.co.uk/history/ww2peopleswar/timeline/factfiles/nonflash/a6649815.shtml (accessed 6 June 2017).

33. Crang, '"Come into the Army, Maud"'.

34. At the service's peak in 1944 the WRNS had 74,620 women in service whereas 206,200 served in the ATS.

35. Noakes, *Women in the British Army*.

36. Crang, '"Come into the Army, Maud"', p. 383.

37. Mass Observation, 952, File Report, ATS Campaign, Women's Attitude to Work and War Work: Preferences for ARP, nursing, munitions work, Land Army, Services, Nov. 1941.

38. Martin Francis, *The Flyer: British Culture and the Royal Air Force, 1939–1945* (Oxford: Oxford University Press, 2011), p. 15.

39. Stone, 'Creating a (Gendered?) Military', pp. 606–7.

40. Francis, *The Flyer*, p. 15.

41. Ibid.

42. Although beyond the three women's services, there was also the FANY (First Aid Nursing Yeomanry) which acted as a parent unit for women who undertook espionage work as part of the SOE (Special Operations Executive). Thirty-nine of the fifty women sent undercover in occupied France were members of the FANY. See Juliette Pattinson, *Behind Enemy Lines: Gender, Passing and the Special Operations Executive in the Second World War* (Manchester: Manchester University Press, 2011). See Chapter 6 for a more detailed assessment of the role of the WRNS in challenging the combat taboo.

43. Some interviewees have been anonymised, although they are originally identified in the author's PhD. Some of the interviewees have since given their permission to be identified in this book, for which the author thanks them and their families.

44. Drawn from the National Maritime Museum (NMM), National Archives (TNA), Royal Naval Museum (NMRN), BBC *People's War*, Sussex University's Mass Observation Archive, and the *Association of WRNS* archives.

45. Geoff Eley, 'Foreword: Memory and the Historians: Ordinary Life, Eventfulness and the Instinctual Past', in Lucy Noakes and Juliette Pattinson (eds), *British Cultural Memory and the Second World War* (London: Bloomsbury Academic, 2013), p.xi–xviii, p. xi.

46. Juliette Pattinson, '"The Thing That Made Me Hesitate ...": Re-Examining Gendered Intersubjectivities in Interviews with British Secret War Veterans', *Women's History Review*, 20/2 (1 April 2011): pp. 245–63, pp. 245–6.

47. BBC *People's War*; Sarah Housden and Jenny Zmroczek, 'Exploring Identity in Later Life through BBC *People's War* Interviews', *Oral History*, 35/2 (2007): pp. 100–8, p. 101.

48. Noakes and Pattinson, *British Cultural Memory*, p. 3.

49. See Penny Summerfield and Corinna Peniston-Bird, *Contesting Home Defence: Men, Women and the Home Guard in the Second World War* (Manchester: Manchester University Press, 2007); Crang, '"Come into the Army Maud"'; Stone, 'Creating a (Gendered?) Military'; Francis, *The Flyer*; Pattinson, *Behind Enemy Lines*; Summerfield, *Women's Wartime Lives*; DeGroot and Peniston-Bird, *A Soldier and a Woman*.

50. Francis, *The Flyer*, p. 5; see bibliography for Marwick's work.

51. Lucy Noakes and Juliette Pattinson, 'Introduction: Keep calm and carry on: The Cultural Memory of the Second World War in Britain', in Lucy Noakes and Juliette Pattinson (eds), *British Cultural Memory and the Second World War* (London: Bloomsbury Academic, 2013), pp. 1–24, p. 5.

52. Mady Wechsler Segal, 'Women's Military Roles Cross-Nationally: Past, Present, and Future', *Gender & Society*, 9/6 (1 December 1995): 757–75; Darlene Iskra et al., 'Women's Participation in Armed Forces Cross-Nationally: Expanding Segal's Model', *Current Sociology*, 50/5 (2002): 771–97.

53. Segal, 'Women's Military Roles Cross-Nationally'.

54. Ibid., p. 758.

55. Iskra et al., 'Women's Participation'.

56. Segal, 'Women's Military Roles', p. 786.

57. Such as Noakes and Pattinson, *British Cultural Memory and the Second World War*; Summerfield, *Reconstructing Women's Wartime Lives*.

58. Marwick, *Total War and Social Change*, p. xii.

59. Braybon and Summerfield, *Out of the Cage*.

Chapter 1   The Creation of the World War I WRNS

1. NMM, DAU 43, Letter from Geddes to Furse, 14 Nov. 1917.

2. Lucy Noakes, *Women in the British Army: War and the Gentle Sex, 1907–1948*, new edn (Oxon: Routledge, 2006), p. 62.

3. Ibid., pp. 69–71; TNA, WO32/5253, *Women's Army Auxiliary Corps – Status of*, May 1917.

4. Ursula Stuart Mason, *The Wrens 1917–77: A History of the Women's Royal Naval Service* (Reading: Educational Explorers, 1977), p. 14; Peter Stansky, *Sassoon: The Worlds of Peter and Sybil* (New Haven: Yale University Press, 2003).

5. Darlene Iskra et al., 'Women's Participation in Armed Forces Cross-Nationally: Expanding Segal's Model', *Current Sociology*, 50/5 (2002): 771–97, p. 786.

6. Arthur Marwick, *Women at War, 1914–18* (Glasgow: Fontana, 1977), p. 11.

7. John Ruskin, 'Sesame and Lilies' (1865), in J. M. Golby (ed.), *Culture and Society in Britain 1850–1890: A Source Book of Contemporary Writings* (Oxford: OUP Oxford, 1986), pp. 70–96, 72–4, 87–95.

8. Arthur Marwick, *Britain in the Century of Total War: Peace and Social Change, 1900–67* (London: Penguin Books Ltd, 1968), p. 45.

9. Robert F. Bales and Talcot Parsons, *Family: Socialization and Interaction Process*, 1st edn (Abingdon, UK: Routledge, 2007).

10. B. Gates, *Kindred Nature: Victorian and Edwardian Women Embrace the Living World* (Chicago, IL: Chicago University Press, 1999).

11. Bernard Cohen, 'Florence Nightingale', *Scientific American*, 250/3 (1984): 128–37.

12. Florence Nightingale Museum, available at: http://www.florence-nightingale.co.uk/the-collection/biography.html (accessed 6 June 2017; link no longer working).

13. Mady Wechsler Segal, 'Women's Military Roles Cross-Nationally: Past, Present, and Future', *Gender & Society*, 9/6 (December 1, 1995): 757–75, p. 758.

14. Jenny Gould, 'Women's Military Services in First World War Britain', in Higonnet and Jenson (eds), *Behind the Lines: Gender and the Two World Wars* (New Haven, CT: Yale University Press, 1989), pp. 114–15.

15. Ibid., p. 116.

16. Noakes, *Women in the British Army*, p. 41.

17. Marwick, *Century of Total War*, p. 45.

18. Gould, 'Women's Military Services', pp. 116–17.

19. Ibid., pp. 118–20.

20. Martin Pugh, *Women and the Women's Movement in Britain, 1914–1999* (Basingstoke: Palgrave Macmillan, 2000), p. 7.

21. Noakes, *Women in the British Army*, p. 41.

22. Marwick, *Women at War*, p. 162.

23. Ibid., p. 12.

24. Noakes, *Women in the British Army*, pp. 52–3.

25. Marwick, *Women at War*, p. 162.

26. G. R. Searle, *A New England? Peace and War 1886–1918* (Oxford: Oxford University Press, 2004), p. 785.

27. Pugh, *Women's Movement*.

28. Marwick, *Century of Total War*, p. 106.
29. Marwick, *Women at War*, p. 12.
30. Marwick, *Century of Total War*, p. 105.
31. Subcultural ideological shift is used here to mean a change in the attitudes and values within an institution.
32. Keith Grieves, *Sir Eric Geddes: Business and Government in War and Peace* (Manchester: Manchester University Press, 1989), p. 11.
33. Ibid., pp. 11–12.
34. Chris Wrigley, 'Ministry of Munitions', in Kathleen Burk (ed.), *War and the State: Transformation of British Government, 1914–19* (London: HarperCollins Publishers Ltd, 1982), pp. 32–56.
35. Marwick, *Century of Total War*, pp. 85–86.
36. Ibid., p. 74.
37. Andrew Marr, *The Making of Modern Britain: From Queen Victoria to V. E. Day* (London: Macmillan, 2009), p. 163.
38. Marwick, *Century of Total War*, p. 85.
39. Marr, *Making of Modern Britain*, p. 163.
40. Grieves, *Geddes*, p. 25.
41. Ibid., p. 12.
42. Searle, *A New England*, p. 704.
43. Ibid., p. 808.
44. Grieves, *Geddes*, p. 19.
45. Marwick, *Women at War*, p. 51.
46. Marwick, *Century of Total War*, p. 105.
47. Alan G. V. Simmonds, *Britain and World War One* (London: Routledge, 2013), p. 58.
48. Marwick, *Women at War*, p. 51.
49. Simmonds, *Britain and World War One*, pp. 132–3.
50. Ibid.
51. Wrigley, 'Ministry of munitions'.
52. Marwick, *Women at War*, p. 11.
53. Dorothy Goldman, *Women and World War 1: The Written Response* (London: Macmillan, 1993), p. 9.
54. Thierry Bonzon, 'The Labour Market and Industrial Mobilization, 1915–1917', in J. Winter & J. Robert (eds), *Capital Cities at War*, Studies in the Social and Cultural History of Modern Warfare (Cambridge: Cambridge University Press, 1997), pp. 164–95, pp. 187–8.
55. Grieves, *Geddes*, pp. 18–19.
56. Ibid., pp. 22–4.
57. In 1917 he was awarded the OBE.
58. *Ardtaraig*, available at: http://www.ardtaraig.net/ardtarig-a-reminiscence/reminiscence-p54/ (accessed 27 September 2010; link not working).
59. Grieves, *Geddes*, p. 39.
60. Segal, 'Women's Military Roles'; Iskra, 'Women's Participation in Armed Forces'.

61. Marwick, *Century of Total War*, p. 91.
62. Marwick, *Women at War*, p. 83.
63. Marr, *Making of Modern Britain*, p. 142.
64. Grieves, *Geddes*, p. 40.
65. Searle, *A New England*, p. 708.
66. Grieves, *Geddes*, pp. 39–41.
67. Ibid., p. 42.
68. Ibid.
69. Ibid., pp. 46–7.
70. Ibid., p. 44.
71. Alfred Temple Patterson, *Jellicoe: A Biography* (London: Macmillan, 1969), pp. 177–202.
72. Grieves, *Geddes*, p. 44, p. 66.
73. Ibid., p. 66.
74. Ibid., p. 44.
75. TNA, ADM 116/1807, memo of Geddes, 6 Mar. 1918.
76. TNA, ADM 116/1804, George Riddell interview with Geddes, 13 Aug. 1917.
77. Patterson, *Jellicoe*, pp. 197–8.
78. Grieves, *Geddes*, p. 44.
79. Ibid., pp. 45–7.
80. Patterson, *Jellicoe*, p. 201.
81. TNA, ADM 116/1807, letter from Geddes to Jellicoe, 24 Dec. 1917.
82. Patterson, *Jellicoe*, p. 181.
83. TNA, ADM 116/1807, Geddes' planned speech to the House of Commons, 6 Mar. 1918.
84. Patterson, *Jellicoe*, p. 180.
85. Lady V. Wemyss, *Life and Letters of Lord Wester Wemyess* (London: Eyre and Spottiswoode, 1935), p. 637, cited in Patterson, *Jellicoe*, p. 204.
86. Grieves, *Geddes*, p. 49.
87. TNA, ADM 116/1807, personal correspondence of Eric Geddes, Vol 4.
88. See Grieves, *Geddes*, pp. 48–9, for the discussion of this historical debate.
89. Iskra et al., 'Women's participation'.
90. Patterson, *Jellicoe*, p. 156.
91. Ibid., p. 180.
92. Stansky, *Sassoon*, p. 83.
93. Mason, *The Wrens*, p. 14.
94. Stansky, *Sassoon*, p. 83.
95. TNA, ADM 116/1806, letter from Geddes to Lloyd George about personnel, 9 Dec. 1917.
96. NMM, DAU/43, 'WRNS Formation' memo, 11 Nov. 1917.
97. Noakes, *Women in the British Army*, pp. 61–5.
98. TNA WO32/5093, Feb 1917, cited in Noakes, *Women in the British Army*, p. 65.
99. Noakes, *Women in the British Army*, p. 66.

100. Gould, 'Women's military services', p. 124.
101. Noakes, *Women in the British Army*, pp. 68–9.

Chapter 2   The World War I WRNS: 1917–19

1. NMM, DAU/24, Furse memo, 30 Jan. 1919.
2. Katharine Furse, *Hearts and Pomegranates – the Story of Forty Five Years 1875–1920* (London: Peter Davies, 1940), pp. 39–68.
3. Ibid., p. 287.
4. Jenny Gould, 'Women's Military Services in First World War Britain', in Higonnet and Jenson (eds), *Behind the Lines: Gender and the Two World Wars* (New Haven, CT: Yale University Press, 1989), p. 123.
5. Such as Frances Durham, a civil servant who worked in both the Board of Trade and the Employment Department of the Department of Labour. Gould, 'Women's military services', p. 123.
6. *Report of Women's Service Committee*, 16 December 1916, PRO Home Office (HO) 185/258, cited in Gould, 'Women's military services', p. 123.
7. NMM, DAU/5, Memo of Furse related to meeting with Fawcett and Chamberlain, 9 Jan. 1917.
8. NMM, DAU/5, Furse memo to Fawcett, 22 Jan. 1917.
9. NMM, DAU/5, Letter from Furse to Chamberlain, 29 Dec. 1916.
10. NMM, DAU/5, Letter from Furse to Chamberlain, 15 Jan. 1917.
11. Furse, *Hearts and Pomegranates*, p. 336.
12. Arthur Marwick, *Women at War, 1914–18* (Glasgow: Fontana, 1977), p. 91 discusses the squeezing of the VAD by the Red Cross and War.
13. Furse, *Hearts and Pomegranates*, p. 358.
14. NMRN, 350/88 31*32, extracts from Mavis Carter's Diary.
15. Ibid., 2 Nov. 1917.
16. NMRN, 350/88 31*16, *The Times*, 16 Nov. 1917.
17. Ibid.
18. NMRN, 350/88, *The WRNS Never at Sea 1917–1919*.
19. NMM, DAU/43, 'WRNS Formation' memo, 11 Nov. 1917.
20. NMM, DAU/43, Furse memo, 11 Nov. 1917.
21. Noakes, *Women in the British Army*, p. 68.
22. Ibid., p. 66.
23. Gould, 'Women's Military Services', p. 124.
24. Furse, *Hearts and Pomegranates*, p. 361.
25. NMM, DAU/43, Letter from Furse to Geddes, 13 Nov. 1917.
26. NMM, DAU/43, Furse memo, 21 Nov. 1917.
27. NMM, DAU/43, Furse memo, 12 Nov. 1917.
28. From Marjorie H. Fletcher, WRNS: A History of the Women's Royal Naval Service (London: Batsford Ltd, 1989), p. 13.
29. NMM, DAU/24, Admiralty memo no. 245, 29 Nov. 1917.

30. This document outlines the organisation of the WAAC and was issued by the War Office on 7 July 1917.
31. TNA, ADM 1/8506/264, memo of Furse related to Scheme of Service, 29 Nov. 1917.
32. National Army Museum WRAC Collection, 94010253–20, cited in Noakes, *Women in the British Army*, p. 75.
33. Noakes, *Women in the British Army*, pp. 75–6.
34. Susan R. Grayzel, *Women's Identities at War: Gender, Motherhood and Politics in Britain and France During the First World War* (Chapel Hill, N.C: The University of North Carolina Press, 1999), p. 77.
35. Noakes, *Women in the British Army*, pp. 75–9.
36. Grayzel, *Women's Identities at War*, p. 54; Janet S. K. Watson, *Fighting Different Wars: Experience, Memory, and the First World War in Britain* (Cambridge: Cambridge University Press, 2004), p. 30.
37. Watson, *Fighting Different* Wars, p. 30.
38. Grayzel, *Women's Identities at War*, p. 157.
39. Noakes, *Women in the British Army*, p. 76.
40. Ibid.
41. Watson, *Fighting Different Wars*, p. 10.
42. Ibid., pp. 20–1.
43. Ibid., p. 29.
44. Marwick, *Women at War*, p. 169.
45. TNA, HO 185/258, memo of Furse, 24 Nov. 1916; Noakes, *Women in the British Army*, p. 69.
46. Watson, *Fighting Different Wars*, p. 29; IWM, letter from Dorothy Pickford to her sister Molly, 14 Mar. 1918, IWM DD Con Shelf.
47. Watson, *Fighting Different Wars*, p. 39.
48. Ibid., pp. 36–9.
49. TNA, ADM 1/8056/264, Formation and Organisation of the WRNS, November 1918.
50. IWM, account of Jean Rawson, Miscellaneous 156 (2422).
51. TNA, ADM 1/8056/264, Formation and Organisation of the WRNS, November 1918.
52. TNA, ADM 116/3739, Vol. 1, Formation of the WRNS, n.d.
53. Watson, *Fighting Different Wars*, p. 35.
54. Furse, *Hearts and Pomegranates*, p. 371.
55. Ibid., pp. 371–2.
56. Charles Walker to Katharine Furse, 16 Nov. 1918, cited in Watson, *Fighting Different Wars*, p. 40.
57. Eric Geddes to Katharine Furse, 18 Nov. 1918, cited in Watson, *Fighting Different Wars*, p. 40.
58. Watson, *Fighting Different Wars*, p. 52.
59. Ibid., p. 55. See her discussion about letters written to the *Morning Post* throughout July 1915.
60. Noakes, *Women in the British Army*, p. 73.

61. Watson, *Fighting Different wars*, p. 35.

62. Furse, *Hearts and Pomegranates*, p. 364.

63. From TNA ADM1/8506/264, Formation and Organisation of the WRNS, Nov. 1918.

64. Ibid.

65. Bailey and Thomas, *WRNS in Camera*, p. 97.

66. Mason, *The Wrens*, p. 25.

67. NMRN, 1988.350.1, Regulations and Instructions for Women's Royal Naval Service to 31 Dec. 1943, 1943.

68. TNA, ADM 116/3739, Vol. 1, Formation of the WRNS, 'Terms and Conditions of Service', 1917.

69. TNA, ADM 1/8056/264, Formation and Organisation of the WRNS, 'Changes to categories', 30 Aug. 1918.

70. Badges for categories, World War I, from TNA ADM1/116/3739, WS39A, 'Uniform Acquaint Ratings'.

71. www.royalnavy.mod.uk/~/media/royal%20navy%20responsive/.../an21c. pdf, Annex 21C, "Ethos Values and Standards", Feb. 2016 (accessed 6 June 2017).

72. http://www.pbenyon.plus.com/KR&AI/Discipline_General.html, *'King's Regulations and Admiralty Instructions'*, 1913 (accessed 6 June 2017).

73. Mason, *The Wrens*, pp. 35–6.

74. Ibid., p. 37.

75. Ibid., p. 39. The lack of references by Mason means it has not been possible to trace this document.

Chapter 3   The Re-Creation of the WRNS

1. Susan Kingsley Kent, *Gender and Power in Britain 1640–1990* (London: Routledge, 2002), pp. 299–300.

2. Martin Pugh, *State and Society: A Social and Political History of Britain, 1870–1997* (London: Hodder Arnold, 1999), p. 202.

3. Susan Kingsley Kent, *Making Peace: The Reconstruction of Gender in Interwar Britain* (Princeton, NJ: Princeton University Press, 1993), pp. 299–300.

4. Gail Braybon and Penny Summerfield, *Out of the Cage*, 1st edn (London: Pandora, 1987), p. 138.

5. Ina Zweiniger-Bargielowska, *Women in Twentieth-Century Britain: Social, Cultural and Political Change*, 1st edn (London: Longman, 2001), p. 266.

6. Ibid.

7. Lesley Hall, *Sex, Gender and Social Change in Britain since 1880* (London: Palgrave Macmillan, 2000), p. 85.

8. Hansard, Debate in House of Commons, Speaker Sir R. Horne, 2 Jun. 1919.

9. Ibid.

10. Arthur Marwick, *Women at War, 1914–18* (Glasgow: Fontana, 1977), p. 162.

11. Arthur Marwick, *Britain in the Century of Total War: Peace and Social Change, 1900–67* (London: Penguin Books Ltd, 1968), p. 167.

12. Braybon and Summerfield, *Out of the Cage*, p. 141.

13. Ibid., pp. 138–9.

14. Pugh, *State and Society*, p. 255.

15. Zweiniger-Bargielowska, *Women in Twentieth Century Britain*, p. 269.

16. Braybon and Summerfield, *Out of the Cage*, p. 131.

17. Lucy Noakes, *Women in the British Army: War and the Gentle Sex, 1907–1948*, new edn (Oxon: Routledge, 2006), p. 86.

18. Braybon and Summerfield, *Out of the Cage*, pp. 122–3.

19. Ibid., p. 143.

20. Noakes, *Women in the British Army*, p. 93.

21. C. Gasquoine Hartley, *Women's Wild Oats Essays on the Re-Fixing of Moral Standards* (London: T Werner Laurie, 1919), p. 54.

22. Braybon and Summerfield, *Out of the Cage*, pp. 146–7.

23. Noakes, *Women in the British Army*, p. 86.

24. Vera Brittain, *Testament of Youth: An Autobiographical Study of the Years 1900–1925*, film tie-in edition (London: Virago, 2014 [1933]).

25. For a more detailed discussion of the proposed Women's Reserve see Noakes, *Women in the British Army*, pp. 90–2.

26. Ibid., p. 92.

27. Jeremy A. Crang, 'The Revival of the British Women's Auxiliary Services in the Late Nineteen-Thirties', *Historical Research*, 83/220 (1 May 2010): 343–57.

28. The magazine is still being produced today. It began in 1920 and was edited by Vera Laughton Mathews until 1939 when she was appointed Director.

29. Ursula Stuart Mason, *The Wrens 1917–77: A History of the Women's Royal Naval Service* (Reading: Educational Explorers, 1977), p. 48.

30. See copies of *The Wren* for this period.

31. Pugh, *State and Society*, p. 224.

32. Arthur Marwick, *Explosion of British Society, 1914–70* (London: Macmillan, 1971), p. 51.

33. Kathy Baker, interviewed 10 February 2010.

34. Hall, *Sex, Gender and Social Change*, p. 99.

35. Zweiniger-Bargielowska, *Women in Twentieth-Century Britain*, chapter 17.

36. Laughton Mathews, *Blue Tapestry*, pp. 25–9.

37. Ibid., p. 31.

38. Ibid., p. 45.

39. Kathy Baker, interviewed 10 February 2010.

40. Laughton Mathews, *Blue Tapestry*, p. 48.

41. Ibid., p. 79.

42. Joe Maiolo, *Cry Havoc: The Arms Race and the Second World War, 1931–41: The Global Arms Race 1931–41* (London: John Murray, 2010), pp. 119–40.

43. N. H. Gibbs, *Grand Strategy: Rearmament Policy* v. 1 (London: Stationery Office Books, 1976), p. 3.

44. Maiolo, *Cry Havoc*, pp. 119–40.

45. Ibid.

46. G. A. H. Gordon, *British Seapower and Procurement between the Wars* (Annapolis, MD: Naval Institute Press, 1988), p. 74.

47. Grieves, *Geddes*, pp. 101–5.

48. Maiolo, *Cry Havoc*, pp. 119–40.

49. Gibbs, *Grand Strategy*, p. 3.

50. Gordon, *British Seapower*, p. 105.

51. Gibbs, *Grand Strategy*, p. 6, p. 44.

52. Gordon, *British Seapower*, p. 107.

53. Maurice Hankey was Secretary to the Cabinet 1916–38 (a role created for him in 1916), the most senior civil servant and policy adviser to the Prime Minister and Cabinet.

54. Lord Chatfield, *It Might Happen Again*, Vol. II, *The Navy And Defence, The Autobiography of Admiral of The Fleet Lord Chatfield* (William Heinemann, 1947), p. 78.

55. Robert Paul Shay, *British Rearmament in the Thirties: Politics and Profits* (Princeton NJ: Princeton University Press, 2015), p. 18.

56. Gordon, *British Seapower*, p. 112.

57. Gibbs, *Grand Strategy*, p. 96.

58. Maiolo, *Cry Havoc*.

59. Gordon, *British Seapower*, pp. 123–5.

60. Ibid., p. 126.

61. Murray Williamson, 'Britain', in Robert Boyce and Joseph A. Maiolo (eds), *The Origins of World War Two: The Debate Continues* (London: Palgrave Macmillan, 2003), pp. 111–34, p. 114.

62. Ibid., p. 124.

63. Ibid., p. 126.

64. Fletcher, *WRNS*, p. 25.

65. Mason, *The Wrens*, p. 49.

66. Crang, 'The Revival of the British Women's Auxiliary Services', p. 347.

67. Association of the Wrens Archive, Portsmouth, *The Wren*, Katharine Furse, 'Use of the WRNS', April 1938.

68. Braybon and Summerfield, *Out of the Cage*, pp. 151–2.

69. Mason, *The Wrens*, p. 49.

70. Maiolo, *Cry Havoc*.

71. TNA, CAB 24/280, Manpower Sub-Committee Final Report, 29 Sept. 1938, p. 173.

72. TNA, CAB 24/280, Memo of Lord Privy Seal Sir John Anderson MP to the Cabinet, 18 Nov. 1938, p. 164.

73. Ibid.

74. TNA, CAB 24/280, Handbook for National Service, Jan. 1939, p. 6.

75. Ibid.
76. TNA, CAB 24/280, Handbook for National Service, Jan. 1939.
77. TNA, ADM 1/9742, Women's Auxiliary Corps Requirements Summarised, 13 Oct. 1938.
78. Mason, *The Wrens*, p. 50.
79. Chris Howard Bailey and Lesley Thomas, *The WRNS in Camera: The Work of the Women's Royal Naval Service in the Second World War* (Stroud: Sutton Publishing Ltd, 2000), p. 101.
80. Ibid., pp. 103−5.
81. There is a great deal of literature on women in the labour force during the war, with much of it having an American focus, such as: Ruth Milkman, *Gender at Work: The Dynamics of Job Segregation by Sex During World War II* (Urbana, IL: University of Illinois Press, 1987); Susan Hartmann, *The Home Front and Beyond: American Women in the 1940s* (Boston, MA: Twayne Publishers Inc., 1983); Penny Colman, *Rosie the Riveter: Women Working on the Home Front in World War II* (Clermont, FL: Paw Prints, 2008).
82. Patricia J. Thomas, 'Women in the Military; America and the British Commonwealth', *Armed Forces & Society*, 4/4 (1 July 1978): 623−46.
83. Ibid.
84. Vera Laughton Mathews, *Blue Tapestry* (London: Hollis and Carter, 1949), p. 47.
85. Gordon Williamson, *World War II German Women's Auxiliary Services* (London: Osprey Publishing, 2003).
86. Marshall Cavendish Corporation (ed.), *History of World War II* (New York, NY: Cavendish Square Publishing, 2004), p. 587.
87. Gerard DeGroot, 'Whose Finger on the Trigger. Mixed Anti-Aircraft Batteries and the Female Combat Taboo', *War in History*, 4/4 (1 October 2016): 434−53.
88. Noakes, *Women in the British Army*, p. 119.
89. Mason, *The Wrens*, p. 50.
90. TNA, ADM 1/9742, notes of C. M. Bruce related to Scheme of Service, 29 Sept. 1938.
91. TNA, ADM 1/8056/264, Formation and Organisation of the WRNS, November 1918.
92. Mason, *The Wrens*, p. 49.
93. TNA, ADM 1/9742, letter from Furse to Eastwood, 25 Sept. 1938.
94. Ibid.
95. Association of the Wrens Archive, *The Wren*, Katharine Furse, 'Use of the WRNS', October 1938.
96. Laughton Mathews, *Blue Tapestry*, p. 50.
97. TNA, ADM 1/9742, letter from Carter to Furse, 29 Sept. 1938.
98. Mason, *The Wrens*, pp. 50−1; see also notes in TNA file, ADM 1/9742.

Chapter 4   April 1939–41: Management and Growth of the 'Civilian' Service

1. Vera Laughton Mathews, *Blue Tapestry* (London: Hollis and Carter, 1949), p. 136.
2. TNA, ADM 1/9742, letter to Laughton Mathews, 13 Feb. 1939.
3. Laughton Mathews, *Blue Tapestry*, p. 53.
4. TNA, ADM 1/9742, Formation of Second World War WRNS, Notes from meeting re formation of service, 22 Feb. 1939.
5. Laughton Mathews, *Blue Tapestry*, p. 53.
6. See documents in TNA, ADM 1/11114 for discussions of issues of stripes.
7. Ursula Stuart Mason, *The Wrens 1917–77: A History of the Women's Royal Naval Service* (Reading: Educational Explorers, 1977), p. 52.
8. Records of Secretary's Department, http://discovery.nationalarchives.gov.uk/SearchUI/details?Uri=C719 (accessed 6 June 2017).
9. http://homepages.warwick.ac.uk/~lysic/1920s/admiralty.htm (accessed 6 June 2017).
10. Laughton Mathews, *Blue Tapestry*, p. 52.
11. NMRN, 350/88 (99*24.35), Letter from Lord Stanhope to the King, 3 Apr. 1939.
12. Mason, *The Wrens*, p. 53.
13. Chris Howard Bailey and Lesley Thomas, *The WRNS in Camera: The Work of the Women's Royal Naval Service in the Second World War* (Stroud: Sutton Publishing Ltd, 2000), pp. 103–5.
14. Laughton Mathews, *Blue Tapestry*, p. 83.
15. From TNA, ADM 1/9742, Formation of Second World War WRNS, n.d.
16. NMRN, 350/88 (99*24.35), Letter from Lord Stanhope to the King asking for approval of uniform, 22 Jun. 1939.
17. Laughton Mathews, *Blue Tapestry*, p. 87.
18. Ibid., p. 114.
19. TNA, ADM 1/1114, letter from Le Maistre to Laughton Mathews, 3 Sep. 1940.
20. TNA, ADM 1/1114, letter from Little to Le Maistre, 3 Oct. 1940.
21. TNA, ADM 1/1114, letter from Mackenzie-Grieve to Laughton Mathews, 20 May 1940.
22. From Marjorie H. Fletcher, *WRNS: A History of the Women's Royal Naval Service* (London: Batsford Ltd, 1989), p. 39.
23. Ibid.
24. Laughton Mathews, *Blue Tapestry*, p. 54.
25. TNA, ADM 1/9742, letter from Carter to Laughton Mathews, 31 Mar. 1939.
26. TNA, ADM 1/9742, letter from Laughton Mathews to Carter, 1 Apr. 1939.
27. Fletcher, *WRNS*, pp. 26–7.
28. Mason, *The Wrens*, p. 53.
29. Laughton Mathews, *Blue Tapestry*, p. 56.
30. Mason, *The Wrens*, p. 64.

31. Laughton Mathews, *Blue Tapestry*, p. 50.
32. Jeremy A. Crang, 'The Revival of the British Women's Auxiliary Services in the Late Nineteen-Thirties', *Historical Research*, 83/220 (1 May 2010): pp. 343–57, p. 351.
33. Laughton Mathews, *Blue Tapestry*, p. 51.
34. So far no originals of these letters have been found.
35. Mason, *The Wrens*, p. 55.
36. Laughton Mathews, *Blue Tapestry*, pp. 56–8.
37. Ibid., p. 60.
38. Ibid., p. 70.
39. Ibid.
40. Jean Atkins, interviewed 24 March 2010.
41. Laughton Mathews, *Blue Tapestry*, p. 58.
42. Ibid., pp. 79–80.
43. TNA, ADM 1/9742, Formation of Second World War WRNS, Newspaper article advertising for WRNS, Apr. 1939.
44. TNA, ADM 1/9742, The Formation of the Women's Royal Naval Service, 12 Oct. 1938.
45. Lucy Noakes, *Women in the British Army: War and the Gentle Sex, 1907–1948*, new edn (Oxon: Routledge, 2006), p. 101.
46. Laughton Mathews, *Blue Tapestry*, p. 65.
47. Mason, *The Wrens*, p. 56.
48. Laughton Mathews, *Blue Tapestry*, pp. 63–7.
49. Ibid., p. 99.
50. Ibid., p. 67.
51. Ibid., p. 70.
52. Mason, *The Wrens*, p. 58.
53. Laughton Mathews, *Blue Tapestry*, p. 72.
54. Ibid., pp. 133–4.
55. Ibid., p. 74.
56. Ibid., p. 77, letter from Captain William Powlett in 1944.
57. Ibid., p. 77.
58. TNA, ADM 1/9742, Women's Royal Naval Service scheme of service amendments, Apr. 1939.
59. TNA, ADM 1/8056/264, Formation and Organisation of the WRNS, Nov. 1918.
60. Laughton Mathews, *Blue Tapestry*, p. 69.
61. Ibid., p. 69.
62. Ibid., p. 93.
63. Gail Braybon and Penny Summerfield, *Out of the Cage* (London: Pandora, 1987), p. 157.
64. Ibid., pp. 155–8.
65. Ibid.
66. Ibid., p. 159.
67. Noakes, *Women in the British Army*, p. 116.

68. Braybon and Summerfield, *Out of the Cage*, p. 165.
69. Arthur Marwick, *Britain in the Century of Total War: Peace and Social Change, 1900–67* (London: Penguin Books Ltd, 1968), pp. 292–3.
70. Noakes, *Women in the British Army*, pp. 116–17.
71. Laughton Mathews, *Blue Tapestry*, p. 90.
72. Penny Summerfield, *Reconstructing Women's Wartime Lives: Discourse and Subjectivity in Oral Histories of the Second World War* (Manchester: Manchester University Press, 1998), p. 78.
73. Ibid., p. 78.
74. From Chris Howard Bailey and Lesley Thomas, The WRNS in Camera: The Work of the Women's Royal Naval Service in the Second World War (Stroud: Sutton Publishing Ltd, 2000), p. 101.
75. Mason, *The Wrens*, p. 62; Kathy Baker, interviewed 10 February 2010.
76. Fletcher, *WRNS*, p. 28.
77. Ibid.
78. NMRN, 1988 350 (58*5), Admiralty letter re: cypher officers, 19 Aug. 1938.
79. Laughton Mathews, *Blue Tapestry*, p. 89.
80. Nancy Jennings, interviewed 8 April 2010.
81. Laughton Mathews, *Blue Tapestry*, p. 89.
82. Mason, *The Wrens*, p. 62.
83. Laughton Mathews, *Blue Tapestry*, p. 147.
84. Jane Waller and Michael Vaughan-Rees, *Women in Uniform 1939–45*, (London: Macmillan Interactive Publishing, 1989), p. 53.
85. Pamela Bates, interviewed 18 May 2010.
86. Ibid.
87. Fletcher, *WRNS*, p. 72.
88. Interview with Janet Dodds (pseudonym) for Hannah Roberts' undergraduate dissertation, 'An Interpretative Biographical Exploration of the Experiences of Women Who Served in the WRNS during World War Two' (London School of Economics and Political Science, 2007).
89. Ibid.
90. Fletcher, *WRNS*, pp. 30–2.
91. IWM, memoir of D. Coyne, 93/2/1.
92. Claire James, interviewed 12 May 2010.
93. Laughton Mathews, *Blue Tapestry*, p. 225.
94. Ibid., p. 224.
95. Jean Atkins, interviewed 24 March 2010.
96. Bunty Marshall, 'The Despatcher's Tale', *Oldie Magazine*, June 2010, p. 34.
97. Ibid.; extract in Waller and Vaughan-Rees, '*Women in Uniform*', p. 54.
98. Laughton Mathews, *Blue Tapestry*, p. 112.
99. Fletcher, *WRNS*, p. 50.
100. Hansard, Vol. 128 cc279–8, House of Lords Debate, 'Women Dispatch Riders', 6 Jul. 1943.
101. Laughton Mathews, *Blue Tapestry*, p. 206.

102. Ibid., p. 201, p. 206.
103. Raynes, *Maid Matelot*.
104. Fletcher, *WRNS*, p. 39.
105. Martha Rose, interviewed 2 June 2010.
106. Laughton Mathews, *Blue Tapestry*, p. 202.
107. Fletcher, *WRNS*, p. 39.
108. Laughton Mathews, *Blue Tapestry*, p. 206.
109. Bailey and Thomas, *The WRNS in Camera*.
110. Mason, *The Wrens*, p. 64.
111. Laughton Mathews, *Blue Tapestry*, pp. 83–4.
112. Crang, 'The British Women's Auxiliary Services', p. 352.
113. Laughton Mathews, *Blue Tapestry*, p. 136.
114. Fletcher, *WRNS*, p. 33–5.
115. NMRN, 988 350 (58* 11–32), Admiral Creasy, Account of Submarine Attack Teacher WRNS, n.d.
116. Jo Stanley, *Cabin 'Boys' to Captains: 250 Years of Women at Sea* (Stroud: The History Press, 2016), p. 34.

Chapter 5   Becoming a Wren: Meritocracy Over Social Position

1. Gail Braybon and Penny Summerfield, *Out of the Cage*, 1st edn (London: Pandora, 1987), p. 198.
2. Mass Observation, 952, File Report, ATS Campaign, Women's Attitude to Work and War Work: Preferences for ARP, nursing, munitions work, Land Army, Services, Nov. 1941.
3. Tessa Stone, 'Creating a (gendered?) Military Identity: The Women's Auxiliary Air Force in Great Britain in the Second World War', *Women's History Review*, 8/4 (1 December 1999): 605–24, pp. 605–6.
4. Martin Francis, *The Flyer: British Culture and the Royal Air Force, 1939–1945* (Oxford: Oxford University Press, 2011), p. 15.
5. Ibid., p. 15.
6. TNA, ADM 1/9742, Draft Conditions of Service, Oct. 1938.
7. IWM, Coyne, 93/2/1.
8. Husband of Sarah Abbott, interviewed 17 May 2010; Amanda Davies, interviewed 4 June 2010.
9. TNA, ADM 1/9742, Draft Conditions of Service, Oct. 1938.
10. Ibid.
11. Lucy Noakes, *Women in the British Army: War and the Gentle Sex, 1907–1948*, new edn (Oxon: Routledge, 2006), pp. 73–5.
12. Ibid., p. 77.
13. Jane Waller and Michael Vaughan-Rees, *Women in Uniform 1939–45* (London: Macmillan Interactive Publishing, 1989), p. 32.
14. TNA, ADM 1/9742, Draft Conditions of Service, Oct. 1938.

15. Ibid.
16. IWM, Coyne, 93/2/1.
17. Noakes, *Women in the British Army*, pp. 117–18; Hansard, Debates in the House of Commons, 'Maximum National Effort', Nov.–Dec. 1941.
18. Noakes, *Women in the British Army*, p. 118.
19. Ibid.
20. Vera Laughton Mathews, *Blue Tapestry* (London: Hollis and Carter, 1949, p. 78.
21. Kathy Baker, interviewed 10 February 2010.
22. Noakes, *Women in the British Army*, p. 110.
23. Ibid., p. 131.
24. Ibid., p. 106.
25. Ibid., p. 110.
26. Braybon and Summerfield, *Out of the Cage*, p. 165.
27. Noakes, *Women in the British Army*, p. 107.
28. Laughton Mathews, *Blue Tapestry*, p. 60.
29. Ibid., p. 54.
30. Noakes, *Women in the British Army*, p. 107.
31. Ibid., p. 118.
32. Hansard, Debate in House of Commons, 'Woman Power', 20 Mar. 1941.
33. Hansard, Debate in House of Commons, 'Women's Royal Naval Service', 10 Mar. 1943.
34. Laughton Mathews, *Blue Tapestry*, p. 50.
35. TNA, ADM 1/1114, Charles Little, 'Status of the WRNS', 9 Sept. 1941.
36. Laughton Mathews, *Blue Tapestry*, pp. 115–16.
37. IWM, diary of V. Boyce, IWM 93/18/1.
38. Mason, *The Wrens*, p. 60.
39. Noakes, *Women in the British Army*, p. 114.
40. Betty Calderara, interviewed 17 March 2010.
41. TNA: ADM 1/21217, Head of Naval Law to Second Sea Lord, 1 Oct. 1948; Kathleen Sherit, 'The Integration of Women into the Royal Navy and the Royal Air Force, Post-World War II to the Mid 1990s', King's College London, 2013, p. 45, available at: https://kclpure.kcl.ac.uk/portal/files/31893847/2013_Sherit_Kathleen_1069333_ethesis.pdf (accessed 11 April 2017).
42. Sherit, 'The Integration of Women into the Royal Navy and the Royal Air Force', pp. 62–4.
43. Fletcher, *WRNS*, pp. 30, 42.
44. Penny Summerfield, *Reconstructing Women's Wartime Lives: Discourse and Subjectivity in Oral Histories of the Second World War* (Manchester: Manchester University Press, 1998), p. 165.
45. Jeremy A. Crang, 'The Revival of the British Women's Auxiliary Services in the Late Nineteen-Thirties', *Historical Research*, 83/220 (1 May 2010): 343–57, p. 351.
46. Summerfield, *Reconstructing Women's Wartime Lives*, p. 164.

47. Laughton Mathews, *Blue Tapestry*, p. 130.
48. 'Join the Wrens and free a man for the fleet', pamphlet contained in documents of IWM, official papers of J. S. B. Swete-Evans, 06/47/1.
49. IWM, Swete-Evans, 06/47/1.
50. TNA, ADM 1/9742, Draft Conditions of Service, Oct. 1938.
51. Nina Adams, interviewed 5 May 2010.
52. TNA, ADM 1/9742, Draft Conditions of Service, Oct. 1938.
53. Nancy Jennings, interviewed 8 April 2010.
54. Jeanette Wakeford, interviewed 4 May 2010.
55. Braybon and Summerfield, *Out of the Cage*, p. 138.
56. NMRN, 1988.350.1, *Regulations and Instructions for Women's Royal Naval Service to 31 December 1943*, 1943.
57. Jean Matthews, interviewed 13 April 2010.
58. Laughton Mathews, *Blue Tapestry*, p. 130.
59. Hansard, Debate in House of Commons, Speaker George Hall, 14 Oct. 1942.
60. Hansard, Debate in House of Commons, Speaker Henry Brooke, 14 Oct. 1942.
61. Kathy Baker, interviewed 10 February 2010.
62. Laughton Mathews, *Blue Tapestry*, p. 130.
63. IWM, Swete-Evans, 06/47/1.
64. IWM, account by S. J. Riley, 96/34/1.
65. Fletcher, *WRNS*, p. 30.
66. Mason, *The Wrens*, p. 120.
67. Ibid., p. 120.
68. NMRN, 1988.350.1, *Regulations and Instructions for Women's Royal Naval Service to 31 December 1943*, 1943.
69. IWM, account of S. Hamnett, 88/3/1.
70. Fletcher, *WRNS*, p. 42.
71. Mason, *The Wrens*, p. 120.
72. Ibid., p. 121.
73. IWM, Miscellaneous, Misc 130 (2006), official forms of Joan Martin.
74. IWM, Ridley, 67/268/1.
75. Ibid.
76. IWM, account of S. Carman, 03/43/1.
77. IWM, memoir and official documents of J. F. Wheatley, 91/36/1.
78. IWM, account of M. Pratt, 99/37/1.
79. BBC *People's War*, A2939646, Margaret Boothroyd, August 2004.
80. Amanda Davies, interviewed 4 June 2010.
81. Jean Atkins, interviewed 24 Mar 2010.
82. Martha Rose, interviewed 2 June 2010.
83. Kathy Baker, interviewed 10 February 2010.
84. IWM, Coyne, 93/2/1.
85. Laughton Mathews, *Blue Tapestry*, p. 165.

86. 'Etiquette violations: eating off your knife', 8 May 2011, available at: https://restaurant-ingthroughhistory.com/2011/05/08/etiquette-violations-eating-off-your-knife/ (accessed 23 July 1916).
87. Hansard, House of Commons Debate, 14 Oct. 1942; Fletcher, *WRNS*, p. 45.
88. Sheila Rodman, interviewed 7 April 2010.
89. Fletcher, *The WRNS*, p. 70.
90. Sheila Rodman, interviewed 7 April 2010.
91. Christian Lamb, *I Only Joined for the Hat: Redoubtable Wrens at War - Their Trials, Tribulations and Triumphs* (London: Bene Factum Publishing Ltd, 2007), p. 5.
92. Summerfield, *Reconstructing Women's Wartime Lives*, p. 175.
93. Betty Calderara, interviewed, 17 March 2010.
94. Summerfield, *Reconstructing Women's Wartime Lives*, pp. 176–7.
95. Waller and Vaughan-Rees, *Women in Uniform*, p. 21.
96. Summerfield, *Reconstructing Women's Wartime Lives*, p. 177.
97. Lamb, *I Only Joined for the Hat*, p. 6.
98. Jeanette Wakeford, interviewed 4 May 2010.
99. Claire James, interviewed 12 May 2010.
100. Laughton Mathews, *Blue Tapestry*, p. 165.
101. Peggy Scott, *British Women in War* (London: Hutchinson, 1940), p. 18.
102. Ibid., p. 17.
103. Laughton Mathews, *Blue Tapestry*, p. 89.
104. Ibid., p. 166.
105. Scott, *British Women in War*, p. 25.
106. Kathy Baker, interviewed 10 February 2010.
107. Lamb, *I Only Joined for the Hat*, p. 16.
108. Laughton Mathews, *Blue Tapestry*, p. 160.
109. Lamb, *I Only Joined for the Hat*, p. 33.
110. Laughton Mathews, *Blue Tapestry*, pp. 162–3.
111. Ibid., pp. 163–6.
112. Ibid., p. 165.
113. Hansard, Debate in House of Commons, 'Navy Estimates', 7 Mar. 1944.
114. Ibid.
115. Laughton Mathews, *Blue Tapestry*, pp. 165–6.
116. IWM, account of S. J. Riley, 96/34/1.
117. Ibid.
118. Laughton Mathews, *Blue Tapestry*, p. 167.
119. IWM, memoir of E. Dunkley, 01/02/10.
120. Mason, *The Wrens*, p. 119.
121. Laughton Mathews, *Blue Tapestry*, p. 168.
122. Summerfield, *Reconstructing Women's Wartime Lives*, p. 187.
123. Betty Calderara, interviewed 17 March 2010.
124. Jean Atkins, interviewed 24 March 2010.
125. Nancy Jennings, interviewed 8 April 2010.
126. Mabel Langdon, interviewed 29 June 2010.

127. Nina Adams, interviewed 5 May 2010.
128. Husband of Sarah Abbott, interviewed 17 May 2010.
129. Jeanette Wakeford, interviewed 4 May 2010.
130. Amanda Davies, interviewed 4 June 2010.
131. Lamb, *I Only Joined for the Hat*, p. 3.
132. Ibid., p. 9.
133. Noakes, *Women in the British Army*, p. 108.
134. Summerfield, *Reconstructing Women's Wartime Lives*, p. xi.
135. Ibid., p. 14.
136. Jean Matthews, interviewed 13 April 2010.
137. Corinna Peniston-Bird, 'The People's War in Personal Testimony and Bronze: Sorority and the Memorial to the Women of World War II', in Lucy Noakes and Juliette Pattinson (eds), *British Cultural Memory and the Second World War* (London: Bloomsbury Academic, 2013), pp. 67–88, p. 67.
138. Corinna Peniston-Bird, 'War and Peace in the Cloakroom: The Controversy over the Memorial to the Women of World War II', in Stephen Gibson and Simon Mollan (eds), *Representations of Peace and Conflict* (Houndmills, Basingstoke, Hampshire: Palgrave Macmillan, 2012), pp. 263–84, pp. 263–4.
139. Peniston-Bird, 'War and Peace in the Cloakroom', pp. 277–8.
140. Pam Marsden, interviewed 3 June 2010.
141. Pamela Bates, interviewed 18 May 2010.
142. Martha Rose, interviewed 2 June 2010.
143. Summerfield, *Reconstructing Women's Wartime Lives*, p. 45.
144. Claire James, interviewed 12 May 2010.
145. Josephine Rayne, interviewed 12 May 2010.
146. IWM, Tapp, Misc 14 (303).
147. Beatrice Parsons, Account of Mrs J Spears. nee Tapp interviewed 10 May 2010.
148. Summerfield, *Reconstructing Women's Wartime Lives*, p. 45.
149. Ibid., pp. 45–6.
150. http://historyinposters.tumblr.com/page/45 (ATS poster) (accessed 6 June 2017).
151. Summerfield, *Reconstructing Women's Wartime Lives*, p. 46.
152. Pam Marsden, interviewed 2 June 2010.
153. Summerfield, *Reconstructing Women's Wartime Lives*, pp. 49–50.
154. Scott, *British Women in War*, p. 11.
155. IWM, Wheatley, 91/36/1.
156. IWM, Pratt, 99/37/1.
157. Raynes, Rozelle, *Maid Matelot: Adventures of a Wren Stoker in World War 2, Featuring D-Day in Southampton*, 3rd edn (Newark: Castweasel Publishing, 2004).
158. Ibid., p. 21.
159. Ibid., pp. 41–2.
160. IWM, memoir of P. Damonte, 95/32/1.

Chapter 6   Disrupting the Combat Taboo

1. Chris Howard Bailey and Lesley Thomas, *The WRNS in Camera: The Work of the Women's Royal Naval Service in the Second World War* (Stroud: Sutton Publishing Ltd, 2000), p. 101.

2. Gerard DeGroot, 'Whose Finger on the Trigger? Mixed Anti-Aircraft Batteries and the Female Combat Taboo', *War in History*, 4/4 (1 October 2016): 434–53, p. 434.

3. Penny Summerfield, '"She Wants a Gun, Not a Dishcloth!": Gender, Service and Citizenship in Britain in the Second World War', in Gerard J. DeGroot and C. Peniston-Bird (eds), *A Soldier and a Woman: Women in the Military*, 1st edn (London: Routledge, 2000), pp. 119–35, p. 119.

4. Cynthia H. Enloe, *Does Khaki Become You?*, new e. edn (London: Pandora P., 1988).

5. DeGroot, 'Whose Finger on the Trigger?', p. 435.

6. Gerard DeGroot, 'Arms and the Woman', in Gerard DeGroot and C. Peniston-Bird (eds), *A Soldier and a Woman: Women in the Military*, 1st edn (London: Routledge, 2000), pp. 3–18, p. 11.

7. Summerfield, Penny, and Corinna Peniston-Bird, 'Women in the Firing Line: The Home Guard and the Defence of Gender Boundaries in Britain in the Second World War', *Women's History Review*, 9/2 (1 June 2000): 231–55, p. 232. doi:10.1080/09612020000200250.

8. Ibid; Penny Summerfield and Corinna Peniston-Bird, *Contesting Home Defence: Men, Women and the Home Guard in the Second World War* (Manchester: Manchester University Press, 2007), p. 65.

9. Juliette Pattinson, *Behind Enemy Lines: Gender, Passing and the Special Operations Executive in the Second World War* (Manchester: Manchester University Press, 2011).

10. BBC *People's War*, A3112219, Antoinette Porter, 10 October 2004.

11. Hansard, Debate in House of Commons, 'Women's Royal Naval Service', 10 Mar. 1943.

12. Vera Laughton Mathews, *Blue Tapestry* (London: Hollis and Carter, 1949), p. 136.

13. Bailey and Thomas, *The WRNS in Camera*, p. 101.

14. Hansard, Debate in House of Commons, 'Women's Royal Naval Service', 10 March 1943. In March 1943, 30 per cent of Wren roles were domestic.

15. Laughton Mathews, *Blue Tapestry*, p. 136.

16. Penny Summerfield, *Reconstructing Women's Wartime Lives: Discourse and Subjectivity in Oral Histories of the Second World War* (Manchester: Manchester University Press, 1998), pp. 85–6.

17. Sheila Rodman, interviewed 7 April 2010.

18. Graham Bebbington, *The Fledglings* (Leek: Churnet Valley Books, 2003), p. 6, p. 19.

19. Ibid., p. 20.

20. Ibid., p. 37.
21. Fletcher, *WRNS*, p. 61.
22. Sheila Rodman, interviewed 7 April 2010.
23. Fletcher, *The WRNS*, pp. 83–4.
24. Pam Marsden, interviewed 3 June 2010.
25. Laughton Mathews, *Blue Tapestry*, p. 187.
26. Beatrice Parsons, interviewed 10 May 2010.
27. Claire James, interviewed 12 June 2010.
28. IWM, Coyne, 93/2/1.
29. Fletcher, *WRNS*, p. 51.
30. Jean Atkins, interviewed 24 March 2010.
31. Mason, *The Wrens*, pp. 104–5.
32. Judy Botting, interviewed for undergraduate dissertation, Roberts, 'An Interpretative Biographical Exploration of the Experiences of Women Who Served in the WRNS during World War Two' (London School of Economics and Political Science, 2007).
33. Mason, *The Wrens*, p. 107.
34. Ibid., p. 107.
35. Laughton Mathews, *Blue Tapestry*, pp. 237–8.
36. Jean Elshtain, *Women and War* (Chicago, IL: University of Chicago, 1995), pp. 3–4.
37. Mason, *The Wrens*, p. 109.
38. Laughton Mathews, *Blue Tapestry*, p. 148.
39. Fletcher, *WRNS*, pp. 41–4.
40. Jane Waller and Michael Vaughan-Rees, *Women in Uniform 1939–45* (London: Macmillan Interactive Publishing, 1989), p. 134.
41. Laughton Mathews, *Blue Tapestry*, p. 266.
42. Bailey and Thomas, *The WRNS*, p. 100.
43. Mason, *The Wrens*, p. 115.
44. Laughton Mathews, *Blue Tapestry*, p. 250.
45. Jean Matthews, interviewed 13 April 2010.
46. Nina Adams, interviewed 5 May 2010.
47. Josephine Rayne, interviewed 12 May 2010.
48. IWM, memoir of P. Martin, 02/36/1.
49. Waller and Vaughan-Rees, *Women in Uniform*, pp. 135–6.
50. NMRN, 1981/351, 198/11.15, 1988/239, 1988/350.19.1–5, Collection of newspaper clippings covering World War II.
51. Mason, *The Wrens*, pp. 110–12.
52. Ibid.
53. Laughton Mathews, *Blue Tapestry*, p. 148.
54. Ibid., p. 149.
55. IWM, Hamnett, 88/3/1.
56. IWM, documents and diary entry of K. B. Tomlin, 05/72/1.
57. IWM, Pratt, 99/37/1.
58. Ibid.

59. Ibid.
60. IWM, Carman, 03/43/1.
61. Jean Matthews, interviewed 13 April 2010.
62. IWM, Hamnett, 88/3/1.
63. Mason, *The Wrens*, p. 112.
64. IWM, Carman, 03/43/1.
65. Waller and Vaughan-Rees, *Women in Uniform*, p. 148.
66. IWM, Carman, 03/43/1.
67. IWM, Hamnett, 88/3/1.
68. Waller and Vaughan-Rees, *Women in Uniform*, p. 149.
69. IWM, Pratt, 99/37/1.
70. IWM, Tomlin, 05/72/1.
71. IWM, Hamnett, 88/3/1.
72. Waller and Vaughan-Rees, *Women in Uniform*, p. 134.
73. IWM, Pratt, 99/37/1.
74. Ibid.
75. Jean Matthews, interviewed 13 April 2010.
76. Ibid.
77. Gwendoline Page, *They Listened in Secret* (Wynmondham: George R. Reeve Ltd, 2003), pp. 71–8.
78. Helen Clarke, interviewed 14 June 2010.
79. Provided by Matthew Richardson (Sophie Richardson), interviewed 24 May 2010.
80. Helen Clarke, interviewed 14 June 2010.
81. Nancy Jennings, interviewed 8 April 2010.
82. IWM, Dunkley, 01/02/10.
83. Fletcher, *WRNS*, p. 59.
84. Laughton Mathews, *Blue Tapestry*, p. 200.
85. Ibid., p. 97.
86. Fletcher, *WRNS*, p. 62.
87. Hansard, Debate in House of Commons, 'Women's Royal Naval Service', 10 March. 1943.
88. Ibid.
89. Christopher Dandeker, 'Women in the Military', available at: http://www.oxfordreference.com/view/10.1093/acref/9780198606963.001.0001/acref-9780198606963-e-1390 (accessed 6 June 2017).
90. Mady Wechsler Segal, 'Women's Military Roles Cross-Nationally: Past, Present, and Future', *Gender & Society*, 9/6 (1 December 1995): pp. 757–75, p. 760.
91. Laughton Mathews, *Blue Tapestry*, p. 227.
92. Tessa Stone, 'Creating a (gendered?) Military Identity: The Women's Auxiliary Air Force in Great Britain in the Second World War', *Women's History Review*, 8/4 (1 December 1999): pp. 605–24, p. 611.
93. IWM, memoir of S. Bywater, 05/62/1; TNA, ADM 199/848, 'Operation "Outward": offensive use of free balloons; clearance of fishing vessels from 'sink at sight' zones: policy', 1941–1946.

94. Ibid.
95. BBC *People's War*, Antoinette Porter, A3112219, 10 October 2004.
96. Fletcher, *WRNS*, p. 45.
97. 'Felixstowe's Secret War Exposed', *Ipswich Star*, available at: www.ipswichs tar.co.uk/news/felixstowe_s_secret_war_exposed_1_94762 (accessed 6 June 2017).
98. Corinna Peniston-Bird, 'Of Hockey Sticks and Sten Guns: British Auxiliaries and Their Weapons in the Second World War'. *Women's History Magazine* Autumn 2014, no. 76 (2014): pp. 13–22, p. 13.
99. IWM, Bywater, 05/62/1.
100. Laughton Mathews, *Blue Tapestry*, p. 226.
101. Gerard DeGroot, 'Arms and the Woman', in Gerard DeGroot and C. Peniston-Bird (eds), *A Soldier and a Woman: Women in the Military*, 1st edn (London: Routledge, 2000), pp. 3–18, p. 11, Lucy Noakes, *Women in the British Army: War and the Gentle Sex, 1907–1948*, new edn (Oxon: Routledge, 2006), p. 119.
102. DeGroot, 'Arms and the Woman', p. 14.
103. Vera Laughton Mathews, *Blue Tapestry* (London: Hollis and Carter, 1949), p. 226.
104. BBC *People's War*, Antoinette Porter, A3112219, 10 October 2004.
105. Gail Braybon and Penny Summerfield, *Out of the Cage*, 1st edn (London: Pandora, 1987), pp. 195–6.
106. Summerfield, *Reconstructing Women's Wartime Lives*, p. 83.
107. Elshtain, *Women and War*, p. 4.
108. Ibid.
109. Bailey and Thomas, *The WRNS in Camera*.
110. Fletcher, *WRNS*, p. 39.
111. Ibid., p. 63.
112. Bailey and Thomas, *The WRNS in Camera*, p. 39.
113. Peniston-Bird, 'Of Hockey Sticks and Sten Guns', p. 13.

Chapter 7   Social Perceptions and Relationships in the Service

1. Penny Summerfield, *Reconstructing Women's Wartime Lives: Discourse and Subjectivity in Oral Histories of the Second World War* (Manchester: Manchester University Press, 1998), p. 116.
2. Gerard DeGroot, 'Arms and the Woman', in Gerard DeGroot and C. Peniston-Bird (eds), *A Soldier and a Woman: Women in the Military*, 1st edn (London: Routledge, 2000), pp. 3–18, p. 14.
3. Gerard DeGroot, 'Lipstick on Her Nipples, Cordite in Her Hair: Sex and Romance among British Servicewomen during the Second World War', in Gerard J. DeGroot and C. Peniston-Bird (eds), *A Soldier and a Woman: Women in the Military* (London: Routledge, 2000), pp. 100–5.

4. Penny Summerfield, '"She Wants a Gun, Not a Dishcloth!"': Gender, Service and Citizenship in Britain in the Second World War', in Gerald J. DeGroot and C. Peniston-Bird (eds), *A Soldier and a Woman: Women in the Military*, 1st edn (London: Routledge, 2000), pp. 119–35, p. 120.

5. DeGroot, 'Arms and the Woman', p. 5.

6. Jean Atkins, interviewed 24 March 2010.

7. Kathy Baker, interviewed 10 February 2010.

8. Nina Adams, interviewed 5 May 2010.

9. Summerfield, *Reconstructing Women's Wartime Lives*, p. 124.

10. Pamela Bates, interviewed 8 June 2010.

11. Jean Atkins, interviewed 24 March 2010.

12. IWM, Hamnett, 88/3/1.

13. Betty Calderara, interviewed 17 March 2010.

14. IWM, Miscellaneous 2422, Misc 156 (2422), responses of appeal for contributions to the book, *Women in Uniform*.

15. DeGroot, 'Lipstick on her Nipples', pp. 100–2.

16. Jean Matthews, interviewed 13 April 2010.

17. IWM, Pratt, 99/37/1.

18. Ibid.

19. Laughton Mathews, *Blue Tapestry*, p. 118.

20. IWM, account of J. K. Neale, Lieutenant Commander DSC, 92/50/1, 'Work of WRNS'.

21. Vera Laughton Mathews, *Blue Tapestry* (London: Hollis and Carter, 1949), p. 120.

22. BBC *People's War*, A2195705, Patricia Manley-Cooper, contributed by Pat Rose, January 2004.

23. IWM, Account of Mrs J Spears, nee Tapp, Misc 14 (303).

24. IWM, Miscellaneous 3461, Misc 251 (3461), letter from a Wren.

25. IWM, memoir of J. Hodges, 99/37/1.

26. IWM, memoir of G. Page, 88/3/1.

27. Sheila Rodman, interviewed 7 April 2010.

28. IWM, Coyne, 93/2/1.

29. Lucy Noakes, *Women in the British Army: War and the Gentle Sex, 1907–1948*, new edn (Oxon: Routledge, 2006), p. 122; TNA, MO File Report 952, ATS campaign, 7 Nov. 1941.

30. Laughton Mathews, *Blue Tapestry*, p. 118.

31. Pamela Bates, interviewed 8 June 2010.

32. IWM, Misc 2422.

33. IWM, Hamnett, 88/3/1.

34. Sheila Rodman, interviewed 7 April 2010.

35. Pamela Bates, interviewed 8 June 2010.

36. Ibid.

37. IWM, Page, 99/37/1.

38. Pamela Bates, interviewed 8 June 2010.

39. IWM, Hodges, 99/37/1.

40. IWM, memoir of M. J. James, 93/30/1.
41. Laughton Mathews, *Blue Tapestry*, p. 120.
42. Ibid., p. 121.
43. Ibid., p. 122.
44. Kathy Baker, interviewed 10 February 2010.
45. Braybon and Summerfield, *Out of the Cage*, p. 217.
46. Ibid., pp. 215–16.
47. IWM, Riley, 96/34/1.
48. Ibid.
49. Betty Calderara, interviewed 17 March 2010.
50. IWM, account of E. J. Openshaw, 88/3/1.
51. Pilcher, *Coming Home*.
52. Jeanette Wakeford, interviewed 4 May 2010.
53. Josephine Rayne, interviewed 12 May 2010.
54. Including Sheila Rodman, interviewed 7 April 2010.
55. IWM, account of De Courey, S B Captain RN, 92/4/1, Conduct of Wrens at Fearn.
56. Laughton Mathews, *Blue Tapestry*, p. 83.
57. Noakes, *Women in the British Army*, pp. 113–14; *Evening Standard*, 25 Sept 1941.
58. Summerfield, *Reconstructing Women's Wartime Lives*, p. 45.
59. DeGroot, 'Lipstick on her Nipples', p. 102.
60. Jeremy A. Crang, '"Come into the Army, Maud": Women, Military Conscription, and the Markham Inquiry,' *Defence Studies* 8/3 (1 September 2008): pp. 381–95, p. 390.
61. Noakes, *Women in the British Army*, p. 122.
62. Ibid; TNA, MO File Report 952, ATS campaign, 7 Nov. 1941.
63. Martin J. Brayley, *World War II Allied Women's Services* (Oxford: Osprey Publishing, 2001), p. 5.
64. Laughton Mathews, *Blue Tapestry*, p. 118.
65. Ibid., pp. 119–20.
66. Graham Bebbington, *The Fledglings* (Leek: Churnet Valley Books, 2003), p. 42.
67. Josephine Rayne, interviewed 12 May 2010.
68. Account of Mrs J Spears née Tapp, IWM, Tapp, Misc 14 (303).
69. Beatrice Parsons, interviewed 10 May 2010.
70. IWM, Page, 88/3/1.
71. Beatrice Parsons, interviewed 10 May 2010.
72. DeGroot, 'Lipstick on her Nipples', p. 104.
73. BBC *People's War*, A2939646, Margaret Boothroyd, August 2004.
74. Summerfield, *Reconstructing Women's Wartime Lives*, pp. 178–9.
75. IWM, Hamnett, 88/3/1.
76. Norma Deering, interviewed 24 February 2010.
77. IWM, Riley, 96/34/1.
78. Jean Matthews, interviewed 13 April 2010.

79. Laughton Mathews, *Blue Tapestry*, p. 96.
80. Ibid., p. 100.
81. Kathy Baker, interviewed 10 February 2010.
82. Ibid.
83. IWM, Riley, 96/34/1.
84. Laughton Mathews, *Blue Tapestry*, p. 94.
85. IWM, Pratt, 99/37/1.
86. Bebbington, *The Fledglings*, p. 42.
87. Summerfield, *Reconstructing Women's Wartime Lives*, p. 124.
88. Kathy Baker, interviewed 10 February 2010.
89. Ibid.
90. Claire James, interviewed 12 May 2010.
91. Nancy Jennings, interviewed 8 April 2010.
92. Pam Marsden, interviewed 3 June 2010.
93. Sheila Rodman, interviewed 7 Apr 2010.
94. Summerfield, *Reconstructing Women's Wartime Lives*, p. 133.
95. Sheila Rodman, interviewed 7 April 2010.
96. Jane Waller and Michael Vaughan-Rees, *Women in Uniform 1939—45* (London: Macmillan Interactive Publishing, 1989), p. 32.
97. Summerfield, *Reconstructing Women's Wartime Lives*, p. 133.
98. Betty Calderara, interviewed 17 March 2010.
99. IWM, Ridley, 67/268/1.
100. Helen Clarke, interviewed 14 June 2010.
101. Waller and Vaughan-Rees, *Women in Uniform*, p. 57.
102. Ibid.
103. IWM, Coyne, 93/2/1.
104. Waller and Vaughan-Rees, *Women in Uniform*, p. 68.
105. Ibid.
106. Kathy Baker, interviewed 10 February 2010.
107. Betty Calderara, interviewed 17 March 2010.
108. Waller and Vaughan-Rees, *Women in Uniform*, p. 71.
109. Pamela Bates, interviewed, 8 June 2010.
110. BBC *People's War*, A2195705, Patricia Manley-Cooper, contributed by Pat Rose, January 2004.
111. Jean Atkins, interviewed 24 March 2010.
112. IWM, Coyne, 93/2/1.
113. Laughton Mathews, *Blue Tapestry*, p. 161.

Postscript   The Service Postwar and the Impact on the Wrens

1. TNA: CAB 131/2, Organisation of the Women's Services in Peace, 8 May 1946.

2. Fletcher, *WRNS*, p. 88.

3. Kathleen Sherit, 'The Integration of Women into the Royal Navy and the Royal Air Force, Post-World War II to the Mid 1990s', King's College London, 2013, p. 33, available at: https://kclpure.kcl.ac.uk/portal/files/31893847/2013_Sherit_Kathleen_1069333_ethesis.pdf (accessed 11 April 2017).

4. TNA: CAB 66/38, Report of the Committee on the Women's Services, 24 Jun. 1943.

5. Sherit, 'The integration of Women into the Royal Navy and the Royal Air Force', p. 37.

6. TNA: ADM 1/18884, Statement for Royal Commission on Equal Pay, 3 Oct. 1945.

7. Sherit, 'The integration of Women into the Royal Navy and the Royal Air Force', p. 38; TNA: ADM 167/124, Admiralty Board Minutes, 21 Dec. 1945; NMRN: 1988.350.57, Permanent Service, 28 Mar 1946.

8. Sherit, 'The integration of Women into the Royal Navy and the Royal Air Force', p. 38.

9. Mady Wechsler Segal, 'Women's Military Roles Cross-Nationally: Past, Present, and Future', *Gender & Society*, 9/6 (1 December 1995): 757–75.

10. Sherit, 'The integration of Women into the Royal Navy and the Royal Air Force', pp. 39–40; TNA: ADM 116/5725, Signal, First Lord to Markham, 17 Apr. 1946.

11. Sherit, 'The integration of Women into the Royal Navy and the Royal Air Force', p. 40; TNA: CAB 131/2, Organisation of the Women's Services in Peace, 8 May 1946.

12. Penny Summerfield, *Reconstructing Women's Wartime Lives: Discourse and Subjectivity in Oral Histories of the Second World War* (Manchester: Manchester University Press, 1998), p. 98.

13. Segal, 'Women's Participation in Armed Forces'.

14. Helena Carreiras, *Gender and the Military: Women in the Armed Forces of Western Democracies* (London; New York: Routledge, 2008), p. 1.

15. Marjorie. H. Fletcher, *WRNS: A History of the Women's Royal Naval Service*, (London: Batsford Ltd, 1989), pp. 112–15.

16. Ursula Stuart Mason, *The Wrens 1917–77: A History of the Women's Royal Naval Service* (Reading: Educational Explorers, 1977), p. 132.

17. Carreiras, *Gender and the Military*.

18. Tessa Stone, 'Creating a (Gendered?) Military Identity: The Women's Auxiliary Air Force in Great Britain in the Second World War', *Women's History Review*, 8/4 (1 December 1999): pp. 605–24, p. 607.

19. Martha Rose, interviewed 2 June 2010.

20. Joan Scott, 'Rewriting History', in Margaret R. Higonnet and Jane Jenson (eds), *Behind Enemy Lines: Gender and the Two World Wars* (New Haven, CT: Yale University Press, 1989), pp. 19–30, p. 25.

21. Arthur Marwick, *Britain in the Century of Total War: Peace and Social Change, 1900−67* (London: Penguin Books Ltd, 1968), p. 11.
22. Ibid., p. xvii.
23. Harold L. Smith, *War and Social Change: British Society in the Second World War* (Manchester: Manchester University Press, 1990), pp. 208−29, p. 217, p. 225.
24. Beatrice Parsons, interviewed 10 May 2010.
25. Josephine Rayne, interviewed 12 May 2010.
26. Helen Clarke, interviewed 14 June 2010.
27. Jean Matthews, interviewed 13 April 2010.
28. Norma Deering, interviewed 24 February 2010.
29. Jeanette Wakeford, interviewed 4 May 2010.
30. Kathy Baker, interviewed 10 February 2010.
31. Jean Atkins, interviewed 24 March 2010.
32. Claire James, interviewed 15 May 2010.
33. Sheila Rodman, interviewed 7 April 2010.
34. Nancy Jennings, interviewed 8 April 2010.
35. Matthew Richardson, interviewed 24 March 2010.
36. Amanda Davies, interviewed 4 June 2010.
37. Betty Calderara, interviewed 17 March 2010.

BIBLIOGRAPHY

PRIMARY MATERIAL

Unpublished material

Interviews (all interviews were conducted by the author and have been transcribed. Some names have been anonymised)

Interviewee	Role in the WRNS
Husband of Sarah Abbott, interviewed 17 May 2010.	Cypher Officer; went to France in 1944.
Nina Adams, interviewed 5 May 2010.	Coder, left as Leading Wren; worked in Palestine for 2 1/2 years.
Jean Atkins, interviewed 24 March 2010. *Not anonymised.*	Met forecaster, left as Third Officer.
Kathy Baker, interviewed 10 February 2010.	Classifier until 25 August 1944 when made Third Officer; became Second Officer.
Pamela Bates, interviewed 18 May 2010. *Not anonymised.*	Bletchley Park as coder, later retrained as MT Driver.
Judy Botting, (pseudonym) interviewed January 2007 by Hannah Roberts for undergraduate dissertation, LSE.	Steward at Worthy Down, later retrained as a motor transport driver
Betty Calderara, interviewed 17 March 2010. *Not anonymised.*	Writer, left as Leading Wren.
Annie Carter, interviewed 12 July 2010.	Motorcycle dispatch rider, was a Leading Wren when left.
Helen Clarke, interviewed 14 June 2010.	Special Duties: Linguistics P/O.
May Collins, interviewed 6 April 2010.	Radar plot, left as Leading Wren.
Amanda Davies, interviewed 4 June 2010.	Bletchley Park – P5 coder.

Norma Deering, interviewed 24 February 2010.
Bletchley Park – P5 coder.

Janet Dodds, interviewed December 2006 for Hannah Roberts's undergraduate dissertation, LSE.
Steward and later M/T driver.

Claire James, interviewed 12 May 2010.
Radio mechanic, 1944 retrained as plotter; left as Leading Wren.

Nancy Jennings, interviewed 8 April 2010.
Cypher Officer, then became Second Officer Signals.

Mabel Langdon, interviewed 29 June 2010.
Shorthand typist; left as Third Officer.

Pam Marsden, interviewed 3 June 2010. *Not anonymised.*
Radar mechanic in Fleet Air Arm.

Jean Matthews, interviewed 13 April 2010.
Bletchley Park – coder. When war ended in Europe was sent to Ceylon as a P/O.

Beatrice Parsons, interviewed 10 May 2010.
Radar fitter, left as P/O.

Josephine Rayne, interviewed 12 May 2010.
Shorthand typist, left as Third Officer.

Matthew Richardson (Sophie Richardson), interviewed 24 May 2010.
Special Duties because could speak German. End of 1945 was transferred to the Nuremburg Trials as an interpreter.

Sheila Rodman, interviewed 7 April 2010. *Not anonymised, with thanks to her family.*
Wren Ordnance (Armourer), later retrained as air mechanic; early 1946 had to retrain as a writer.

Martha Rose, interviewed 2 June 2010.
Boats Crew Wren, 1945 retrained as a writer.

Jeanette Wakeford, interviewed 4 May 2010. *Not anonymised.*
Writer, left as Ordinary Wren.

Official documents and correspondence
Official Documents

'Employment of Women's Royal Naval Service (WRNS) Personnel in the Royal Navy', Executive Summary. Freedom of Information Request 2007, Annex A of 1990 Memorandum by the Second Sea Lord, March 1989.

'Employment of WRNS Personnel in the RN', Freedom of Information Request 2007, Memorandum by the Second Sea Lord, January 1990.

'Ministry of Defence: Control and Use of Manpower', National Audit Office Report, 27 April 1989.

The National Museum of the Royal Navy, Portsmouth (NMRN)

NMRN, 988 350 (58* 11–32), Admiral Creasy, Account of Submarine Attack Teacher WRNS, n.d.

NMRN, 1988 350 (58*5), Admiralty letter re cypher officers, 19 Aug. 1938.

NMRN, 350/88 (99*24.35), Letter from Lord Stanhope to the King, 3 April 1939.

NMRN, 350/88 (99*24.35), Letter from Lord Stanhope to the King asking for approval of uniform, 22 Jun. 1939.

NMRN, 1988.350.1, Regulations and Instructions for Women's Royal Naval Service to 31 Dec. 1943, 1943.

The National Archives, Kew (TNA)

TNA, WO32/5253, Women's Army Auxiliary Corps-Status of, May 1917.

TNA, ADM 166/1806, Letter from Eric Geddes to Lloyd George about personnel, 9 Dec. 1917.

TNA, ADM 1/11303, Representation of the People Act, 1918.

TNA, ADM 116/1807, Geddes planned speech (not used), 6 Mar. 1918.

TNA, ADM 1/8056/264, Formation and Organisation of the WRNS, Nov. 1918.

TNA, ADM 116/1917, Location of WRNS 1919, 1919.

TNA, ADM 116/3739, Vol. 1, Formation of the WRNS, n.d.

TNA, ADM 116/3740, Vol. 2, Formation of the WRNS, n.d.

TNA, ADM 116/3741, Vol. 3, Formation of the WRNS, n.d.

TNA, ADM 116/3739, WS 39A, 'Uniform Acquaint Ratings'.

TNA, ADM 1/9742, Formation of Second World War WRNS, n.d.

TNA, ADM 1/9742, Draft Conditions of Service, Oct. 1938.

TNA, ADM 1/9742, The formation of the Women's Royal Naval Service, 12 Oct. 1938.

TNA, ADM 1/9742, Women's Auxiliary Corps Requirements Summarised, 13 Oct. 1938.

TNA, CAB 24/280, Handbook for National Service, Jan. 1939, p. 6.

TNA, ADM 1/9742, Women's Royal Naval Service scheme of service amendments, April. 1939.

TNA, ADM 199/848, 'Operation "Outward": offensive use of free balloons; clearance of fishing vessels from "sink at sight" zones: policy', 1941–46.

TNA, ADM 1/8508/281, Revisions to FO 414 Formation of WRNS, n.d.

TNA, ADM 1/11114, 'Status and Rank of WRNS Officers 1941', 1941.

TNA, ADM 1/11114, Charles Little, 'Status of the WRNS', 9 Sep. 1941.

TNA, ADM 1/15102, WRNS service certificates and conduct sheets, 1939–45.

TNA, MO File Report 952, ATS campaign, 7 Nov. 1941.

TNA, ADM 1/12764, Officers Recruitment, n.d.

TNA, ADM 1/25860, Policy on unsuitable marriages, n.d.

TNA, ADM 1/10320, Appointments of Commanders, letters about appointing the Queen as Commandant in Chief and the Duchess of Kent as Commandant, n.d.

TNA, CAB 66/38, Report of the Committee on the Women's Services, 24 Jun. 1943.

TNA, ADM 1/21949, 'Badge Design and Issue', 1939–45.

TNA: ADM 1/18884, Statement for Royal Commission on Equal Pay, 3 Oct. 1945.

TNA: ADM 167/124, Admiralty Board Minutes, 21 Dec. 1945.

TNA: CAB 131/2, Organisation of the Women's Services in Peace, 8 May 1946.

TNA: ADM 1/21217, Head of Naval Law to Second Sea Lord, 1 Oct. 1948.

Private correspondence, diaries and memoirs
The National Archives, Kew (TNA)
TNA, HO 185/258, memo of Furse, 24 Nov. 1916.
TNA, WO 162/30, Sir George Newman, Report of the Women's Services Committee, p. 6, 14 Dec. 1916.
TNA, ADM 116/1804, personal correspondence of Eric Geddes, Vol 1.
TNA, ADM 116/1805, personal correspondence of Eric Geddes, Vol 2.
TNA, ADM 116/1806, personal correspondence of Eric Geddes, Vol 3.
TNA, WO162/31, Conclusions by Adjutant-General Leith Wood, 5 Jan. 1917.
TNA, ADM 1/8506/264, memo of Furse related to Scheme of Service, 29 Nov. 1917.
TNA, ADM 116/1806, letter from Geddes to Lloyd George about personnel, 9 Dec. 1917.
TNA, ADM 116/1807, letter from Geddes to Jellicoe, 24 Dec. 1917.
TNA, ADM 116/1807, personal correspondence of Eric Geddes, Vol 4.
TNA, ADM 116/1807, memo of Geddes, 6 Mar. 1918.
TNA, ADM 116/1807, Geddes planned speech (not used), 6 Mar. 1918.
TNA, ADM 116/1808, personal correspondence of Eric Geddes, Vol 5.
TNA, ADM 116/1809, personal correspondence of Eric Geddes, Vol 6.
TNA, ADM 116/1810, personal correspondence of Eric Geddes, Vol 7.
TNA, ADM 1/9742, letter from Furse to Eastwood, 25 Sep. 1938.
TNA, ADM 1/9742, letter from Carter to Furse, 29 Sep. 1938.
TNA, ADM 1/9742, notes of C. M. Bruce related to Scheme of Service, 29 Sep. 1938.
TNA, CAB 24/280, Memo of Lord Privy Seal Sir John Anderson MP to the Cabinet, 18 Nov. 1938.
TNA, ADM 1/9742, letter to Laughton Mathews, 13 Feb. 1939.
TNA, ADM 1/9742, notes from meeting re reformation of service, 22 Feb. 1939.
TNA, ADM 1/9742, letter from Carter to Laughton Mathews, 31 Mar. 1939.
TNA, ADM 1/9742, letter from Laughton Mathews to Carter, 1 Apr. 1939.
TNA, ADM 1/1114, letter from Mackenzie-Grieve to Laughton Mathews, 20 May 1940.
TNA, ADM 1/1114, letter from Le Maistre to Laughton Mathews, 3 Sep. 1940.
TNA, ADM 1/1114, letter from Little to Le Maistre, 3 Oct. 1940.
TNA, ADM 1/1114, letter from Mackenzie-Grieve to Laughton Mathews, 20 May. 1940.
TNA: ADM 116/5725, Signal, First Lord to Markham, 17 Apr. 1946.

Imperial War Museum, Department of Documents,
London (IWM)
IWM, account of M. Ackroyd, 88/3/191/4/1, 35 accounts of Wrens who served in Y stations.
IWM, diary of P. Arnold, 88/3/1.
IWM, account of D. Barker, 91/4/1, working in a 'Y' station during the war.
IWM, diary of V. Boyce, IWM 93/18/1.

IWM, memoir of S. Bywater, 05/62/1.

IWM, account of S. Carman, 03/43/1.

IWM, account of V. Chenery, 88/3/1.

IWM, account of J. Cochrane, 88/3/1.

IWM, account of E. Cooper, 02/36/1.

IWM, memoir of D. Coyne, 93/2/1.

IWM, account of M. Crisford, 91/27/1.

IWM, memoir of P. Damonte, 95/32/1.

IWM, account of De Courey, S B Captain RN, 92/4/1, Conduct of Wrens at Fearn.

IWM, memoir of G. Dix, 05/62/1.

IWM, memoir of E. Dunkley, 01/02/10.

IWM, memoir of H. Fullick, 87/21/1, June 1943.

IWM, documents of B. Gordon, 71/43/1, WW1 documents.

IWM, documents of P. M. Green, 91/4/1.

IWM, account of S. Hamnett, 88/3/1.

IWM, memoir of J. Hodges, 99/37/1.

IWM, account of H. F. Hooper, Lieutenant RNVR, 95/5/1, disparaging comments towards WRNS.

IWM, memoir of M. J. James, 93/30/1.

IWM, scrapbook of M. J. Kennedy, 03/45/1.

IWM letters of J. M. Kirby, Con shelf, 1943–1945.

IWM, memoir of J. Kruisselbrink, 91/27/1, Jun. 1943–46, only Wren in gunnery school.

IWM, memoir of J. E. Loughton, 86/29/1, 1942–1945.

IWM, memoir of C. M. Lowry, 86/12/1, 1940–1944.

IWM, memoir of P. Martin, 02/36/1.

IWM, Miscellaneous, Misc 130 (2006), official forms of Joan Martin.

IWM, Miscellaneous 2422, Misc 156 (2422), responses of appeal for contributions to the book, *Women in Uniform*.

IWM, Miscellaneous 2842, Misc 188 (2842), collection of documents relating to Constance Morris.

IWM, Miscellaneous 2912, Misc 197/1–3 (2912), memoirs.

IWM, Miscellaneous 303, Misc 14 (303), account of J. Spears née Tapp.

IWM, Miscellaneous 3461, Misc 251 (3461), letter from a Wren.

IWM, Miscellaneous 3720, Misc 276 (3720), collection of memoirs.

IWM, Miscellaneous 513, Misc 28 (513), First World War items.

IWM, account of A. Napier-Smith, PP/MCR/277 67/162/1.

IWM, account of J. K. Neale, Lieutenant Commander DSC, 92/50/1, work of WRNS.

IWM, account of E. J. Openshaw, 88/3/1.

IWM, account of V. M. Owen, Con Shelf, problems facing married women.

IWM, memoir of G. Page, 88/3/1.

IWM, memoir of A. Parkhurst, 94/27/1.

IWM, letter from Dorothy Pickford to her sister Molly, 14 Mar. 1918, IWM DD Con Shelf.

IWM, account of M. Pratt, 99/37/1.

IWM, account of Jean Rawson, Miscellaneous 156 (2422).

IWM, memoir of B. G. Rhodes, 95/14/1.

IWM, account of E. M. Ridley, 67/268/1.

IWM, account of S. J. Riley, 96/34/1.
IWM, account of E. Shuter, 05/62/1.
IWM, official papers of D. C. Stow, 76/25/1.
IWM, official papers of J. S. B. Swete-Evans, 06/47/1.
IWM, documents and diary entry of K. B. Tomlin, 05/72/1, 1946.
IWM, account of C. Waterhouse, 97/34/1.
IWM, memoir and official documents of J. F. Wheatley, 91/36/1.
IWM, memoir of M. Winter, 91/27/1.

National Maritime Museum, London (NMM)
NMM, DAU/5, Letter from Furse to Chamberlain, 29 Dec. 1916.
NMM, DAU/5, Memo of Furse related to meeting with Fawcett and Chamberlain, 9 Jan. 1917.
NMM, DAU/5, Letter from Furse to Chamberlain, 15 Jan. 1917.
NMM, DAU/5, Furse memo to Fawcett, 22 Jan. 1917.
NMM, DAU/43, 'WRNS Formation' memo, 11 Nov. 1917.
NMM, DAU/43, Furse memo, 11 Nov. 1917.
NMM, DAU/43, Furse memo, 12 Nov. 1917.
NMM, DAU/43, Letter from Furse to Geddes, 13 Nov. 1917.
NMM, DAU 43, Letter from Geddes to Furse, 14 Nov. 1917.
NMM, DAU/43, Furse memo, 21 Nov. 1917.
NMM, DAU/24, Admiralty memo no.245, 29 Nov. 1917.
NMM, DAU/55, Letter from Furse to Bridgeman, 3 Jan. 1919.
NMM, DAU/24, Furse memo, 30 Jan. 1919.

The National Museum Royal Navy, Portsmouth (NMRN)
NMRN, 350/88 31*32, Extracts from Mavis Carter's Diary, 1917.
NMRN, 350/88, 'The WRNS Never at Sea 1917–1919', 1919.
NMRN, 1981/351, 198/11.15, 1988/239, 1988/350.19.1–5, Collection of newspaper clippings covering World War II.
NMRN, *Sea Your History*, interview 4 Jul. 2006, interviewer: Katy Elliott.
NMRN: 1988.350.57, 'Permanent Service', 28 Mar. 1946.

Theses
Roberts, Hannah, 'An Interpretative Biographical Exploration of the Experiences of Women Who Served in the WRNS during World War Two', undergraduate dissertation, London School of Economics and Political Science, 2007.
————, 'Why Was the Decision Made to Implement Female Sea Service in the Royal Navy in 1990', Master's dissertation, Kings College London, 2008.
Sherit, Kathleen, 'The Integration of Women into the Royal Navy and the Royal Air Force, Post-World War II to the Mid 1990s', King's College London, 2013, p. 45, available at: https://kclpure.kcl.ac.uk/portal/files/31893847/2013_Sherit_Kathleen_1069333_ethesis.pdf (accessed 11 April 2017).

Published works

Official documents, correspondence, proceedings of Parliament

Hansard, Proceedings of the House of Commons and House of Lords.

Hansard, Debate in House of Commons, Speaker Sir R. Horne, 2 Jun. 1919.

Hansard, Debate in House of Commons, 'Woman Power', 20 Mar. 1941.

Hansard, Debates in the House of Commons, 'Maximum National Effort', Nov.–Dec. 1941.

Hansard, Debate in House of Commons, Speaker George Hall, 14 Oct. 1942.

Hansard, Debate in House of Commons, Speaker Henry Brooke, 14 Oct. 1942.

Hansard, Debate in House of Commons, 'Navy Estimates', 7 Mar. 1944.

Hansard, Debate in House of Commons, 'Women's Royal Naval Service', 10 Mar. 1943.

Hansard, Vol. 128 cc279–8, House of Lords Debate, 'Women Dispatch Riders', 6 Jul. 1943.

The National Archives, Kew

TNA, CAB 24/280, Manpower Sub-Committee final report, 29 Sept. 1938.

TNA, CAB 24/280, Handbook for National Service, Jan. 1939.

Mass Observation Archive, University of Sussex

Mass Observation, 952, File Report, ATS Campaign, Women's Attitude to Work and War Work: Preferences for ARP, nursing, munitions work, Land Army, Services, Nov. 1941.

Collections of speeches, pamphlets, newspapers, memoirs etc

BBC People's War

BBC *People's War*, A2067248, Anonymous, 'Cigarettes and Alcohol', 21 Nov. 2003.

BBC *People's War*, A2187056, Kath Dooley, 'Wartime Wren', 9 Jan. 2004.

BBC *People's War*, A2195705, Patricia Manley-Cooper, contributed by Pat Rose, 'World War II: My Memories of School and the WRNS', 12 Jan. 2004.

BBC *People's War*, A25244032, Ginger Thomas, 'D-Day: Working for Cossac', 16 Apr. 2004.

BBC *People's War*, A2939646, Margaret Boothroyd, 'In the WRNS with Laura Ashley', 23 Aug. 2004.

BBC *People's War*, A3112219, Antoinette Porter, 'Tuppence a Day Danger Money', 10 Oct. 2004.

BBC *People's War*, A3429209, Olive Partridge, contributed by Wyre Forest Volunteer Bureau, 'One Wren's War', 20 Dec. 2004.

BBC *People's War*, A3699606, Maureen Ascott's grandmother, 'World War Two Plane Stories', 22 Feb. 2005.

BBC *People's War*, A4336012, Joan Schwartz, 'A Bird's Eye View of the Yalta Conference by a Wren', 3 Jul. 2005.

BBC *People's War*, A4445101, Marjorie Cook, contributed by Angela Ng, 'What the WRNS did in North Shields', 13 Jul. 2005.

Newspaper articles

ATS Advertisement, *Evening Standard*, 25 September 1941.

Furse, Katharine, 'Use of the WRNS'. *The Wren*, April 1938, Association of the Wrens Archive, Portsmouth.

————, 'Use of the WRNS', *The Wren*, October 1938, Association of the Wrens Archive, Portsmouth.

Hamilton, Archie, 'Interview with Lord Hamilton', by Katy Elliot, 4 July 2006, *Sea your History*, NMRN.

'Lord Hamilton Comments', *Navy News*, October 2007.

Marshall, Bunty, 'The Despatcher's Tale', *Oldie Magazine*, June 2010.

NMRN, 350/88 31*16, *The Times*, 15 Nov. 1917.

NMRN, 350/88 31*16, *The Times*, 16 Nov. 1917.

TNA, ADM 116/1804, George Riddell interview with Geddes, 13 Aug. 1917.

TNA, ADM 1/9742, newspaper article advertising for WRNS, Apr. 1939.

Books: autobiographies and published memoirs

Chatfield, Lord, *It Might Happen Again,* Vol. II, *The Navy And Defence, The Autobiography of Admiral of The Fleet Lord Chatfield* (William Heinemann, 1947).

Furse, Katharine, *Hearts and Pomegranates – the Story of Forty Five Years 1875–1920* (London: Peter Davies, 1940).

Houston, Roxanne, *Changing Course: The Wartime Experiences of a Member of the Women's Royal Naval Service, 1939–1945* (London: Grub Street, 2005).

Lamb, Christian, *I Only Joined for the Hat: Redoubtable Wrens at War - Their Trials, Tribulations and Triumphs* (London: Bene Factum Publishing Ltd, 2007).

Laughton Mathews, Vera, *Blue Tapestry* (London: Hollis and Carter, 1949).

Raynes, Rozelle, *Maid Matelot: Adventures of a Wren Stoker in World War 2, Featuring D-Day in Southampton*, 3rd edn (Newark: Castweasel Publishing, 2004).

Wells, Maureen, *Entertaining Eric: A Wartime Love Story* (London: Ebury Press, 2007).

Wemyss, Lady V., *Life and Letters of Lord Wester Wemyss* (London: Eyre and Spottiswoode, 1935).

SECONDARY MATERIAL

Books

Abbott, Pamela, and Claire Wallace, *An Introduction to Sociology: Feminist Perspectives* (London: Routledge, 1990).

Bailey, Chris Howard, and Lesley Thomas, *The WRNS in Camera: The Work of the Women's Royal Naval Service in the Second World War* (Stroud: Sutton Publishing Ltd, 2000).

Bales, Robert F., and Talcot Parsons, *Family: Socialization and Interaction Process*, 1st edn (Abingdon, UK: Routledge, 2007).

Baum, Willa K., *Oral History: An Interdisciplinary Anthology*, 2nd rev. edn (London: SAGE Publications Ltd, 1996).

Bebbington, Graham, *The Fledglings* (Leek: Churnet Valley Books, 2003).

Bonzon, Thierry, 'The Labour Market and Industrial Mobilization, 1915–1917', in J. Winter & J. Robert (eds), *Capital Cities at War*, Studies in the Social and

Cultural History of Modern Warfare (Cambridge: Cambridge University Press, 1997), pp. 164–95.

Boyce, Robert, and Joseph A. Maiolo, (eds), *The Origins of World War Two: The Debate Continues*, (London: Palgrave Macmillan, 2003).

Braybon, Gail, *Women Workers in the First World War* (London: Routledge, 1989).

Braybon, Gail, and Penny Summerfield, *Out of the Cage*, 1st edn (London: Pandora, 1987).

Brayley, Martin J., *World War II Allied Women's Services* (Oxford: Osprey Publishing, 2001).

Brewer, John D., *C. Wright Mills and the Ending of Violence* (Basingstoke: Palgrave Macmillan, 2003).

Brittain, Vera, *Testament of Youth: An Autobiographical Study of the Years 1900–1925* (London: Virago, 2014 [1933]).

Buhle, Paul, *The Concise History of Woman Suffrage: Selections from History of Woman Suffrage by Elizabeth Cady Stanton, Susan B. Anthony, Matilda Joslyn Gage*, ed. by Mary Jo Buhle (Urbana, IL: University of Illinois Press, 2005).

Burk, Kathleen, (ed.), *War and the State: Transformation of British Government, 1914–19* (London: HarperCollins Publishers Ltd, 1982).

Burke, Peter, *History and Social Theory* (Cambridge: Polity Press, 2005).

Calder, Angus, *The People's War: Britain 1939–1945: Britain, 1939–45* (London: Pimlico, 1992).

Carreiras, Helena, *Gender and the Military: Women in the Armed Forces of Western Democracies* (London; New York: Routledge, 2008).

Colman, Penny, *Rosie the Riveter: Women Working on the Home Front in World War II* (Clermont, FL: Paw Prints, 2008).

Connerton, Paul, *How Societies Remember* (Cambridge: Cambridge University Press, 1989).

Creswell, J.W., *Qualitative Inquiry and Research Design: Choosing among Five Traditions* (London: Sage, 1998).

DeGroot, Gerard, 'Arms and the Woman', in Gerard DeGroot and C. Peniston-Bird (eds), *A Soldier and a Woman: Women in the Military*, 1st edn (London: Routledge, 2000), pp. 3–18.

———, 'Lipstick on Her Nipples, Cordite in Her Hair: Sex and Romance among British Servicewomen during the Second World War', in Gerard J. DeGroot and C. Peniston-Bird (eds), *A Soldier and a Woman: Women in the Military* (London: Routledge, 2000), pp. 100–5.

DeGroot, Gerard, and C. Peniston-Bird, (eds), *A Soldier and a Woman: Women in the Military*, 1st edn (London: Routledge, 2000).

Denzin, Norman, *Interpretative Biography: Qualitative Research Methods Series 17* (Newbury Park, CA: Sage, 1989).

Drummond, John D. *Blue for a Girl: The Story of the WRNS* (London: Cox and Wyman, 1960).

Eley, Geoff, 'Foreword: Memory and the Historians: Ordinary Life, Eventfulness and the Instinctual Past', in Lucy Noakes and Juliette Pattinson (eds), *British Cultural Memory and the Second World War* (London: Bloomsbury Academic, 2013), p.xi–xviii.

Elshtain, Jean, *Women and War* (Chicago, IL: University of Chicago, 1995).

Enloe, Cynthia H., *Does Khaki Become You?*, new e. edn (London: Pandora Press, 1988).

——, *Maneuvers: The International Politics of Militarizing Women's Lives* (Berkeley, CA: University of California Press, 2000).

Fletcher, Marjorie. H. *WRNS: A History of the Women's Royal Naval Service* (London: Batsford Ltd, 1989).

Francis, Martin, *The Flyer: British Culture and the Royal Air Force, 1939–1945* (Oxford: Oxford University Press, 2011).

Gates, B.T., *Kindred Nature: Victorian and Edwardian Women Embrace the Living World* (Chicago, IL: Chicago University Press, 1999).

Gibbs, N.H., *Grand Strategy: Rearmament Policy* v. 1 (London: Stationery Office Books, 1976).

Gibson, Dr Stephen, and Dr Simon Mollan, (eds) *Representations of Peace and Conflict* (Houndmills, Basingstoke, Hampshire: Palgrave Macmillan, 2012).

Golby, J.M., *Culture and Society in Britain 1850–1890: A Source Book of Contemporary Writings* (Oxford: Oxford University Press, 1986).

Goldman, Dorothy, *Women and World War 1: The Written Response* (London: Macmillan, 1993).

Gordon, G.A.H., *British Seapower and Procurement between the Wars* (Annapolis, MD: Naval Institute Press, 1988).

Gould, Jenny, 'Women's Military Services in First World War Britain', in Higonnet and Jenson (eds), *Behind the Lines: Gender and the Two World Wars* (New Haven, CT: Yale University Press, 1989), pp. 114–15.

Grayzel, Susan R., *Women's Identities at War: Gender, Motherhood and Politics in Britain and France During the First World War* (Chapel Hill, NC: The University of North Carolina Press, 1999).

——, *Women and the First World War*, 1st edn (London: Longman, 2002).

Green, Barbara, *Girls in Khaki: A History of the ATS in the Second World War* (Stroud: The History Press Ltd, 2012).

Grieves, Keith, *Sir Eric Geddes: Business and Government in War and Peace* (Manchester: Manchester University Press, 1989).

Gubar, Susan, 'This Is My Rifle, This Is My Gun: World War II and the Blitz on Women' in Margaret R. Higonnet and Jane Jenson (eds), *Behind the Lines: Gender and the Two World Wars* (New Haven, CT: Yale University Press, 1989), pp. 227–60.

Hacker, Barton, 'Women and Military Institutions in Early Modern Europe', *Signs*, 6/4 (1981): 643–71.

Hall, Lesley, *Sex, Gender and Social Change in Britain since 1880* (London: Palgrave Macmillan, 2000).

Hartley, C. Gasquoine, *Women's Wild Oats Essays on the Re-Fixing of Moral Standards* (London: T Werner Laurie, 1919).

Hartmann, Susan, *The Home Front and Beyond: American Women in the 1940s* (Boston, MA: Twayne Publishers Inc., 1983).

Hattersley, Roy, *David Lloyd George: The Great Outsider* (London: Little, Brown & Company, 2010).

Higonnet, Margaret R., and Jane Jenson, (eds), *Behind the Lines: Gender and the Two World Wars* (New Haven: Yale University Press, 1989).

Isaksson, Eva (ed.), *Women in the Military System* (Worcester: Billing and Sons, 1988).

Keegan, John, *A History Of Warfare* (London: Pimlico, 2004).

Kent, Susan Kingsley, *Making Peace: The Reconstruction of Gender in Interwar Britain* (Princeton, NJ: Princeton University Press, 1993).

———, *Gender and Power in Britain 1640–1990* (London: Routledge, 2002).

Maiolo, Joe, *Cry Havoc: The Arms Race and the Second World War, 1931–41: The Global Arms Race 1931–41* (London: John Murray, 2010).

Marr, Andrew, *The Making of Modern Britain: From Queen Victoria to V.E. Day* (London: Macmillan, 2009).

Marshall Cavendish Corporation (ed.), *History of World War II* (New York NY: Cavendish Square Publishing, 2004).

Marwick, Arthur, *Britain in the Century of Total War: Peace and Social Change, 1900–67* (London: Penguin Books Ltd, 1968).

———, *Explosion of British Society, 1914–70* (London: Macmillan, 1971).

———, *War and Social Change in the Twentieth Century: A Comparative Study of Britain, France, Germany, Russia and the United States* (London: Palgrave Macmillan, 1974).

———, *Women at War, 1914–18* (Glasgow: Fontana, 1977).

———, *Total War and Social Change* (Basingstoke: Macmillan Press Ltd, 1988).

———, *The Deluge: British Society and the First World War* (London: Palgrave Macmillan, 2006).

Mason, Ursula Stuart, *The Wrens 1917–77: A History of the Women's Royal Naval Service* (Reading: Educational Explorers, 1977).

McKay, Sinclair, *The Secret Life of Bletchley Park: The History of the Wartime Codebreaking Centre by the Men and Women Who Were There* (London: Aurum Press Ltd, 2011).

McLaine, Ian, *Ministry of Morale: Home Front Morale and the Ministry of Information in World War II* (London and Boston: Allen & Unwin, 1979).

Milkman, Ruth, *Gender at Work: The Dynamics of Job Segregation by Sex During World War II* (Urbana, IL: University of Illinois Press, 1987).

Mills, C. Wright, *Sociological Imagination*, new edn, (Middlesex: Penguin, 1999).

Moskos, Charles C., and F.R. Wood, *The Military: More Than Just a Job?* (Washington, DC: Brassey's Inc., 1988).

Myrdal, Alva Reimer, and Viola Klein, *Women's Two Roles, Home and Work* (London: Routledge & Paul, 1956).

Nicholson, Virginia, *Millions Like Us: Women's Lives During the Second World War* (London: Penguin, 2012).

Nightingale, Florence, *Cassandra: An Essay*, new edn (New York, NY: Feminist Press at The City University of New York, 1979 [1852]).

Noakes, Lucy, *Women in the British Army: War and the Gentle Sex, 1907–1948*, new edn (Oxon: Routledge, 2006).

Noakes, Lucy, and Juliette Pattinson, 'Introduction: Keep calm and carry on: The Cultural Memory of the Second World War in Britain', in Lucy Noakes and Juliette Pattinson (eds), *British Cultural Memory and the Second World War* (London: Bloomsbury Academic, 2013), pp. 1–24.

Noakes, Lucy, and Juliette Pattinson (eds), *British Cultural Memory and the Second World War*, London: Bloomsbury Academic, 2013.

Oakley, Ann, *Father and Daughter: Patriarchy, Gender and Social Science* (Bristol: Policy Press, 2014).

Page, Gwendoline, *They Listened in Secret* (Wynmondham: George R Reeve Ltd, 2003).

Passerini, Luisa, 'Work Ideology and Consensus under Italian Fascism', in Robert Perks and Alistair Thomson (eds), *The Oral History Reader* (London and New York, NY: Routledge, 1997), pp. 53–63.

Patterson, Alfred Temple, *Jellicoe: A Biography* (London: Macmillan, 1969).

Pattinson, Juliette, *Behind Enemy Lines: Gender, Passing and the Special Operations Executive in the Second World War* (Manchester: Manchester University Press, 2011).

Peniston-Bird, Corinna, 'War and Peace in the Cloakroom: The Controversy over the Memorial to the Women of World War II', in Stephen Gibson and Simon Mollan (eds), *Representations of Peace and Conflict* (Houndmills, Basingstoke, Hampshire: Palgrave Macmillan, 2012), pp. 263–84.

——, 'The People's War in Personal Testimony and Bronze: Sorority and the Memorial to the Women of World War II', in Lucy Noakes and Juliette Pattinson (eds), *British Cultural Memory and the Second World War* (London: Bloomsbury Academic, 2013).

Perks, Robert, and Alistair Thomson (eds), *The Oral History Reader* (London?and New York, NY: Routledge, 1997).

Pierson, R.R., 'The Military, More than Just a Job?' in Eva Isaksson (ed.), *Women in the Military System* (Worcester: Billing and Sons, 1988).

Pilcher, Rosamunde, *Coming Home* (London: Hodder & Stoughton, 2005).

Pope, Dudley, *Life in Nelson's Navy*, new edn (London: Chatham Publishing, 1997).

Pugh, Martin, *State and Society: A Social and Political History of Britain, 1870–1997* (London: Hodder Arnold, 1999).

——, *Women and the Women's Movement in Britain, 1914–1999* (Basingstoke: Palgrave Macmillan, 2000).

Riley, Denise, *War in The Nursery: Theories of the Child and Mother* (London: Virago, 1983).

——, *Am I That Name?: Feminism and the Category of Women in History* (Minneapolis, MN: University of Minnesota Press, 2003).

Roberts, Michael, *The Military Revolution, 1560–1660; An Inaugural Lecture Delivered before the Queen's University of Belfast* (Belfast: M. Boyd, 1956).

Rodger, N.A.M., *The Wooden World: Anatomy of the Georgian Navy* (London: Fontana Press, 1988).

Ruskin, John, 'Sesame and Lilies' (1865), in J.M. Golby (ed.), *Culture and Society in Britain 1850–1890: A Source Book of Contemporary Writings* (Oxford: OUP Oxford, 1986), pp. 70–96.

Scott, Joan Wallach, 'Rewriting History', in Margaret R. Higonnet and Jane Jenson (eds), *Behind Enemy Lines: Gender and the Two World Wars* (New Haven, CT: Yale University Press, 1989), pp. 19–30.

—— (ed.), *Feminism and History* (New York, NY and Oxford: Oxford University Press, 1996).

Scott, Peggy, *British Women in War* (London: Hutchinson, 1940).

Searle, G.R., *A New England? Peace and War 1886–1918* (Oxford: Oxford University Press, 2004).

Shay, Robert Paul, *British Rearmament in the Thirties: Politics and Profits* (Princeton NJ: Princeton University Press, 2015).

Simmonds, Alan G.V., *Britain and World War One* (London: Routledge, 2013).

Skocpol, Theda, *Vision and Method in Historical Sociology* (Cambridge: Cambridge University Press, 1984).

Smith, Harold L., *War and Social Change: British Society in the Second World War* (Manchester: Manchester University Press, 1990), pp. 208–29.

Smith, Michael, *The Debs of Bletchley Park* (Aurum Press Ltd, 2015).

Stanley, Jo, *Cabin 'Boys' to Captains: 250 Years of Women at Sea* (Stroud: The History Press, 2016).

Stanley, Liz, *The Auto/biographical I: Theory and Practice of Feminist Auto/biography*, v. 1 (Manchester: Manchester University Press, 1995).

Stansky, Peter, *Sassoon: The Worlds of Peter and Sybil* (New Haven: Yale University Press, 2003).

Stark, Suzanne, *Female Tars: Women Aboard Ship in the Age of Sail* (London: Constable and Company Ltd, 1996).

Summerfield, Penny, 'Women, War and Social Change: Women in Britain in World War Two', in Arthur Marwick (ed.), *Total War and Social Change* (Basingstoke: Macmillan Press Ltd, 1988).

———, *Women Workers in the Second World War: Production and Patriarchy in Conflict* (London: Routledge, 1989).

———, *Reconstructing Women's Wartime Lives: Discourse and Subjectivity in Oral Histories of the Second World War* (Manchester: Manchester University Press, 1998).

———, '"She Wants a Gun, Not a Dishcloth!": Gender, Service and Citizenship in Britain in the Second World War', in Gerard J. DeGroot and C. Peniston-Bird (eds), *A Soldier and a Woman: Women in the Military*, 1st edn (London: Routledge, 2000), pp. 119–35.

———, 'The Generation of Memory: Gender and the Popular Memory of the Second World War in Britain', in Lucy Noakes and Juliette Pattinson (eds), *British Cultural Memory and the Second World War* (London: Bloomsbury Academic, 2013).

Summerfield, Penny, and Corinna Peniston-Bird, *Contesting Home Defence: Men, Women and the Home Guard in the Second World War* (Manchester: Manchester University Press, 2007).

Terry, Roy, *Women in Khaki: The Story of the British Woman Soldier* (Columbus: Columbus, 1988).

Thom, Deborah, *Nice Girls and Rude Girls: Women Workers in World War 1*, illustrated edn (London: I.B.Tauris & Co Ltd, 1998).

Tilly, Charles, *As Sociology Meets History* (Cambridge MT:Academic Press Inc., 1982).

Tosh, John, *The Pursuit of History: Aims, Methods and New Directions in the Study of Modern History*, 4th edn (Harlow: Longman, 2006).

Tucker, Jedidiah Stephens (ed.), *Memoirs of Admiral the Right Honorable, the Earl of St. Vincent* (London: Richard Bentley, 1942).

Wadge, D. Collett, *Women in Uniform* (London: Imperial War Museum, 1946).

Waller, Jane, and Michael Vaughan-Rees, *Women in Uniform 1939–45*, (London: Macmillan Interactive Publishing, 1989).

Watson, Janet S.K., *Fighting Different Wars: Experience, Memory, and the First World War in Britain* (Cambridge: Cambridge University Press, 2004).

Williamson, Gordon, *World War II German Women's Auxiliary Services* (London: Osprey Publishing, 2003).

Williamson, Murray, 'Britain', in Robert Boyce and Joseph A. Maiolo (eds), *The Origins of World War Two: The Debate Continues* (London: Palgrave Macmillan, 2003), pp. 111–34.

Winter, Jay M., and Jean-Louis Robert (eds), *Capital Cities at War: Paris, London, Berlin, 1914 –1919.* Vol. 1. Studies in the Social and Cultural History of Modern Warfare 2 (Cambridge: Cambridge University Press, 1999).

Wrigley, Chris, 'Ministry of Munitions', in Kathleen Burk (ed.), *War and the State: Transformation of British Government, 1914–19* (London: HarperCollins Publishers Ltd, 1982) pp. 32–56.

Zweiniger-Bargielowska, Ina, *Women in Twentieth-Century Britain: Social, Cultural and Political Change*, 1st edn (London: Longman, 2001).

Journal articles

Cohen, I. Bernard, 'Florence Nightingale', *Scientific American*, 250/3 (1984): 128–37.

Crang, Jeremy A., '"Come into the Army, Maud": Women, Military Conscription, and the Markham Inquiry', *Defence Studies*, 8/3 (1 September 2008): 381–95.

———, 'The Revival of the British Women's Auxiliary Services in the Late Nineteen-Thirties', *Historical Research*, 83/220 (1 May 2010): 343–57. doi:10.1111/j.1468-2281.2008.00478.x.

Dandeker, Christopher, and Mady Segal, 'Gender Integration in the Armed Forces: Recent Policy Developments in the United Kingdom', *Armed Forces and Society*, 23 (1996): 29–47.

DeGroot, Gerard J., 'Combatants or Non-combatants? Women in Mixed Anti-aircraft Batteries during the Second World War', *The RUSI Journal*, 140/5 (1 October 1995): 65–70. doi:10.1080/03071849508445958.

———, 'Whose Finger on the Trigger? Mixed Anti-Aircraft Batteries and the Female Combat Taboo', *War in History*, 4/4 (1 October 2016): 434–53. doi:10.1177/096834459700400404.

Hacker, Barton, 'Women and Military Institutions in Early Modern Europe', *Signs*, 6/4 (1981): 643–71.

Housden, Sarah, and Jenny Zmroczek, 'Exploring Identity in Later Life through BBC *People's War* Interviews', *Oral History*, 35/2 (2007): 100–8.

Iskra, Darlene, Stephen Trainor, Marcia Leithauser, and Mady Wechsler Segal, 'Women's Participation in Armed Forces Cross-Nationally: Expanding Segal's Model', *Current Sociology*, 50/5 (2002): 771–97. doi:10.1177/0011392102050005009.

Kennedy-Pipe, Caroline, 'Women and the Military', *The Journal of Strategic Studies*, 23/4 (2000): 32–50.

Pattinson, Juliette, '"Playing the Daft Lassie with Them": Gender, Captivity and the Special Operations Executive during the Second World War', *European Review of History: Revue Européenne D'histoire*, 13/2 (1 June 2006): 271–92. doi:10.1080/13507480600785955.

———, '"The Thing That Made Me Hesitate ...": Re-Examining Gendered Intersubjectivities in Interviews with British Secret War Veterans', *Women's History Review*, 20/2 (1 April 2011): 245–63. doi:10.1080/09612025.2011.556322.

Peniston-Bird, Corinna, 'Classifying the Body in the Second World War: British Men in and Out of Uniform', *Body & Society*, 9/4 (1 December 2003): 31–48. doi:10.1177/135703403773684630.

———, 'Of Hockey Sticks and Sten Guns: British Auxiliaries and Their Weapons in the Second World War', *Women's History Magazine*, 2014, no. 76 (Autumn 2014): 13–22.

———, 'The Grieving Male in Memorialization: Monuments of Discretion', *Journal of War & Culture Studies*, 8/1 (February 1, 2015): 41–56. doi:10.1179/1752628014Y.0000000017.

Peniston-Bird, Corinna, and Wendy Ugolini, 'Introduction', *Journal of War & Culture Studies*, 8/1 (1 February 2015): 1–6. doi:10.1179/1752627214Z.00000000057.

Segal, Mady Wechsler, 'Women's Military Roles Cross-Nationally: Past, Present, and Future', *Gender & Society*, 9/6 (1 December 1995): 757–75. doi:10.1177/089124395009006008.

Stone, Tessa, 'Creating a (gendered?) Military Identity: The Women's Auxiliary Air Force in Great Britain in the Second World War', *Women's History Review*, 8/4 (1 December 1999): 605–24. doi:10.1080/09612029900200227.

Summerfield, Penny, and Corinna Peniston-Bird, 'Women in the Firing Line: The Home Guard and the Defence of Gender Boundaries in Britain in the Second World War', *Women's History Review*, 9/2 (1 June 2000): 231–55. doi:10.1080/09612020000200250.

Thomas, Patricia J., 'Women in the Military; America and the British Commonwealth', *Armed Forces & Society*, 4/4 (1 July 1978): 623–46. doi:10.1177/0095327X7800400406.

Van-Crevald, Martin, 'Less than We Can Be: Men, Women and the Modern Military', *The Journal of Strategic Studies*, 23/4 (2000): 1–20.

Websites

The Admiralty, available at: http://homepages.warwick.ac.uk/ ~ lysic/1920s/admiralty.htm (accessed 6 June 2017).

Ardtaraig, available at: http://www.ardtaraig.net/ardtarig-a-reminiscence/reminiscence-p54/ (accessed 27 September 2010; link not working).

ATS poster, available at: http://historyinposters.tumblr.com/page/45 (accessed 6 June 2017).

BBC *People's War, Fact File: Royal Navy*, available at: http://www.bbc.co.uk/history/ww2peopleswar/timeline/factfiles/nonflash/a6649815.shtml (accessed 6 June 2017).

Dandeker, Christopher, 'Women in the Military', available at: http://www.oxfordreference.com/view/10.1093/acref/9780198606963.001.0001/acref-9780198606963-e-1390 (accessed 6 June 2017).

'Etiquette violations: eating off your knife', 8 May 2011, available at: https://restaurant-ingthroughhistory.com/2011/05/08/etiquette-violations-eating-off-your-knife/ (accessed 23 July 1916).

Farndale, Nigel, 'The Imitation Game: Who Were the Real Bletchley Park Codebreakers?', *Telegraph*, 31 July 2016, available at: http://www.telegraph.co.uk/films/2016/07/31/the-imitation-game-who-were-the-real-bletchley-park-codebreakers/ (accessed 6 June 2017).

'Felixstowe's Secret War Exposed', *Ipswich Star*, available at: www.ipswichstar.co.
uk/news/felixstowe_s_secret_war_exposed_1_94762 (accessed 6 June
2017).

Florence Nightingale Museum, available at: http://www.florence-nightingale.co.
uk/the-collection/biography.html (accessed 6 June 2017; link no longer
working).

Imperial War Museum, Collections, available at: http://www.iwm.org.uk/collecti
ons/item/object/29092 (accessed 6 June 2017).

'King's Regulations and Admiralty Instructions', 1913, available at: http://www.
pbenyon.plus.com/KR&AI/Discipline_General.html (accessed 6 June 2017).

National Archives, available at: http://discovery.nationalarchives.gov.uk/SearchUI/
details?Uri=C719 (accessed 6 June 2017).

Royal Navy, Annex 21C, 'Ethos Values and Standards', available at: http://www.
royalnavy.mod.uk/-/media/royal-navy-responsive/documents/reference-
library/br-3-vol-1/chapter-21.pdf, Feb. 2016 (accessed 6 June 2017).

TV programmes

Moore, Roland, 'Land Girls', BBC, 2009.

INDEX

Plate 1   Dame Katharine Furse inspecting VAD officers. Credit: Alamy.

Plate 2   Sir Eric Geddes. Credit: Alamy.

Plate 3 WRNS on German U-boat, November 1918. Courtesy of WRNS Benevolent Trust.

Plate 4 World War I recruitment poster for WAAC and WRNS. Credit: Alamy.

Plate 5   Betty Calderara. Courtesy of Betty Calderara.

Plate 6   Jean Atkins née Aitchison and her sister Mary, a topographical Wren. Courtesy of Jean Atkins.

Plate 7 Jean Atkins née Aitchison having completed her Officer's training at Stoke Pogues (first from right at the back). Courtesy of Jean Atkins.

Plate 8 Met Office Staff at Machrihanish, Scotland. Jean Atkins née Aitchison with Commander John Simmonds, better known as 'Seaweed'. Courtesy of Jean Atkins.

Plate 9 Sheila Rodman. Courtesy of Sheila Rodman.

Plate 10 Third Officer Wren interviewed for this book. Courtesy of the interviewee.

Plate 11   Norwegian Wrens on training exercise in the destroyer HMS *Glaisdale*, September 1943. Courtesy of Eve Tar Collection.

Plate 12   Wren maintaining gun. Courtesy of WRNS Benevolent Trust.

Plate 13   Airey Neave with Sophie Richardson. Courtesy of the interviewees.

Plate 14   Dame Vera Laughton Mathews with her children. Credit: Getty Images.